The
100
greatest Watford wins

PELOTON PUBLISHING
WWW.LIONELBIRNIE.COM

First published in Great Britain in 2011
by Peloton Publishing
© 2011 Lionel Birnie

Typeset by Peloton Publishing
Printed and bound in England by SS Media

Cover design by Lionel Birnie
Photography courtesy of the Watford Observer,
Press Association and Alan Cozzi.

Peloton Publishing Ltd
Registered in England
32 Ridge Street, Watford, WD24 6BP
Registered company number: 7353619
www.lionelbirnie.com
info@lionelbirnie.com

For Watford supporters everywhere
Keep the faith

BY THE SAME AUTHOR

Enjoy the game
The story of Watford's greatest ever decade told by the people who made it happen. The players and management reveal what really happened as the club rose through the divisions to finish runners-up to Liverpool. Almost a hundred exclusive interviews have been woven expertly together to offer unique insight into a fantastic era.

It's a very, very good book – Graham Taylor

The best football book I've read by a long way – John McClelland

The book triumphs in identifying a compelling angle and pursuing it doggedly. It's a blinding read. The richness of the anecdotes, the candour of the interviewees, and the author's skill at hanging the story around the dramatic storyline make this a vital read for all Watford supporters of any vintage – Matt Rowson

Four Seasons
A lavish hardback edition combining Alan Cozzi's superb photography and a deftly-written commentary to dramatically document Graham Taylor's second spell as Watford manager. Lightning doesn't strike twice, they say, but once again Taylor steered the Hornets from lower division obscurity to the top flight.

See www.lionelbirnie.com for more details or to order both books.

Introduction

The joy of being a Watford fan is that victory is not guaranteed and success is not viewed as a birthright. We are used to taking the rough with the smooth and the highs feel all the better simply because they do not come along every day.

This book is intended to be a celebration of some of the greatest days. It is a countdown of the team's hundred most significant and enjoyable post-war wins.

Hopefully, each match will give you a reason to smile and the book may become the perfect antidote to any bleak goalless draws or numbing home defeats that come our way.

Think of it like this – if you were to pull this book from the shelf and remind yourself of one glorious victory every time Watford were to lose a game, it should see you through the next six seasons.

Of course, I don't expect anyone to agree entirely with the order I've chosen. Perhaps there are other matches you feel should have been included. But this book is not intended to be a definitive record. The games are not supposed to be set in stone. Rather, I hope it sparks debate and, more importantly, revives memories.

Some of the matches you will remember as if they were yesterday but I hope that others explain, particularly to younger fans, why this club of ours is so special. Perhaps a few people will gain a new perspective on the stories told by their mums, dads and other older fans and realise that yes, we really did do that.

As such, the book is unashamedly populist and necessarily biased. It is supposed to be a crowd-pleaser.

What is important is that every game featured in this book meant something. It was either hugely important, such as a promotion clincher, a cup triumph, or a relegation escape act. Or it was a right hammering that came out of the blue and lifted everyone's spirits.

There are quite a few people to thank for their help, in particular Sam Suresh at SS Media, Richard Walker at Watford FC, Peter Wilson-Leary and Anthony Matthews at the Watford Observer, Simon Ricketts, Alan Cozzi and Edward Pickering.

I hope that everyone who reads this book enjoys it, and if you do, please tell your fellow Watford fans about it. **Lionel Birnie, September 2011**

The Championship, Friday August 6 2010

Mackay's relegation favourites pass their trial by television

John Eustace leads the celebrations after scoring the first goal against Norwich City.

The script was written. Norwich City, the division's new boys, had won the League One title in a manner that had the experts cooing. Now, Paul Lambert, the Canaries' manager and the latest cause célèbre, was ready to make an impression in The Championship.

Watford were in the grip of yet another financial crisis. Favourites for relegation. Again. With a squad described as 'threadbare and painfully inexperienced' by *The Guardian*.

The pundits and bookmakers are rarely wrong, are they? As has so often been the case with televised fixtures in recent years, the Hornets were not supposed to be the stars of the show. They were merely extras to support the overall narrative.

The opening match of the season was moved to Friday evening so it could be shown live. It served as the curtain raiser for the entire English league. Sky's pundits hyped up the home team and their commentator's opening words were: 'Welcome to the crazy, unpredictable world of The Championship.' You might have thought they'd seen this coming.

Once again, Watford looked like the *Rossoneri* in their red and black-striped away shirts. Once again, they played like them. The Hornets almost lost John Eustace to Leeds during the summer. How relieved they were to keep their increasingly influential skipper.

Eustace dominated the midfield. He got the first goal, bringing the ball down and lashing it low into the net.

Ten minutes later, Danny Graham got the second. He chested the ball down to Marvin Sordell then ran into space to receive the through ball.

Graham's finish was sublime. He took the ball on with a touch of his left foot and then fired a powerful shot that caught John Ruddy cold.

He was about to prove himself the most complete forward Watford have had since the days of John Barnes.

Norwich pulled one back when Andrew Crofts scored early in the second half. But Watford continued to batter the Canaries. Adrian Mariappa should have scored when Ruddy could only parry a long-range shot. Mariappa's header fell the wrong side of the post.

Graham scored his second nine minutes from time. Receiving the ball on the left-hand corner of the 18-yard box, he was allowed time to pick his spot. He threaded the ball towards the far post and although Ruddy got a hand to it, the ball went in.

Norwich got another goal back at the death but Watford fully deserved their win. Another one in the eye for the experts.

Loach, Hodson, M Taylor, Mariappa, Doyley, Cowie, Eustace, McGinn, Buckley (Jenkins 59), Graham, Sordell (Deeney 58)
Manager Malky Mackay
Scorers Eustace 14, Graham 24, 81
Norwich scorers Crofts 52, Nelson 90
Attendance 24,348

THE HORNETS ON THE OPENING DAY

Ten other opening day wins to remember				
1958	Southport	H	5-1	4th
1977	Stockport County	A	3-1	4th
1978	Walsall	A	4-2	3rd
1981	Newcastle United	A	1-0	2nd
1982	Everton	H	2-0	1st
1986	Oxford United	H	3-0	1st
1987	Wimbledon	H	1-0	1st
1992	Millwall	H	3-1	1st
1997	Burnley	H	1-0	2nd
2007	Wolves	A	2-1	Ch

...And eight to forget				
1950	Southend United	A	1-5	3S
1969	Bristol City	A	0-1	2nd
1971	Fulham	A	0-3	2nd
1983	Coventry City	H	2-3	1st
1985	Tottenham	A	0-4	1st
1993	Luton Town	A	1-2	1st
1994	Sheffield United	A	0-3	1st
2001	Manchester City	A	0-3	1st

Watford's post-war opening day record
P 66 W 28 D 11 L 26 F 92 A 92

Keep an eye on their number three, we may be seeing him again

Watford probably should have scored ten. Into his third full season at the helm, Ken Furphy was on the verge of crafting a team capable of reaching Division Two. Not much longer to wait now. Be patient.

In the Sixties, Vicarage Road wasn't quite a fortress but it was a very difficult place for opposition teams to visit.

Unbeaten at home since the opening day of the season, Watford were primed to give someone a good hiding.

Grimsby Town were the ones on the receiving end. Dixie Hale, who arrived from Cardiff City during the summer, opened the scoring then Terry Garbett and Tony Currie hit the target. Stewart Scullion, the winger, was in superb form. Earlier that week, he had turned down a transfer to Sheffield United.

On his day, he could turn a defence inside out and he was in particularly cruel form this afternoon. The Mariners' defenders were unable to cope.

Currie, the 17-year-old striker, was another star in the making. He looked destined for greatness the moment he pulled on a gold shirt. He scored two on his league debut against Bristol Rovers, got a hat-trick against Peterborough in only his third start and then got another three against Grimsby. On February 1,

he was gone, sold with indecent haste to the Blades for £26,500.

While Furphy was trying to arrange the goods to best effect, Jim Bonser was selling the assets out of the stock room's back door.

Watford ripped into Grimsby early in the second half. Hale got his second, as did Garbett and then Currie followed suit. Grimsby did manage to get one goal but Currie completed his hat-trick with 15 minutes remaining.

Currie left before Watford had even had a chance to fully appreciate his gift. He went on to play for England.

Scullion became a Hornets hero before he was sold to Sheffield United.

But there was a player on the pitch that afternoon who was to have a greater impact on Watford's fortunes than anyone else.

Grimsby's left-back was a 23-year-old former schoolboy international called Graham Taylor. And the negative approach of his Grimsby boss, and perhaps even this hammering, were to influence his approach to the game.

Slater, Welbourne, Williams, Hale, Garvey, Walley, Scullion, Currie, Garbett, Farrell, Lewis
Manager Ken Furphy
Scorers Hale 19, 46, Garbett 39, 54, Currie 44, 56, 75
Grimsby scorer Ross 60
Attendance 9,074

WATFORD............ 5 LUTON TOWN................ 2

Division One, Monday April 4 1983

Sometimes, Graham Taylor's audacity could be breathtaking. Luton Town, the old enemy, were visiting Vicarage Road on Easter Monday. The ground would be packed and there was far more than local pride at stake.

The Hornets were third in the table, chasing a place in Europe, while the Hatters were second from bottom, scrabbling to avoid a quick return to the Second Division. Promoted together the previous season, with Luton as champions, naturally, it was Watford who had adjusted to life in the top flight more comfortably.

That didn't mean their wretched run of poor results against their local rivals had improved. On December 27, they lost 1-0 at Kenilworth Road, which was enough to spoil Christmas. Now it was Easter. Time for a resurrection.

Luton had won five of the previous meetings 1-0, but Watford proved that there's no substitute for style.

When the teams were announced before the game, Watford's supporters must have imagined Steve Sims and Ian Bolton had been involved in a collision on the training ground the previous day. They'd been the regular partnership at the heart of the defence since October. They'd barely put a foot wrong and were the solid foundations upon which the team was built.

But Taylor decided to rest them both. Instead, he paired 20-year-old Steve Terry with 21-year-old Kenny Jackett for the first time in two years.

They still had nightmares about one of the final appearances alongside each other in defence. They had been ruthlessly exposed by Garry Thompson and Mark Hateley during a 5-0 drubbing at Coventry City in the League Cup in December 1980.

Taylor had decided Jackett's best position was in midfield and Terry, who had started the season at centre half, had lost his place to Sims after Aston Villa's Peter Withe dominated him.

Now the manager wanted to see how the youngsters coped in a high-pressure game. 'I deliberately chose the Luton match,' Taylor said. 'Bolton and Sims have proved they can handle Division One. Can the others?'

This was a full-blooded derby game. Luther Blissett scored early but Trevor Aylott and Brian Horton put Luton in front. Terry and Jackett had some shaky moments but Watford managed to level just before half-time.

After the break, it was a different story. The frustration of not having beaten Luton since 1971 gave way to delight as Watford scored twice in two minutes and then added a fifth near the end, showing that attack is the best form of defence.

This was a good old-fashioned drubbing and Watford's most comprehensive win over Luton for 50 years.

Sherwood, Rice, Rostron, Taylor, Terry, Jackett, Callaghan (Armstrong 82), Blissett, Barnes, Jobson, Lohman
Manager Graham Taylor
Scorers Blissett 6, 48 pen, Jobson 42, Barnes 49, Callaghan 78
Luton scorers Aylott 16, Horton 29
Attendance 20,120

TOTTENHAM HOTSPUR.......2 WATFORD.......3

Coca-Cola Cup second round, second leg
Tuesday October 4 1994

Like kids in a sweet shop, Hornets raid White Hart Lane

Most of the Watford fans had already bought their tickets for the second leg before the 6-3 defeat in the first match, so they had to go.

The Premiership was only in its third season but already football at the top was changing. It was becoming clear that those at the top didn't want the likes of Watford around.

Let's not be churlish about it. Ossie Ardiles, in his brief time as Tottenham manager, encouraged his team to play with the sort of carefree abandon you see in the school playground.

The Argentinian played with five attacking players – Jürgen Klinsmann, Darren Anderton, Nick Barmby, Teddy Sheringham and Illie Dumitrescu.

If he could have played with a 'rush goalie' you get the feeling he would have done. Fortunately, Spurs couldn't defend, otherwise the first leg could have been humiliating.

Craig Ramage scored in the first minute but by half-time Watford were 4-1 down and reeling. Klinsmann scored a hat-trick. Vicarage Road had not seen such a display of potent and fluid forward play for years. One thing was certain, the tie was dead.

White Hart Lane seemed to have lost its soul in the six years since Watford had last visited. It didn't help that the ground was half full and those Spurs fans who did turn up gave the impression that second leg League Cup matches were beneath them these days.

Watford may not have pulled off the impossible but this was still a famous victory. A night when they managed to bloody noses against the odds. The Hornets traded blows with Spurs on an equal footing. Colin Foster put them ahead, Barmby equalised. Lee Nogan made it 2-1 just after half-time, then Klinsmann levelled.

Nogan scored the winner and the visitors threw everyone forward in the vain hope of forcing extra time.

Afterwards, Glenn Roeder said he believed his side deserved another couple of goals and an extra 30 minutes to finish the job, which was perhaps stretching things a bit.

It was an evening to savour. At a time when the delights of the Premiership's candy store seemed a million miles away, Watford made the most of their opportunity. Besides, any victory over the pampered Spurs tastes sweet.

Miller, Lavin, Bazeley (Nogan 8), Foster, Holdsworth, Ramage, Hessenthaler, Johnson, Moralee, Porter, Mooney
Manager Glenn Roeder
Scorers Foster 14, Nogan 47, 74
Tottenham scorers Barmby 30, Klinsmann 63
Attendance 17,798

Division Two, Saturday December 16 1989

Vicarage Road bids farewell to the Eighties in fine fashion

How fitting it was that Vicarage Road should sign off at the end of the club's most successful decade in such emphatic style.

At the start of the Eighties, Watford were just getting to grips with the Second Division. With the decade drawing to a close, the man who had been the team's left-back then was now the manager.

Steve Harrison's programme notes drew inspiration from the success that had gone before.

This match could almost be seen as symbolic of the entire decade but, sadly, rather than being a catalyst for further success, the result was just a pleasant blip on a chart that showed mostly a downward trend.

After ten years of feast came ten of famine.

By his own admission, Harrison was not cut out for the manager's chair. His first full season in charge had seen the team fall agonisingly short of a return to the top division. They were the first club to be knocked out of the play-offs without losing a match. Two draws against Blackburn Rovers in the semifinal meant they were eliminated on the away goals rule.

Although there was optimism for the new campaign, Harrison continued to wrestle with the demands of the job. A brilliant coach who found it easy to strike up a rapport with players, even if his exuberance strayed over the boundaries of taste once or twice, he found the distance a manager had to keep from his squad artificial. He didn't cope with the stress and although he had no problem making decisions, he found the dialogue with disappointed players exhausting. Too often, he was confrontational. 'By the end, I didn't even like myself,' he says.

Then there were the comparisons to the Taylor era. Desperate to be his own man, he felt pressure to recreate the dynamic wing play of his predecessor's most successful team.

Barely a week went by without the local paper making a reference to Taylor's old team. Glyn Hodges had his strengths and shortcomings weighed up against those of John Barnes.

With the team sliding down the table, Harrison decided to change his approach and do things his way. He signed Gary Penrice, a forward from Bristol Rovers. Penrice had a moustache

that captured the imagination of the fans, which perhaps betrayed their nocturnal viewing habits. But he also had a touch and vision that were far more subtle than some of the battering-ram centre forwards Harrison had previously employed alongside Paul Wilkinson.

The start of the season had been quite encouraging. But two home wins and two away draws were undone by a heavy defeat at Sunderland before the Hornets unravelled alarmingly in the autumn. They went ten games without a win and slumped to 19th place.

That was when Harrison decided to change things. Rather than playing Hodges as an out-and-out winger, he gave the Welshman a looser role. Lee Richardson, a young midfielder who had joined from Halifax towards the end of the previous season, was improving. Harrison used him to hold the midfield together, allowing Gary Porter and Liburd Henry to get forward from deeper positions, while Hodges and Penrice roamed.

Everything slotted perfectly into place to give the Watford supporters an early Christmas present. As Gary Porter said afterwards, the signs that someone was about to get a hammering had been there. Watford had won three in a row. They were fast out of the blocks, scoring after just three minutes when Penrice set up Paul Wilkinson.

Richardson scored with a delightful chip and two minutes later Porter made it 3-0 with a searing shot.

Penrice scored his sixth goal in as many games before Barry Ashby made it 5-0 just before half-time.

David Campbell and Jimmy Quinn pulled goals back for Bradford in the second half before Wilkinson and Henry added the sixth and seventh.

There was a great sense of optimism as the players left the field that evening but it was to prove misplaced. They never quite got going, spluttering and jerking like a diesel engine that has been treated to a gallon of unleaded.

They reached the heady heights of eighth place after a win at Barnsley the following week before slipping back to mid-table anonymity.

But that could not detract from the joy of seeing such a wholehearted and skilful display. It was different to the days of that irresistible front four but it was no less exciting.

And as the supporters turned to leave the stadium, they could have been forgiven for thinking they saw ghosts in the shadows cast by the floodlights.

They were the figures of the Eighties, of Barnes and Blissett, Rostron and Callaghan. This was a different team but it was still so hard to let go. If an entire decade could be summed up by a single score, it would be this. Seven-two.

Coton, Gibbs, Ashby, Richardson, Holdsworth, Roeder, Henry, Wilkinson, Penrice, Porter Hodges
Manager Steve Harrison
Watford scorers Wilkinson 3, 71, Richardson 17, Porter 19, Penrice 28, Ashby 43, Henry 76
Bradford scorers Campbell 60, Quinn 66
Attendance 8,554

Super Kev – the best ten grand I ever spent

Division One, Saturday December 2 1995

Glenn Roeder can remember seeing Kevin Phillips for the first time and knowing within minutes he was good enough for him.

'I used to let Nigel Callaghan come in and train with us once a week because he was a nice lad. Nigel was playing at Baldock Town at the time and I asked him what the training was like up there. They used to finish up each session with a game of five-a-side. Nigel told me that if he wasn't on the same team as a lad called Kevin Phillips, he'd go in and get showered and changed. This lad was the only one on Nigel's wavelength.'

Roeder made a trip to north Hertfordshire one night to see Baldock play. 'It was a freezing cold night and they were playing Fisher Athletic. There were no teamsheets and they didn't announce the line-up but I knew who Kevin Phillips was just by seeing the way he warmed up the goalkeeper,' he says. 'There were two or three of them taking shots at the keeper before the match and each time this lad had a go, I thought "that's got to be him". He was hitting the ball so sweetly and with so much power.

'My one concern was his size. He was stocky but he was small. As much as we don't like to admit it, size is a factor in league football.

'It was 0-0 at half-time and he hadn't had a clear-cut chance but I'd seen enough. We got him in the next day for a trial and to play a couple of reserve matches. Although he didn't score in either there was no doubt about it, we had to take him. His ball retention was excellent. I shouldn't have worried about his size because he had an unbelievable leap on him and was a terrific header of the ball. Teams always put their smaller central defender on him, which was their first mistake. He could shield the ball well and his movement was excellent. He was a real find.

'We paid Baldock £10,000 and we gave them an extra £10,000 for every ten first team games. In the end, we paid £30,000 for him.'

Roeder's search for a striker to replace Paul Furlong defined his time as Watford manager. Although he picked up some superb bargains, such as goalkeeper Kevin Miller, defenders Colin Foster and Keith Millen, the mercurial midfielder Craig Ramage, and, of course, one of the club's most

Kevin Phillips went from working in a warehouse to the Premiership in five years.

popular players, Tommy Mooney, his attempt to recruit a prolific centre forward was exhausting and frustrating.

At the end of Roeder's first season in charge, the chairman Jack Petchey sold Paul Furlong to Chelsea for £2.3million. By his standards, Petchey was generous with the transfer budget and allowed Roeder to pay Millwall £450,000 for Jamie Moralee.

It turned out to be a costly mistake and one that hampered Roeder when it came to doing further deals. 'At the time I don't think many people thought it was a bad buy,' he says. 'He had scored a lot of goals for Millwall. But I didn't do enough homework on the boy. I don't want to be too critical but he wasn't the right type of person for me.

'I never complained about the transfer budget. I know the supporters thought Jack was too tight but he ran the club to turn over a profit. He had to bring the ground up to the regulations and he

BEFORE THE MATCH

Top of Division One

		P	W	D	L	F	A	Pts
1	Millwall	19	9	7	3	23	17	34
2	Norwich City	19	9	6	4	30	20	33
3	Grimsby Town	19	9	6	4	23	19	33
4	Leicester City	19	9	5	5	31	26	32
5	Birmingham	19	8	7	4	30	22	31

Bottom of Division One

		P	W	D	L	F	A	Pts
20	Wolves	19	4	6	9	22	28	18
21	Watford	19	3	8	8	22	28	17
22	Portsmouth	19	3	7	9	26	34	16
23	Luton Town	19	3	6	10	12	25	15
24	Port Vale	19	2	8	9	20	28	14

END OF THE SEASON

Bottom of Division One

		P	W	D	L	F	A	Pts
20	Wolves	46	13	16	17	56	62	55
21	Portsmouth	46	13	13	20	61	69	52
22	Millwall	46	13	13	20	43	63	52
23	Watford	46	10	18	18	62	70	48
24	Luton Town	46	11	12	23	40	64	45

built two new stands by selling Furlong and Bruce Dyer. Whatever people think of him, he was a very clever business-man. He came out of the navy at the end of the Second World War with nothing and created a business that made him an awful lot of money. I have no idea how much it was but it was rumoured to be hundreds of millions.

'He made it clear to me from the start that there weren't going to be vast sums of money. He taught me a lot about wheeling and dealing, although that makes it sound like it was beneath the counter. What I mean is he taught me how to get the best price possible.

'We got Craig Ramage for £90,000. That was an excellent deal. Millen and Foster were not expensive. We got people in for not a lot of money and they added a lot to the squad.

'But I will never spend a better £10,000 than I did on Kevin Phillips.'

Roeder's third season as manager had not started well. Far from building on the previous season's seventh place, they found they were getting sucked into a relegation battle.

At the start of December, they headed to the New Den to face Millwall, who were top of the table. Two weeks earlier, Roeder had sold Gerard Lavin to the Lions for £425,000.

Roeder thought he had found the perfect target man to spend the money on. Sigur Rushfeldt, a Norwegian, was keen to join Watford but the deal fell through when Birmingham's Barry Fry showed interested at the eleventh hour. It was a recurring theme. Every time Roeder was close to getting someone, Fry would make a call and the price would be driven out of Watford's league. Even if the players weren't ending up at St Andrew's they weren't coming to Vicarage Road.

The manager was getting desperate. Moralee's form was worse than ever. Despite Phillips' obvious qualities, Roeder needed someone experienced to play alongside him.

In the end, he got Paul Wilkinson on loan from Middlesbrough. He had scored a lot of goals during his three seasons at Watford, and had been caught offside with even greater frequency.

Roeder's experiments in the loan market were erratic and it could be said they were his undoing.

'I signed a few who weren't really Glenn Roeder signings,' he says. 'It was very hard to get the right players.'

Darren Caskey, a midfielder from Spurs, and Wilkinson were reasonable short-term measures. Gary Penrice came back too, but without the same success. However, Roeder's final few throws of the dice all landed on ones and twos, rather than fives or sixes.

Steve Hodge and Warren Neill weren't up to it. Bringing in Kerry Dixon, a former Luton favourite, had the fans turning on each other and against Roeder. Devon White and Danny Hill came in for what turned out to be Roeder's final game, a dismal 4-0 defeat at Crystal Palace.

Hill, another midfielder from Spurs, looked as if he'd only been introduced to the concept of kicking a ball that very morning. The manager was sacked after that defeat at Selhurst Park and he accepted that the signing of Moralee had undermined him in the end.

A transfer fee can be a weight on a player's shoulders but it can be a noose around a manager's neck, poised to be pulled tight at any moment.

'It was a mistake,' he says. 'But overall, I don't think my record in the transfer market was too bad. If you look at Moralee and Phillips, one of them looked to be worth £420,000, and the other looked about ten grand.'

'We didn't have any luck at all that season,' says Roeder. 'I always felt we would turn the corner and we'd wriggle out of it. There was still plenty of time and there were signs that things were getting better.'

No match at Millwall looks inviting but there was a glimmer of hope that cold afternoon. Mick McCarthy's side were top but they were wobbling slightly. They were on a run of three without a win. Watford were exactly the sort of side they needed to face to get themselves back on track.

Wilkinson took the small band of travelling supporters on a wistful trip down memory lane.

He was caught offside after just 20 seconds. The Watford supporters cheered and Wilkinson turned to berate the linesman. It was just like old times.

Watford had a lucky break, perhaps their first of the season, when Kasey Keller fumbled a long clearance. Even Millwall's defenders had turned to run upfield, thinking their keeper had it under control. Phillips, alert like a fox spotting a gap in the hen house fence, pounced and walked it into the net.

Not long before half-time Phillips scored again, as Watford continued to have success on the counter-attack. Although Chris Makin pulled one back just before the referee blew for the break, Watford's nerves held in the second half. What a fine and unexpected victory to offer hope of a revival. Of course, there was to be no revival.

As away fans ran the gauntlet in the hostile backstreets of Bermondsey, Roeder faced the press. He brushed off the rumours from a national newspaper reporter that Graham Taylor was being lined up to replace him.

Although the signs that bleak winter afternoon in that bleak corner of London had been encouraging, there was to be no recovery.

However, few could have predicted that Millwall would go into freefall and would be relegated alongside the Hornets the following May. And no one would have believed that Graham Taylor was on his way back.

Miller, Bazeley, Johnson, Foster, Holdsworth, Palmer, Hessenthaler, Wilkinson, Mooney, Porter (Payne 64) Phillips
Manager Glenn Roeder
Scorer Phillips 24, 38
Millwall scorer Makin 45
Attendance 8,389

Division One, Saturday December 3 1983

Reilly and Johnston strike up perfect partnership on and off the pitch

Panic was beginning to set in. So much so that Graham Taylor had to reassure Watford's supporters their team would not 'do a Swansea'.

The Welsh side and Watford had been engaged in a race through the divisions. When Watford won the Fourth Division title in 1978, Swansea went up with them. They were both promoted again the following year.

Swansea reached the top flight a year before Watford. The meteoric rise by both clubs captured the imagination. John Toshack's side finished sixth in Division One at the first attempt but were relegated the following season.

Watford did even better than the Swans, clinching the runners-up spot. By December 1983, the Swans were sinking again and Watford looked like they were following them. The sense of déja-vu was uncanny.

As it turned out, Swansea's equally rapid return to the basement was well underway. They would be back where they started by 1986. But Taylor had no intention of following them.

However, the 1983-84 season was Watford's equivalent of the difficult second album. The first year had been hit after hit. But the team was barely recognisable. Pat Rice, the captain, had been forced to accept that his legs had gone. Ian Bolton, who was undergoing a difficult marriage break-up, went to Brentford hoping it would be a fresh start. Luther Blissett, Ross Jenkins and Gerry Armstrong had all moved on.

The rebuilding work was underway but it was not a speedy process. The team that played in the Uefa Cup looked more like a reserve line-up and though they performed heroics in Europe, Taylor had his doubts that they were the long-term solution to his problems.

Initially, he had considered playing John Barnes as a centre forward, as he had impressed so much in the role alongside Blissett the previous season. But that plan had to be shelved when

BEFORE THE MATCH

More than a third of the season gone and only two wins on the board, things were not looking good. Watford pulled away from trouble in the New Year and finished 11th. Wolves never looked like recovering and went down with just 29 points.

		P	W	D	L	F	A	Pts
17	Everton	15	5	3	7	9	17	18
18	Notts County	15	4	2	9	18	26	14
19	Leicester City	16	3	4	9	18	31	13
20	Stoke City	15	2	6	7	15	26	12
21	**Watford**	15	2	4	9	20	30	10
22	Wolves	15	1	4	10	11	35	7

Paul Atkinson, who Taylor had signed from Oldham and earmarked for a role wide on the left, broke his ankle in his first practice match for the club.

It wasn't as if the manager had been sitting on his hands. In the summer, he bought George Reilly, a forward in the same mould as Jenkins. Reilly cost £90,000 from Cambridge United. Some supporters were not impressed. They'd seen Blissett leave for a million and his replacement was someone who'd never played in Division One.

Taylor also used his role as England youth manager to cherrypick a couple of promising defenders. He got 18-year-old Lee Sinnott from Walsall and David Bardsley, a 19-year-old from Blackpool.

The most expensive new arrival was Maurice Johnston, who was a raw but undoubtedly exciting striker from Partick Thistle. While Everton and Spurs hesitated about the 21-year-old's ability to step up from the Scottish First Division, Taylor took a chance and paid Partick £200,000.

Johnston made his debut at Old Trafford, two days after he joined the club, partnering Barnes in attack. They lost 4-1 to Manchester United and

AN UNSETTLED TEAM

Injuries played havoc with Graham Taylor's team selection throughout the 1983-84 season. He rarely managed to field the same team twice. As a result the partnerships at the heart of the defence and up front were continually changing. The Johnston-Reilly strikeforce established itself quickly. But at the back, Sims and Franklin both got bad injuries. Had they been fit they would probably have played in the FA Cup final.

Central defensive partnerships

No.5	No.6	Games
Steve Sims	Ian Bolton	1
Ian Bolton	Paul Franklin	1
Steve Terry	Paul Franklin	5
Steve Sims	Paul Franklin	28
Steve Terry	Kenny Jackett	2
Steve Terry	Ian Bolton	5
Steve Sims	Charlie Palmer	1
Steve Terry	Lee Sinnott	11
Kenny Jackett	Lee Sinnott	1
Lee Sinnott	Wilf Rostron	1
George Reilly	Lee Sinnott	1

Striking partnerships

No.8	No.9	Games
Jimmy Gilligan	Steve Terry	1
John Barnes	George Reilly	7
John Barnes	Jimmy Gilligan	4
David Johnson	Jimmy Gilligan	1
Ian Richardson	John Barnes	4
Ian Richardson	Jimmy Gilligan	1
Ian Richardson	George Reilly	3
Maurice Johnston	John Barnes	5
Maurice Johnston	George Reilly	23
Maurice Johnston	Jimmy Gilligan	6
Ian Richardson	George Reilly	1
Maurice Johnston	Worrell Sterling	1

dropped into the relegation zone for the first time. Watford's defence was porous, to say the least. They'd thrown away the lead against Leicester, drawing 3-3 and they were thrashed 3-0 at Sunderland before the United defeat.

The next week, there was a Uefa Cup tie against Sparta Prague. Johnston and Reilly had been signed after the registration deadline for European competition so were not in the squad.

They had a whole week to train together. They worked hour after hour with the reserve team, perfecting their runs and learning each other's moves.

On the Saturday, Watford lost 2-1 at home to Luton. It was the nadir and the supporters were getting nervous. But there were signs that the two Scottish forwards were dovetailing nicely.

Taylor revealed a fan had written to him, urging him to drop the attacking 4-2-4 formation, arguing in favour of 4-3-3, saying that an extra midfielder would make the team less vulnerable.

No chance, said Taylor. He was going to stick to his guns. He told the *Watford Observer* the Hornets would not go down. 'I know the league table does not make pleasant reading,' he said. 'We are still relatively new to Division One. We were never going to continue in the same way as last season. Our job is to consolidate and establish ourselves as a First Division club. We will not go down.'

Wolves were also in dire straits. They had managed just one win, which came the previous week at the home of their fierce rivals, West Brom.

This was early December, a bit soon to start talking about relegation six-pointers, but defeat would have been a severe blow to Watford. The gaps above them were starting to open.

Johnston, in only his third match for the club, made himself an instant hero. He scored his first after 13 minutes and eight minutes later he had a hat-trick.

The Wolves defence simply couldn't handle the physical threat of Reilly, the movement of Johnston or the way the wingers and midfielders played the ball in behind them.

Sherwood made a great save when it was 3-0 to steady the ship when Wolves were threatening a revival. Given Watford's defensive woes, this was a more significant stop than the score might have indicated. In the second half, Reilly scored twice and a famous, if short-lived, partnership was born.

Wolves chairman Derek Dougan said afterwards: 'That was a travesty. There were never five goals between the teams.' Taylor replied: 'I won't say anything. I don't want to add to Derek's problems. He has enough.'

For Taylor, victory at Molineux – still the club's biggest ever top flight away win – was the turning point he had been so confident would come.

Sherwood, Bardsley, Price, Jackett, Sims, Franklin, Callaghan, Johnston, Reilly (Porter 72), Rostron, Barnes
Manager Graham Taylor
Scorers Johnston 13, 21, 22, Reilly 58, 61
Attendance 11,905

WATFORD............ 2   WEST HAM UNITED 0

FA Cup fourth round, Saturday January 23 1982

Cally's cheeky backheel is the Hammer blow to Brooking and Co

If there is one moment that sums up the brilliance of Nigel Callaghan it would have to be his goal against West Ham. It was a second of quick-thinking genius that sealed another cup upset.

Watford were already 1-0 up when they won a corner at the Vicarage Road end. Keith Pritchett prepared to take the corner from the right with his left foot. Callaghan took up his position on the far post.

Gerry Armstrong headed the ball down and it fell to Callaghan in the six-yard box, with his back to goal. Instinctively, he backheeled it past Hammers goalkeeper Phil Parkes.

It was cheeky, it was delightful and it was proof that for all the growing talk about Watford favouring a formulaic style, they had individuals who could conjure moments of inspiration.

Callaghan wasn't lurking at the far post by accident. Taylor made sure that at set-pieces his players took up positions based on where the ball might end up if it was headed on or cleared. And it's notable that West Ham didn't have anyone on the post defending.

Watford had already knocked out Manchester United. Now they did for West Ham, who had won the FA Cup two years earlier, while still in the Second Division.

This was the Hammers side of Billy Bonds, Alvin Martin, Frank Lampard senior and Trevor Brooking. They were the self-styled academy of football and just the sort of team to prove to Watford that their so-called kick-and-rush game had no place among the elite.

But they had no answer to Watford, either in terms of industry or invention. This was one of the finest displays by Callaghan. He set up the first goal for Armstrong with a carefully-placed header back across goal.

But Callaghan's goal was the one we remember even if it didn't get the credit it deserved. Imagine the hullabaloo if Brooking had scored one like it.

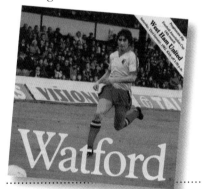

Sherwood, Rice, Pritchett, Blissett, Terry, Bolton, Callaghan, Armstrong, Jenkins (Rostron 77), Lohman, Barnes
Manager Graham Taylor
Scorers Armstrong 47, Callaghan 74.
Attendance 27,004

Division One, Saturday April 16 1994

Tommy Mooney thinks he knows the reason for his popularity. 'The fans took to me because I played the game like they would if they had the chance to pull on the shirt,' he says.

In the spring of 1994, when the 22-year-old first arrived on loan, Watford had a relegation battle on their hands. Mooney was one of a number of men Glenn Roeder brought in just before transfer deadline day in a bid to avoid the drop.

Mooney came from Southend on loan while Dennis Bailey, who was a product of Watford's youth system in the Eighties, came from QPR.

Although both players were short-term measures, Roeder hoped to sign one on a permanent basis in the summer. Early on, the smart money was on that man being Bailey, who had scored from the bench in three consecutive matches. He was a poacher, and with Paul Furlong certain to leave, the more potent replacement.

But Mooney had qualities that few players possessed. He was a fighter. The fans did identify with him because he was their representative on the pitch. He chased lost causes, he clenched his fists, he bulldozed through opposition defences. And over the next seven years, he was to establish himself as one of Vicarage Road's modern heroes. However, the love affair between player and supporters almost didn't happen.

Roeder first noticed Mooney when he was player-manager at Gillingham. 'I was 37 or 38 and I played six games for them because we were so short,' says Roeder. 'I found it very tough but I could use my experience and my know-how to get out of trouble. I was always a good reader of the game and I found most strikers in the bottom division were quite predictable.

'We played Scarborough and I was very impressed with Mooney. He played very well but he wasn't just strong, he did things that players in the Third Division didn't usually do. He was a cut above that division anyway.'

At first, Roeder missed out because

'It took all my willpower not to go and celebrate in Peter Taylor's face'

Mooney joined Southend for £100,000, which was more than Watford would have paid. Things went sour at Roots Hall after Barry Fry left. Peter Taylor arrived and he didn't rate Mooney.

'It was pretty clear that Peter wanted to sell me and get someone else in even though I had scored a few goals for them,' says Mooney. 'Around Christmas time a couple of clubs came in for me, looking to take me on loan. One was Watford, the other was Middlesbrough, my home town club. Now, I would have jumped at a move to Middlesbrough because I had no allegiance to Watford

Walking in a Mooney wonderland. The birth of a terrace hero

at that time. Peter stopped me from going but he still didn't put me in the team.'

As transfer deadline day drew near, Mooney could see his season fizzling out. 'Glenn was ringing me to say he was still interested but Peter wouldn't let me go so I went into the manager's office and had to threaten him. I said: "Look, I am going to kick off here if I don't go somewhere I can play football. It's going to spoil everything. You're going to ruin my career, I've already lost six months."'

Taylor relented and Mooney joined Watford on loan, until the end of the season. His first match was a 2-0 defeat at Sunderland, dropping the Hornets to 23rd place in the table. Relegation was looking increasingly likely.

'That trip to Sunderland was the best way for me to start, even though we lost the game,' says Mooney. 'It was an overnight trip so I had a couple of days to get to know the lads.'

Although it was a difficult first month, Mooney felt things were slowly improving. But there was one date looming on the fixture list and Mooney wanted to be a part of it.

'Nowadays, players who are on loan cannot play against their parent club,' says Roeder. 'But then, you could do it if you got permission.'

Mooney remembers Taylor trying to stop him playing against them but Roeder says it was not an issue. 'Peter is

a very fair and honest man. He wouldn't have been vindictive about it.'

Mooney was in no doubt. 'There was nothing written in the contract, so there was no way they were going to stop me playing.'

With Furlong suspended, the two loanees played up front together. Watford had the dream start, with Bailey scoring after 44 seconds.

Twelve minutes later, the inevitable happened. Mooney scored. 'I had been doing quite well but I hadn't managed to get a goal,' he says. 'As a forward, the longer you go without scoring, the more pressure you feel. To get one against my own club was special.

'It took all my willpower not to run over to the bench and celebrate right in Peter Taylor's face. I'd promised my dad I wouldn't do it. He said it would look more gentlemanly.'

This was the day a terrace chant was born. From now on, we'd always be walking in a Mooney wonderland.

Two minutes later, Colin Foster scored the third and all the anxiety ebbed away.

They weren't safe yet but for the first time during an impossibly tense run-in, people began to believe that Watford were going to get out of trouble.

Digweed, Lavin, Drysdale, Foster, Millen, Dublin, Mooney (Bazeley 85), Hessenthaler, Bailey, Porter, Johnson
Manager Glenn Roeder
Scorers Bailey 44sec, Mooney 12, Foster 14
Attendance 8,554

WANTED
New manager to cut the wage bill by £7million.
Transfer budget: £0
Oh, and keep us up

Ray Lewington was under no illusions about the task he was taking on. He knew the club's finances were in a terrible state.

The Gianluca Vialli experiment had failed spectacularly. Watford's board had gambled on a return to the Premiership, where they would be rewarded handsomely for their vision and courage.

They had put all their chips on red and the roulette wheel came up black.

The collapse of ITV Digital, the broadcaster that appeared to have done its sums on the back of a beer mat, only made matters worse.

ITV Digital had signed a deal with the Football League worth £315million. With the company in administration, Watford's bank wanted its money back.

Lewington had come to Watford as Vialli's reserve team manager, a curious job because the Italian did not like his first-team players turning out for the second eleven.

'That's what happens abroad,' says Lewington. 'These days it's quite common. It allows young players to come through but it does mean you have first team players who are not playing a lot of football.'

Watford knew they had to get Vialli out. They could no longer afford him, his players or the overnight stays at Sopwell House, the hotel in St Albans, before home matches.

Vialli was not prepared to jump, he was waiting to be pushed. 'I thought they'd give the job to Ray Wilkins,' says Lewington. 'But in the end they sacked Ray as a tactic to get Luca out. It didn't work so they had to sack Vialli anyway.'

Lewington was set to go back as reserve team manager when he got a call from Graham Simpson, the chairman, who asked him if he was interested in applying. 'I said I would if I had a chance. Graham told me I had some support on the board. I never did apply, I just went for an interview, then a second interview, then a third.'

Paul Robinson scored the fifth in a delightfully unexpected televised win over Coventry.

During the interview process the full extent of Watford's woes were explained to Lewington.

'They told me a big part of the job would be to reduce the wage bill. We had to cut it from £10.7million to under three million and we had to do it quickly, within 18 months.

'The bank was demanding it and there were no other options. I was told there wouldn't be any money for players. We'd be getting rid of people as quickly as possible, even if it meant selling for less than they were worth. We just had to get them off the books. And we wouldn't be paying agents a penny.

'There were a lot of applicants. It was an attractive job, although I don't know how much the others were told about the financial situation. In the end it went down to a choice between me and Peter Taylor.'

Many of the high earners were let go, including Espen Baardsen, Patrick Blondeau, Stephen Hughes, Ramon Vega, Pierre Issa and Paul Okon. Filippo Galli, the 39-year-old central defender from Italy was one of the few successes of the Vialli season but he was too old and too costly.

However, it left Watford without any experienced centre halves.

'We converted Marcus Gayle from a forward to a defender because I felt he could read the game very well,' says Lewington. 'He needed someone who was experienced alongside him, so I managed to get Sean Dyche on a free transfer from Millwall. I wanted Sean for his personality as much as anything. He is the sort of person who will never, ever give up. He wasn't the quickest but I always looked at what a player could give you, rather than what he doesn't give you.

'In the cold light of day, when I looked at it, we had a decent team. There was Paul Robinson, Stephen Glass, Micah Hyde and Allan Nielsen, Heidar Helguson and Tommy Smith. My concern was that we didn't have strength in depth. A few injuries would hurt us so I felt we needed a good start.'

Things changed overnight. The training schedules would no longer be fitted around the whims of foreign players who wanted to jet home for a few days.

Only six months earlier, the club had managed to buy Vicarage Road, now they had to sell it again.

'There were times when it looked like we'd lose the training ground and the academy and they fought very hard to keep hold of them,' says Lewington. 'But every aspect of how the club operated was looked at from a financial point of view.'

Lewington had been a manager at Fulham and Brentford before, as well as a caretaker at Crystal Palace, but he had not kidded himself that he was the fans' choice. 'Oliver Phillips told me I got one per cent in a poll done by the *Watford Observer*,' he says. 'So it's nice to know my family were voting for me.

'The chairman made it clear that on the pitch the most important thing was to keep us up. Relegation would have been absolutely disastrous.'

In adversity, the club regained its soul. Vialli had replaced hard-working, reliable players with people who were on huge wages.

'If we are honest about it, he didn't know much about the division or the teams we'd be playing,' says goalkeeper Alec Chamberlain. 'That showed by some of the signings he made. Some

of them were on unbelievable contracts and that caused a bit of bad feeling in the dressing room. You look back now and you have to say, what were they thinking?

'I am led to believe the club spent all the ITV Digital money in one go. It was reckless and it put the whole club in jeopardy.

'Some of the players were good but there were those who weren't pulling their weight, in games or training.'

Paul Robinson, a player who would roll his sleeves up and fight with his last ounce of strength, was exasperated. 'These players had been at top clubs. They'd played for their countries but they didn't want to go to tough grounds and battle for a result. It can be hard to get motivated if you're used to being at

ALL CHANGE

A year is an eternity in football. The glitz and glamour of the Vialli era distracted people from the underlying truth that he had created a mostly bad football team.

The line up for the Italian's first match in charge, at Manchester City on August 11 2001 was: Espen Baardsen, Patrick Blondeau, Paul Robinson, Ramon Vega, Filippo Galli, Allan Nielsen, Micah Hyde, Paolo Vernazza, Stephen Hughes, Marcus Gayle, Tommy Smith.

Twelve months on, half of them had gone. Ray Lewington's first selection, at Leicester City on August 10, 2002, was: Alec Chamberlain, Neil Cox, Sean Dyche, Marcus Gayle, Lloyd Doyley, Paul Robinson, Allan Nielsen, Jamie Hand, Micah Hyde, Dominic Foley, Tommy Smith.

the top but in that division you have to battle for every point. They were happy to take the money, though.'

Watford lost their opening game of the season, at Leicester City's brand new Walkers Stadium. They then drew 0-0 with Millwall and beat Wimbledon 3-2 before losing 3-0 at Portsmouth.

'People inside the club were a bit edgy about how the season might pan out,' says Lewington. 'We had a lot going on behind the scenes but, as much as possible, I wanted the players to be positive.'

Lewington managed to persuade Sir Alex Ferguson to lend him Danny Webber, who had spent a month on loan at the end of Vialli's season.

The Coventry game was live on Sky and the Hornets put on a show for the cameras. Webber's movement was exemplary. He caused problems for Calum Davenport and Steve Walsh and forced the Sky Blues player-manager, Gary McAllister, to change his formation to protect his hapless defenders.

If the 3-0 surrender at Fratton Park just two days earlier had deflated the fans, it certainly hadn't done the team any lasting damage.

Glass opened the scoring after just five minutes. Watford then had a number of great chances before they did manage to extend their advantage.

Smith and Webber made it 3-0 before half-time. Then Nielsen and Robinson got on the mark in the second half to make it five with 19 minutes still remaining.

Robinson's goal came at the end of a slick move that demonstrated just how much Watford had dominated. The full back linked up with Smith, continued his run into the box and lashed a shot home with his left foot.

'I didn't score many so it was great to get forward,' he says. 'People were expecting us to struggle but that day we played really well. Who knows what might have happened if there hadn't been all the problems off the pitch?'

Coventry had been thrashed but they did manage to score two late goals to reduce their embarrassment. Gary McSheffrey got the first and John Eustace, who would later become very familiar to the Watford crowd, got the second in injury time.

'It was spoilt a bit by the two late goals because 5-0 looks so much better than 5-2,' says Lewington. 'It was real relief to play so well and be rewarded for it, especially with the TV cameras there. As a manager you never make promises you can't keep, you just do your best, but I do remember seeing Graham Simpson afterwards. Everyone was nervous but that result reassured people a bit.'

Lewington saw Simpson in the corridor, winked, smiled and said calmly: 'Don't worry, we'll be alright.'

Chamberlain, Cox, Dyche, Gayle, Ardley, Hyde, Nielsen, Glass, Robinson, Smith, Webber
Manager Ray Lewington
Scorer Glass 5, Smith 34, Webber 40, Nielsen 63, Robinson 71
Coventry scorers McSheffrey 86, Eustace 90
Attendance 11,136

Division One, Saturday April 30 1994

Captain fantastic plays his get out of jail free card

Going into their final home game of the season, Watford knew they had to win. Defeat or a draw would take their fate out of their own hands. And they didn't want to travel to Selhurst Park on the last day depending on results elsewhere.

At one stage they had looked dead and buried but a late revival had given them a chance.

One of the three relegation places had already been taken. Peterborough were down but six clubs were still in grave danger.

Watford thought three points from their final two games might be enough. Crystal Palace, their final opponents, were already up, but they still didn't want to leave it to the last minute.

There had been some funny results of late. Oxford won at Sunderland in midweek when most people had banked on them losing. West Brom also had a game in hand. It was incredibly tight.

Watford's visitors were Portsmouth, who were nice and cosy in mid-table.

'We were on a good run,' says Andy Hessenthaler, the team's captain. 'We were very fortunate that the players Glenn Roeder brought in settled quickly and made a difference.'

Pompey may have had little to play for but they weren't in any mood to roll over. They went very close early on before Hessenthaler scored. Jason Drysdale hit a ball down the left channel and Hessenthaler timed his run perfectly to spring the offside trap.

After a quick glance over at the linesman, he steadied himself and hit a curling shot past Alan Knight.

Late on, Hessenthaler was injured in a collision and had to be stretchered off. 'It was very tense those last few minutes because we knew an equaliser would undo all that hard work and put us in a very difficult position again,' he says.

Watford did hold on and then there was the wait for other results. Oxford lost at Derby and Birmingham could only draw at Bolton.

Barring a miracle, Watford were safe. It would take a heavy defeat at Palace and a cricket score for Birmingham to send them down now. Vicarage Road could breathe a sigh of relief.

Digweed, Lavin, Drysdale, Dublin, Millen, Foster, Hessenthaler (Ramage 80), Johnson, Furlong, Porter, Mooney (Bailey 61)
Manager Glenn Roeder
Scorer Hessenthaler 18
Attendance 10,141

WATFORD............ 2 HUDDERSFIELD TOWN...... 0

Division Four, Saturday April 16 1977

It isn't often that a manager is sacked after seeing his team win 2-0 with nine men but, in truth, the Watford board had made up their mind about Mike Keen long before.

Keen knew his job depended on Watford winning promotion from the Fourth Division. And he knew that a bizarre run of matches over Easter had probably done for him.

Watford spurned penalties, gave away leads and ended up with just one point from their games against Brentford, Stockport and Aldershot.

Now they were ninth in the table and although there were still seven games to go, the writing was on the wall.

Keen's final game was an extraordinary win over Huddersfield Town. An eccentric display of refereeing meant Watford had two players sent off. First to be shown the red card was Tony Geidmintis, who retaliated after one of a number of bad challenges the referee appeared to miss. Later on Alan Mayes joined him for an early bath and Keen's tenure looked to be over.

Keen was so enraged by the referee's display he considered asking the chairman's permission to take his team off the pitch. But Keen didn't want to give up. He may not have been a successful or a lucky Watford manager but he was not a quitter.

The Vicarage Road crowd rose to the occasion. For once they weren't chanting 'Keen out', which had become something of a terrace anthem as the season wore on. Instead, they roared their nine men to an unlikely victory. Keith Mercer scored twice in the final 19 minutes as Watford showed the sort of fighting spirit Keen could have done with more often. The previous week the players had asked for a meeting with Elton John to plead the case for giving Keen more time. Now they rallied for their manager but it was too late.

On the Monday morning, the board gave Keen the news he had been braced for. He took it well and his final column in the *Watford Observer* was a dignified exit from a man who was aware of his shortcomings but always tried his best.

With Elton's money at their disposal, Watford knew they could take their time selecting a new manager and let coach John Collins take the team for the final games of the season.

The list of candidates was lengthy. As soon as he heard the news, Ken Furphy phoned from his holiday in Barbados to say he was interested. Ron Atkinson, who was leading Cambridge United to the Fourth Division championship, was another name that was suggested.

But as we now know, the job went to a chap at Lincoln City. Graham something. And that everything was about to change.

Sherwood, Geidmintis, Pritchett, Bond, Garner, Walley, Downes, Coffill, Mercer, Horsfield, Mayes
Manager Mike Keen
Scorer Keith Mercer 2
Attendance 6,181

NEWCASTLE UNITED......0 WATFORD............1

Division Two, Saturday August 29 1981

It's time to move on as Super Cally goes ballistic

On the eve of the season, their third since promotion, Graham Taylor said: 'There is this atmosphere, this air among the Watford playing staff that we have established ourselves as a Division Two club in every way and it is time we were moving on.'

The fixture list couldn't have handed the Hornets a much tougher opening game than a trip to St James's Park.

Newcastle United were one of the so-called 'sleeping giants' playing below their natural level.

Watford rode their luck at times and it took a moment of brilliance from Nigel Callaghan to break the deadlock. But they got their promotion challenge off to a flying start, even if the next two games, a defeat at home to Grimsby and a draw against Oldham, reminded them that it was going to be a long haul.

Newcastle's manager Arthur Cox, who later tried to sign Callaghan, called his goal 'one in a million'. The strike, although witnessed by only a small number of travelling fans, was voted goal of the season.

Callaghan volleyed home from 25 yards, connecting sweetly with a lofted crossfield pass from Gerry Armstrong.

Luther Blissett had been kicked and hacked repeatedly and, towards the end, his patience snapped and he lashed out.

Kenny Wharton lunged at him three times in quick succession, trying to cut him down before David Barton finally got him.

The referee blew his whistle to give Watford a free-kick but it was too late. Blissett had already reacted, kicking Barton. He was sent off.

Blissett had to sit in the dressing room hoping his team-mates would hold out. He knew he'd bear the brunt of the manager's frustration if Watford surrendered the points because they had been reduced to ten men.

Newcastle piled on the pressure but couldn't get the equaliser. Watford held on for a terrific opening day victory. Blissett was spared the hairdryer treatment and accepted his £50 fine.

After the match, Callaghan was heading to the team coach for the journey home when a big Newcastle fan stopped him.

'I thought he was going to hit me,' says Callaghan. 'But he gave me his programme and asked me to sign it.'

Callaghan took the programme and the man said, in a strong Geordie accent: 'Just sign it flukey basstid.'

Sherwood, Rice, Henderson, Taylor, Sims, Bolton, Callaghan, Blissett, Armstrong, Jackett, Poskett
Manager Graham Taylor
Scorer Callaghan 25
Attendance 19,376

SOUTHAMPTON.......0 WATFORD....................3

The Championship, October 18 2008

It was somehow fitting that this bizarre match at the St Mary's Stadium turned out to be the last Watford victory Aidy Boothroyd presided over.

Of all Boothroyd's ugly but glorious triumphs, this was one of the most eventful.

Richard Lee saved two penalties, the first in the second minute, and the Hornets put the game beyond doubt before half-time.

The first spot kick was awarded after David McGoldrick went down as Lee and Darren Ward sandwiched him.

Lee only had to fall to his left to stop McGoldrick's feeble penalty kick.

Eight mintues later, Tamas Priskin put the visitors ahead, firing home from Jon Harley's cross.

Incredibly, the referee gave Saints another penalty when Adrian Mariappa was ruled to have fouled in the box. This time Paul Wotton took the kick and Lee pulled off a magnificent save.

John Eustace and Priskin scored to stun the hosts but despite this fine win, time was running out for Boothroyd. A fortnight and three defeats later, his fiery three-year reign was over.

Lee, Mariappa (Doyley 89), Ward, Bromby, Sadler, Smith, Eustace, Williamson, Harley, Hoskins (O'Toole 81), Priskin (Henderson 81)
Manager Aidy Boothroyd
Scorer Priskin 10, 40, Eustace 30
Attendance 17,454

A HALF-CENTURY OF WATFORD MANAGERS

	In	From	Out	To	P	W	D	L	Win %
Ron Burgess	Feb 59	coach	May 63	sacked	200	80	45	75	40
Bill McGarry	July 63	Bournemouth	Oct 64	resigned	57	26	17	14	45.61
Ken Furphy	Nov 64	Workington	Jul 71	Blackburn	295	115	79	101	38.98
George Kirby	Aug 71	Halifax	May 73	sacked	88	17	26	45	19.32
Mike Keen	Jun 73	player	Apr 77	sacked	178	67	48	63	37.64
Graham Taylor	Jun 77	Lincoln	May 87	Aston Villa	428	191	105	132	44.63
Dave Bassett	May 87	Wimbledon	Jan 88	sacked	23	4	6	13	17.39
Steve Harrison	Jan 88	Villa coach	Mar 90	resigned	80	36	29	35	45
Colin Lee	Mar 90	Brentford	Nov 90	sacked	28	5	9	14	17.86
Steve Perryman	Nov 90	Brentford	Jul 93	Spurs	121	42	35	44	34.71
Glenn Roeder	Jul 93	Gillingham	Feb 96	sacked	120	39	32	49	32.50
Graham Taylor	Feb 96		Jun 96		18	5	8	5	27.78
Kenny Jackett	Jun 96	coach	Jun 97	coach	46	16	19	11	34.78
Graham Taylor	Jun 97		May 01	retired	176	71	45	60	40.34
Gianluca Vialli	May 01		Jun 02	sacked	46	16	11	19	34.78
Ray Lewington	Jun 02	coach	Mar 05	sacked	131	42	37	52	32.06
Aidy Boothroyd	Mar 05	coach at Leeds	Nov 08	sacked	176	65	51	60	36.93
Malky Mackay	*Nov 08*	*coach*	*Nov 08*	*coach*	*4*	*2*	*0*	*2*	*50*
Brendan Rodgers	Nov 08		Jun 09	Reading	31	13	6	12	41.94
Malky Mackay	Jun 09	coach	Jun 11	Cardiff	99	33	25	41	33.33

Notes: Steve Perryman joined Tottenham as assistant manager in 1993. When Graham Taylor returned in February 1996, he was appointed general manager and worked with Kenny Jackett and Luther Blissett

CRYSTAL PALACE .... 0 WATFORD 2

Division One, Sunday May 8 1994

Uninvited guests gatecrash the Palace and spoil their party

This was supposed to be Crystal Palace's day. The Eagles had already won the title and were on their way to the Premier League.

The Palace players were presented with the trophy and medals before the kick-off. It was also the last time the old Holmesdale Road terrace would look out on a Palace match before it was replaced by a new stand, so there was a carnival atmosphere in this often surly part of south London.

Their fans sang 'We'll never play you again,' although that, sadly, didn't turn out to be the case.

Tommy Mooney, who had already won a place in Watford's hearts with his commitment and determination, was hoping he'd done enough to secure a permanent move in the summer.

It was no longer just a case of wanting to leave Southend, he was now desperate to join Watford. He wanted one more memorable performance to convince Glenn Roeder to sign him.

'I was playing up front with Paul Furlong and I was really up for the game,' he says.

'It's a horrible ground. I hated going there, apart from on that day.'

As far as Palace were concerned, Watford were not the ideal party guests. They did the equivalent of guzzling all the champagne before knocking over a tray of vol-au-vents. The match was live on television and the hosts were being shown up.

Andy Hessenthaler scored the first and Mooney bundled in the second near the end.

'A few days after the match Glenn took us to Jack Petchey's place in Albufeira as a bit of a well done for how we'd done at the end of the season,' says Mooney. 'I couldn't really relax because I was on the phone to Peter Taylor, my manager at Southend, telling him I wanted this move to happen.

'I had two years to run on my contract, which I wanted paying up, or at least partly paying up. But Southend knew what I was going to get at Watford and they were refusing to pay.

'The Watford fans think it was just a case of Glenn signing me, it wasn't. That was a very stressful summer and it wasn't sorted out until two days before pre-season. I had to walk away and forfeit every penny of my contract so I could join Watford. That's not something many footballers would do.'

Digweed, Lavin, Drysdale, Dublin, Millen, Foster, Hessenthaler, Johnson (Ramage 45), Furlong, Porter, Mooney
Manager Glenn Roeder
Scorers Hessenthaler 59, Mooney 87
Attendance 28,749

Worthington Cup third round, October 9 2001

It was the glimmers of hope like this that made Gianluca Vialli's ill-fated season as Watford manager so much harder to take.

From the start, the Italian looked poorly suited to the rough and tumble of the second tier.

The cashmere sweater and fat tie knot looked out of place in a division that's always been more suited to hobnail boots and workman's overalls.

But there were flashes that suggested the money hadn't been entirely wasted. A thumping cup win over Bradford, who were adjusting to life in the First Division after outlasting the Hornets in the Premiership, was one of those rare nights.

After a run of five league games without a win, many Watford fans were urging patience. Don't panic, they said,

the team just needs time to gel. This was one of the fleeting occasions that they looked like a team rather than a cut-and-shut motor. Even Ramon Vega scored.

Unfortunately, it did not signal an upturn in fortunes. Vialli failed to settle on a team and his men often appeared to over-complicate things.

But this was a night that offered a glimpse of what might have been. Watford played with such freedom and at times the passing and movement looked effortless.

It was also the only time Watford scored four in a match while Vialli was in charge.

Baardsen, Blondeau, Vega, Cox, Robinson, Noble, Hyde, Hughes, Glass, Noel-Williams, Smith
Manager Gianluca Vialli
Scorers Hyde 32, Noel-Williams 45, 67, Vega 50
Bradford scorer Ward 76 pen
Attendance 8,613

Vialli's hits...

Gianluca Vialli's win-or-bust bid to return Watford to the Premiership was costly and unsuccessful but it wasn't all bad. Here are the players who didn't flop.

Filippo Galli
Although 38 when he arrived, the Italian showed why he'd played 200 games for Milan. Oozed class and composure. A shame he wasn't ten years younger.

Marcus Gayle
Cost £900,000 from Glasgow Rangers. Signed as a striker but scored only seven goals. Was later successfully converted to centre-half by Ray Lewington.

Stephen Glass
Wide midfielder with a nice range of passes. Was a free from Newcastle. Stayed another year but joined Hibernian in the next round of cost-cutting.

Wayne Brown
Centre-half came on loan from Ipswich, suggesting Vialli had finally worked out what Division One was about. Joined on a permanent basis the following season.

Gavin Mahon
Played for Lewington at Brentford. Cost £150,000 from Brentford and starred in the play-off success four years later.

Jermaine Pennant
Did well enough on loan from Arsenal. Returned the following season.

Danny Webber
Another loanee who did well enough to earn another visit under Lewington. Later joined from Manchester United on a permanent basis and had a good scoring record.

See match number 65 for Vialli's misses

Fairbrother tries to fill the Big Cliff-shaped hole in Watford's attack

Cliff Holton was the first hero to dominate Vicarage Road by force of his personality.

He drew crowds and gasps in equal measure. He was physically imposing and he led from the front. Even those who did not see him play can sense his aura in a simple black and white photo. Hair immaculately Brylcreemed. Jawline square and strong like Desperate Dan from the comics. Chest jutting out with pride and defiance.

Those who knew him vouch for his character. Holton was a gentleman and a man of his word but he preferred to be a doer of deeds rather than a talker.

As Watford banished the Blues and ushered in a golden era, Holton shone more brightly than their new shirts.

As a goalscoring forward he could do things that made him seem like a real life Roy of the Rovers. When he fired that heavy leather ball at goal he did so with such power. If Holton smacked the ball, it stayed smacked.

When Neil McBain signed Holton in October 1958, it was a real coup, certainly the most extraordinary signing the club had ever made.

Holton had been a league champion. He scored 19 goals as Arsenal won the title in 1953. Now he was dropping down to the Fourth Division, partly so he could develop some business interests that would earn him a living when he finished playing.

Watford's prospects were not so bright. They missed the cut when the Football League expanded in summer 1958 and so started the next season in the Fourth Division. The promised land of Division Two seemed further away than ever.

Holton was not an instant hit. His first season was steady, with a goal every three games and McBain was sacked. It wasn't until new manager Ron Burgess signed Dennis Uphill from Mansfield Town that Holton flourished.

Holton scored 42 league goals as Watford won the Fourth Division title in 1960. He got another 32 in the Third Division and although Watford missed out on a second successive promotion, the progress was unmistakable. And then, a month into the 1961-62 season, he was gone. Just like that.

On Wednesday, September 6 the Watford board committed what most of their supporters thought was high treason. They sold Holton.

Perhaps if he had moved to a club in the First or Second Division the fans would have understood. But they didn't. They flogged him to Northampton Town for just £7,000. Even for a 31-year-old it was a rock bottom price.

The deal was done at a hotel in Kenton, north London. After signing the contract, Holton travelled with the Northampton manager, Dave Bowen, to Selhurst Park. Just three hours after signing for the Cobblers, he scored a hat-trick for his new team in a 4-1 win.

The first many Watford supporters knew was when they opened their newspaper the following morning and saw that Holton had scored three for someone else. It was like discovering the wife had run off with the milkman.

News didn't travel as quickly in those days. Even the radio didn't report much football transfer news. It was a huge shock and the reaction was furious.

Someone left a note on the gate at Vicarage Road. It read: 'Poor old Cliff. Fired by the Gunners, Stung by the Hornets and Caught by the Cobblers.'

Supporters writing to the *Watford Observer* were livid. 'The supporters have been sold up the river,' said one.

'It's the worst thing the board has ever done,' said another. Holton refused to elaborate on the transfer but his wife told the press he didn't want to leave. 'Perhaps it's because he didn't play for Tottenham,' she said, referring to the fact Burgess had played for Spurs.

The chairman, Jim Bonser, was accused of deliberately sabotaging the team's chances of winning promotion.

Holton had picked up an injury in his final game for Watford, a 3-3 draw against Lincoln. Afterwards Burgess had told him to report to the club on Monday morning for treatment. Holton didn't turn up, later claiming he had not heard the manager's instructions.

There were rumbles that Watford were irritated that Holton's business interests were getting in the way of his football. He was a part-timer, whereas most of the rest of the squad were by now full-time.

Bonser said that Northampton had made an approach for Holton and that when he'd put it to the board, they had been unanimous in agreement.

'I was the one who decided to go,' said Holton. 'I went after having a chat with Mr Burgess and Mr Bonser. I realised that as far as I was concerned there was a bee in their bonnets. I felt they wanted me out.'

Why does the story of Cliff Holton dominate a match he didn't even play in? Simply because the consequences of his departure were still reverberating nearly three weeks later. The letters continued to arrive at the club and the local paper. Disappointed supporters threatened never to set foot inside Vicarage Road again.

There was talk of boycotting the next home match and the crowd of 10,339 for Swindon's visit was 5,000 down on the previous gate.

Like Watford, Queens Park Rangers were one of the teams fancied to win promotion. QPR were also their closest rivals in the division and almost always got the better of the exchanges. Watford had not beaten QPR at home since 1938.

The anger was still simmering and a bumper crowd had come to see if Watford could beat their rivals. If they couldn't, they were going to take it out on Jim Bonser.

After Holton was injured against Lincoln, Tommy Williams and Ron Crisp deputised. Both did well. Crisp scored twice in a 4-3 defeat at Peterborough, then Williams got a hat-trick of headers in a 4-3 win at Torquay.

But they were only temporary replacements. Now there was a giant, Holton-sized gap in the forward line.

Step forward John Fairbrother, who had been as prolific for the reserves as Holton was for the first team. The 20-year-old got 40 goals during his first season for the second string and he'd done pretty well when given a chance in Division Three the previous season.

Coming into the team as Holton's direct replacement was another matter.

Things didn't go well at the start. Rangers scored after just 12 minutes when John McClelland, no relation to the Northern Irish defender who played for Watford in the Eighties, slammed home from close range.

A moment of hesitation from Bobby Bell gifted QPR their second. Jim Towers seized the chance, while the Vicarage Road crowd seethed.

With half an hour to go, the crowd made their feelings clear. They began the slow handclap. These were more genteel times but all directors feared the slow handclap, teeming with contempt. It was far more savage then than an inarticulate mouthful of abuse is today.

And it went on. Clap-clap-clap. It wasn't just directed at the team's inept display but at Bonser and Burgess for selling their hero.

The final 20 minutes were superb. John Ryder got the first from a Freddie Bunce cross. Then Fairbrother swivelled on a pass from Peter Walker to smash the equaliser into the roof of the net.

With eight minutes left, Fairbrother headed the winner. The crowd cheered him as if he'd been their hero for years. It helped them forget Cliff, for that afternoon, at least. Cliff who?

In the end, though, selling Holton, or more to the point, failing to replace him, cost Burgess his job.

Underwood, Bell, Nicholas, Ryden, McNeice, Porter, Williams, Walker, Fairbrother, Stokes, Bunce
Manager Ron Burgess
Scorers Ryden 71, Fairbrother 76, 82
QPR scorers McClelland 12, Towers 35
Attendance 15,555

NOTTS COUNTY .... 3 WATFORD 5

Division One, Saturday February 11 1984

When Trevor Christie scored Notts County's second goal after nine minutes, it looked like Watford's superb revival had been stopped in its tracks.

A team that had looked relegation favourites up until December had hit its stride and was now playing with just as much style as the one that had finished as runners-up the previous season.

Watford had a new 'front four' to strike fear into the hearts of any defence even if they were also a trifle profligate at the back.

Rachid Harkouk caught them cold in the fourth minute and they still hadn't regained their composure when Christie scored the second.

The Magpies were in serious trouble, nine points adrift of safety and were playing with the urgency of a team that feared for its lives.

A stroke of good fortune quickly got Watford back into the match.

A lofted free-kick was taken by David Bardsley. George Reilly flicked it on and Kenny Jackett ran in behind the County defence to fire a shot against goalkeeper Jim McDonough. The ball rebounded off David Hunt and went into the net.

There was nothing lucky about the equaliser. Wilf Rostron's centre was knocked down by Les Taylor and Nigel Callaghan lashed it home with his left foot from the corner of the six-yard box. It was a sensational strike but he managed to hit an even better one two minutes before half-time. Watford flooded forward and spread the ball wide to Callaghan. From further out and from a tighter angle this time, Callaghan unleashed a right-foot shot that ended up in the same corner of McDonough's net as his first.

The second strike won the goal of the month competition on the BBC's *Match of the Day* but both were worthy contenders.

Reilly, who dominated County's big centre half Brian Kilcline, made it 4-2 at the start of the second half., following up after Barnes had hit the bar with a header.

As County's manager, Larry Lloyd said of Reilly: 'He's ungainly and awkward but he's very effective.' Reilly's confidence had finally grown to match his towering stature.

After a difficult start to the season, this was Reilly's best display in a Watford shirt. So much more than a target man, Reilly was the focal point of almost every Hornets attack.

County pulled one back but the visitors wrapped it up late on when Les Taylor burst through the defence and cut the cross back so Maurice Johnston could score with a diving header.

Sherwood, Bardsley, Rostron, Taylor, Terry, Franklin, Callaghan, Johnston, Reilly, Jackett, Barnes (Sterling)
Manager Graham Taylor
Scorers Hunt og 14, Callaghan 28, 43, Reilly 46, Johnston 82
Notts County scorers Harkouk 4, Christie 9, 56
Attendance 8,078

SOUTHEND UNITED......... 0 WATFORD............... 3

Division Two, Tuesday November 4 1997

Once Graham Taylor had decided to get his hands dirty and take the managerial reins again, he knew his reputation for talent-spotting in the lower divisions would go before him.

During a conversation with Gerry Armstrong, he remarked that it was not getting any easier to find good left footed players. In fact, it was getting harder.

Armstrong said there was a lad from Northern Ireland who had a left foot almost as sweet as Liam Brady's.

But he also said that the owner of that left foot, Peter Kennedy, was hardly pulling up trees at Notts County.

Taylor watched him and thought the 23-year-old might fit into his jigsaw. Kennedy cost £130,000, a fair sum for a player who'd only started 20 league matches.

'I was going nowhere at County,' says Kennedy. 'I'd come over from Portadown but it just hadn't worked. I didn't really know why and they didn't seem to know why.

'I wanted a fresh start and if I am honest, I'd have gone anywhere to get one. It could've just as easily been Belgium as Watford.'

Taylor had a specific role in mind for Kennedy as an attacking wing-back who was encouraged to get forward.

He was to become one of the most important figures in the team that went from the Second Division to the Premiership in successive seasons.

'I can't really put my finger on anything specific but things just clicked at Watford,' says Kennedy. 'I suppose the biggest factor was that there was a place for me in the team and Graham was so good at explaining what it was he wanted you to do.'

Watford had got out of the block very fast. Ronnie Rosenthal had starred in a 4-1 win against Blackpool the previous weekend to stretch their lead at the top to eight points.

The Hornets were brimming with confidence when they travelled to Roots Hall to face struggling Southend.

Kennedy scored all three goals. The first was a fantastic shot with his weaker right foot, the second was a free-kick that curled over and around the wall and hit the net with neat precision. For the third he cut inside the defender and hit the shot across him so the keeper had little time to deal with it.

'I hadn't even scored a goal in the league before I joined Watford. Now I was scoring a hat-trick. It's an old cliché, but the team was more important than individual performances. But I look back on that with real pride,' he says. 'I still have the ball at home and I look at it every now and then. To be part of such a good team and to score all three goals... You don't really appreciate at the time how good that is.'

Chamberlain, Gibbs, Kennedy, Page, Millen, Mooney, Noel-Williams (Thomas 67), Palmer, Lee, Johnson, Rosenthal
Manager Graham Taylor
Scorers Kennedy 13, 36, 67
Attendance 4,001

WATFORD............... 6 DERBY COUNTY 1

Division Two, Tuesday January 26 1982

Rams hit for six as Hornets close in on the top flight

Three days after knocking West Ham out of the FA Cup to confirm that Watford could live with the top sides, they handed Derby County the sort of merciless beating they'd been threatening for a while.

Astonishingly, Nigel Callaghan was dropped to the bench, despite his superb backheeled goal against the Hammers. Even more astonishing was the story behind the decision.

Exasperated at the way the young winger chose to conduct himself at times, Graham Taylor asked him to live with him and his family for a couple of weeks. Callaghan did as he was asked but refused to stay any longer.

Taylor wanted to rest Callaghan as he had done some of the other young players but Callaghan perceived it as a punishment.

Watford demolished the Rams, with Gerry Armstrong scoring twice in the opening quarter of an hour.

Luther Blissett added a third before half-time and Ian Bolton piled on the misery early in the second half.

Barnes scored Watford's fifth and Callaghan, on as a sub, got the sixth no sooner had Paul Emson grabbed a slim consolation effort for the Rams.

Early in the second half came a moment that was to prove as pivotal to Watford's future fortunes as any that season. Keith Pritchett, the left-back, got injured and had to go off. He was replaced by Callaghan but the job of filling his position on a more permanent basis was not so easy.

Taylor tried the right-back, Mick Henderson, in the next match at Rotherham, but was not convinced.

Had Pritchett not got injured, it is likely that Watford would never have seen the best of Wilf Rostron, who had failed to impress as either a winger or a striker. Languishing in the reserves, he would almost certainly have been moved on at the end of the season had he not embraced a new role.

Taylor tested him out at left-back in training, then put Rostron in the team against Chelsea. He won the man of the match award and never looked back, becoming one of the team's most reliable performers and taking over the captaincy from Pat Rice.

By now Watford were third in the table and firmly in the promotion hunt. This thumping victory signalled the beginning of the big push. Meanwhile, people were beginning to take notice.

Sherwood, Rice, Pritchett (Callaghan 49), Taylor, Terry, Bolton, Blissett, Armstrong, Jenkins, Lohman, Barnes
Manager Graham Taylor
Scorers Armstrong 3, 14, Blissett 27, Bolton 48, Barnes 50, Callaghan 71
Derby scorer Emson 70
Attendance 12,643

WATFORD.............6 GRIMSBY TOWN 3

Division One, Tuesday April 23 1996

With one foot already stuck in the relegation trapdoor, Watford were still kicking, but only just.

Bottom of the league when they sacked Glenn Roeder in mid-February, the anticipated revival under Graham Taylor, Luther Blissett and Kenny Jackett had not really materialised.

The triumvirate presided over just one win in their first 12 games in charge. The rot had set in too deep. This time there was to be no miracle.

But that didn't stop them throwing caution to the wind. If they were to slip out of the division, they were going to fight until their last breath.

Rock bottom, 11 points adrift of safety with six games to go, it was surely all over. But in the space of four days they beat Port Vale 5-2 and Reading 4-2 at home.

David Connolly and Devon White suddenly started scoring. Connolly got a hat-trick against Vale, White scored twice in each game.

A 0-0 draw at Luton, who were also destined for the drop, slowed the charge a bit but Watford resumed with a gung-ho spirit that echoed happier days.

Although they were in the last-chance saloon and time had been called, Watford refused to give up.

They thrashed Grimsby, racing into a 4-0 lead after 21 minutes.

Craig Ramage, exasperating and infuriating at times, but with a touch of genius few could match, scored in the first 60 seconds. Connolly, the lad from

Bushey Rangers who didn't endear himself to the Watford crowd by the manner of his departure a year later, scored the next two.

Grimsby scored either side of half-time and the nerves were jangling, particularly because Watford were set up to play so offensively.

They had three at the back, with Darren Bazeley and Dominic Ludden encouraged to attack. Robert Page pulled out of the Wales squad in order to play, a decision which reportedly cost him a £5,000 appearance fee.

Connolly was first to complete his hat-trick and Ramage followed suit three minutes later.

With two games to go, safety was now just four points away. It was still a tall order but it was not impossible.

Scoring six meant they were level with Portsmouth on goals scored, giving them even more encouragement,

As Blissett said, 'Someone said to me as we came off that it was like the old days. There was wave after wave of attack and that is what Watford was about. If you keep going forward, keep creating chances, you will at least entertain the supporters.

'All we can do is attack and try to win the games and see if that is enough at the end of the season.'

Miller, Bazeley, Ludden, Page, Palmer, Hessenthaler, Ramage, Porter, Mooney, Connolly, White
Manager Graham Taylor
Scorers Ramage 1, 21, 73, Connolly 13, 19, 70
Grimsby scorers Groves 34, Livingstone 49, Walker 82
Attendance 8,909

Milk Cup fourth round, Tuesday November 20 1984

Wembley on the horizon as bruising West Brom are battered

All of a sudden, Watford could sense a quick return to Wembley. The way they brushed aside an aggressive West Brom team to reach the quarter-finals of the Milk Cup suggested that another trip to the Twin Towers was on the cards.

The league campaign had begun in abysmal style. They had bumped along in the bottom three until November, when the arrival of John McClelland acted like a bung to plug the division's leakiest defence.

And while the league form slowly recovered, the Milk Cup offered a welcome distraction.

They won 4-0 against Leeds at Elland Road in the previous round and then came up against the ghosts of Dirty Leeds in the teeming rain at Vicarage Road.

Managed by ex-Leeds star Johnny Giles, who was assisted by Norman Hunter, Albion displayed all the aggression and ill-discipline of their notorious Elland Road side from the Seventies.

Albion took an early lead and as Watford struck back with a rat-a-tat of goals from George Reilly and Luther Blissett, the visitors resorted to some pretty rough tactics. The likes of Derek Statham, Ali Robertson and Tony Grealish employed every trick in the book but their attempts at intimidation failed.

Les Taylor fired the Hornets further ahead before half-time. By the time Steve Terry got the fourth, West Brom had lost the match and their composure. Watford, wise to their guests' tricks, beat them at their own game.

'We were winding them up something rotten,' says Reilly. 'They had been kicking and elbowing us, so we were giving it back. The thing was, we were in control of the match and that just made them madder. We were passing the ball and saying 'Olé' with every touch.'

At the end, Albion were in no mood to congratulate the victors. 'It all kicked off in the tunnel,' says Reilly. 'When I turned round, everyone had gone in the dressing room and shut the door, leaving me to it. Ali Robertson was about to hit me so I poked him in the eye.'

Watford were drawn at home, to either Sunderland or Tottenham, in the quarter-finals. When Spurs were knocked out, suddenly it seemed destined to be Watford's year but they slipped to defeat on an icy pitch. 'That was a lesson to us never to get ahead of ourselves,' said Graham Taylor.

Coton, Sinnott, Jackett, Taylor, Terry, McClelland, Sterling, Blissett, Reilly, Rostron, Barnes
Manager Graham Taylor
Scorers Reilly 18, Blissett 22, Taylor 34, Terry 63
West Brom scorer Cross 3
Attendance 16,378

WATFORD..........2 WOLVES.....................1

Division One, Tuesday August 30 1994

Taylor's not so happy return

Graham Taylor had been mocked and vilified for his failure to lead England to the 1994 World Cup. The fact that he had at his disposal arguably the worst group of England players in a generation was conveniently overlooked by a tabloid press that thought depicting someone's head as a root vegetable was the height of satire.

But there was still one place in the country where he would be guaranteed a warm welcome, although that's not to say Watford weren't determined to send him and his team home empty-handed.

This was Taylor's first return to Vicarage Road as an opposition manager for a competitive fixture.

'The fact we were up against Graham Taylor's team was a great motivator for us that night,' says Glenn Roeder. 'There were people like Gary Porter and David Holdsworth who had been at the club when Graham was here but everyone wanted to impress someone who had been manager of their country.

'We were all set and then a policeman put his head round the dressing room door and said the game was being delayed for 15 minutes because there had been an accident on the motorway.

'Suddenly, all my preparations were ruined because we didn't have an awful lot left to say. Our work was done and the players were in the zone. I was trying to think of what we could do to kill time.

'One by one, I made everyone in the dressing room tell a joke. I'd read about someone doing it before and it was the only thing I could think of.

'So we went round and they took turns. Some of the jokes were awful, some of them were very funny. As you can imagine almost none of them are printable. Some of the lads were in their element and wanted to do more than one, others were crapping themselves.

'But 15 minutes went just like that and all of a sudden it was time to go out. They were relaxed and laughing and probably in the ideal frame of mind for the game.'

As expected, Taylor was given the warmest of receptions, which brought a tear to the eye. The stadium had changed a fair bit since he'd last sat on the bench but it was difficult for the Watford supporters not to think back to some of the glory nights of yesteryear.

But their allegiance was to the men in yellow shirts, not to Graham Taylor and once the game was underway, there was no room for sentiment.

Besides, Wolves were not many people's cup of tea in the Nineties. They seemed to think having a big stadium meant they had a divine right to a place in the Premiership.

Colin Foster, one of the heroes of

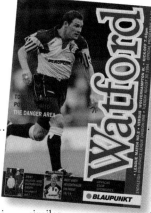

the previous season, gave Watford the lead after just seven minutes.

Roeder treated Foster in a similar way to how Taylor had handled the injury-hit Paul McGrath at Aston Villa.

Foster had been plagued by injuries throughout his career and needed careful management. 'Colin Foster is a great lesson for any manager,' says Roeder. Not all players are the same. 'I wanted to sign Foster from West Ham about six weeks before he eventually joined but I took Kenny Jackett with me to watch their reserves at Bristol City.

'This is not a slight on Kenny but he wasn't impressed. He said he'd seen faster tortoises, which was a fair point.

'Foster then went to Notts County and we went to see him again and he was superb. The lesson was, don't judge experienced players on reserve team football. Very few people manage to motivate themselves for the reserves in the same way.

'Colin was a bit different. He liked to rest a lot at the beginning of the week and train on Thursday and Friday and then play. And when he played he was superb for us.

'He could stop things happening by doing very little. He was always fire-fighting, stopping the little things before the flames got out of control. His anticipation was tremendous. Some of the best defenders think negatively. They think every situation is going to turn out badly in a minute and they are always planning for the worst.'

Watford defended well until five minutes from time, when Neil Emblen headed home from a Paul Birch corner.

Just two minutes later, Richard Johnson unleashed a terrific shot from 25 yards that flew into the net for the Watford winner. It was the type of effort that was to become the Australian's trademark and prompted Watford's fans to shout 'Shoooot' whenever he got the ball on the edge of the box.

Roeder, who reprimanded him for his wayward shooting from way out in the 1-0 defeat at Swindon, now admitted Johnson had found his range.

Taylor avoided the post-match press conference, later saying: 'The England squad had just been announced and John Barnes was in it. I didn't want to be asked about it or get involved.'

The reception from the Watford fans had touched him. 'It was very nice. When the Rookery is finished it will be a different ground to the one I knew. It made me feel quite wistful.'

Miller, Bazeley, Johnson, Foster, Holdsworth, Ramage, Hessenthaler, Payne, Moralee, Porter, Mooney
Manager Glenn Roeder
Scorers Foster 7, Johnson 87
Wolves scorer Emblen 85
Attendance 10,108

FA Cup fourth round replay, February 2 1960

Burgess does his homework to stop Saints in their tracks

Having beaten Birmingham City in the third round, Watford were disappointed to get an away draw for the next round match.

Southampton were going very well in the Third Division and had thrashed First Division Manchester City 5-1 at Maine Road in the previous round.

Watford's manager Ron Burgess knew he had to pull off another tactical masterstroke if they were to avoid defeat at The Dell and bring the Saints back to Vicarage Road.

Worried about Southampton's pair of wingers, John Sydenham and Terry Paine, Burgess spent the week before the match working out how to stop them. He told Bobby Bell to make sure he hugged the touchline so Sydenham had to cut inside, rather than go outside where he could use his left foot to great effect. It worked, Watford escaped with a hard-earned 2-2 draw thanks to a Cliff Holton strike and an own goal.

Cup fever gripped the town again as more than 28,000 supporters turned up to see if Watford could reach the fifth round for the first time since 1932.

Burgess was concerned that his containment tactics might not be so effective on the wider Vicarage Road pitch.

Watford grabbed the first goal and then defended it doggedly. It was Barry Hartle who scored, hooking the ball back over a mass of players from a Freddie Bunce corner.

After that came an hour of nerve-wracking, backs-to-the-wall stuff for Watford. Jimmy Linton made three excellent saves to preserve their lead.

On the counter-attack, Dennis Uphill cut through the Saints defence twice, only to be brought down heavily when poised to shoot. Holton almost scored a second when he hit the post in the second half. The Hornets held on.

The *Watford Observer* printed the pictures of the 11 players on the front page with the headline: 'Here are the men of the week. The heroes who brought honour to Watford.'

1959-60 FA CUP

1st round	Cheltenham Town A	0-0
1st round replay	Cheltenham Town H	3-0
2nd round	Wycombe Wanderers H	5-1
3rd round	Birmingham City H	2-1
4th round	Southampton A	2-2
4th round replay	Southampton H	1-0
5th round	Sheffield United A	2-3

Linton, Bell, Nicholas, Catleugh, McNeice, Chung, Benning, Holton, Uphill, Hartle, Bunce
Manager Ron Burgess
Scorer Hartle 31
Attendance 27,925

WOLVES 0   WATFORD 3

FA Cup fifth round, Saturday February 16 1980

Four days after reaching the League Cup final with a semi-final win over Swindon, Wolves had to face Watford in the FA Cup.

The Hornets had narrowly escaped an upset in the previous round, when they trailed non-league Harlow Town then survived a gutsy fightback before scraping through 4-3.

Watford's survival in the Second Division was by no means assured but when they went to Molineux, they looked more like a First Division team than Wolves did.

They utterly dominated the match, although they didn't score their first goal until 15 minutes from the end.

John Barnwell, the Wolves manager, said his players were tired after their League Cup exploits but the simple fact was that they were outclassed.

Ian Bolton and Steve Sims tucked the Wolves strikers David Richards and Andy Gray (yes, that Andy Gray) neatly in their back pockets for the duration of the match. Barnwell's snarky comment that 'Ian Bolton looked like a world-class player, which we know he is not,' was nothing more than sour grapes.

It may have been a cup tie but this victory was as important to Watford's rise through the divisions as any other.

The way they played was proof that they could outplay top flight teams.

In midfield, Martin Patching, playing against his old team, was inspired. Up front, Ross Jenkins and Malcolm Poskett were too physical and too mobile for the former Liverpool and England defender Emlyn Hughes. However, it took Watford a while to break through.

Wolves brought on John McAlle to rough Sims and Bolton up a bit but the ploy backfired. An awful lunging tackle on Sims gave McAlle a broken leg.

Having used their substitute, Wolves had to play the final part of the game with ten men.

When Watford finally made their deserved breakthrough, the floodgates opened. Poskett scored twice in five minutes, then Blissett added the third before the end.

After Poskett grabbed the second, Graham Taylor left the bench and watched the final ten minutes with the fans on the terrace, something he liked to do when the outcome was no longer in doubt so he could see the game from another perspective.

Watford added another First Division name to their growing list of scalps although they were to come up short against Arsenal in the quarter-finals.

Steele, Henderson, Harrison, Patching, Sims, Bolton, Train, Poskett, Jenkins, Blissett, Rostron
Manager Graham Taylor
Scorer Poskett 75, 79, Blissett 85
Attendance 32,881

Division One, Saturday August 22 1998

Watford and Bristol City had spent the previous season locked in a race for the Second Division championship. It was a race the Hornets won on the final day of the season.

The fact the Robins were managed by Graham Taylor's very good friend and former assistant John Ward made it almost a sibling rivalry. Taylor and Ward had been friends since their Lincoln City days. In the Eighties, when Ward was learning how to be a coach, Taylor mentored him and confided in him.

Although it was a friendly rivalry, both men burned to win. The fixture list meant the two promoted teams met each other early in the new season, at Ashton Gate. Bristol City had spent millions on two strikers, Ade Akinbiyi and Tony Thorpe. Watford had been shopping in the bargain bin again. There was a sense of optimism at Bristol City that was not matched at Watford.

The Watford fans were putting a brave face on things, reminding the City supporters who had won the silverware in May but there was a fear that if they were not careful, the Hornets could be in for a rough afternoon.

Despite two wins in the league, at Portsmouth and at home to Bradford, Watford's most recent match was a truly dreadful 1-1 draw against Cambridge in the League Cup, which saw them slip out of the competition on aggregate.

The score at Ashton Gate suggests

WHERE'S YOUR BANNER GONE?
At the showdown four months earlier, Bristol City's fans unveiled a banner proclaiming them champions. Watford's supporters were quick to ask them why it had mysteriously disappeared.

that Bristol City wilted but that is far from the case. Watford took the lead after eight minutes when Richard Johnson, playing his first game of the season after injury, blasted a volley with fearsome strength from at least 30 yards.

After that, City gave as good as they got. There were chances at both ends in a game played at a frenetic pace.

In the second half, Dean Yates prodded home the second when City failed to deal with a corner but within a minute Soren Andersen had got them back in it. Johnson hit another thunderbolt and then Alon Hazan finished off a superb, fluent move that spread across the pitch and found him in space.

If his finish was ice cool, his celebration defied rational sense. Who can blame him? Hazan's goal rounded off a brilliant team performance. Watford had dismantled a side that had looked dangerous. They simply outplayed City.

Ward left Ashton Gate in October and was replaced by Benny Lennartson. Bristol City finished bottom of the table. Watford won the play-offs.

Here endeth two valuable lessons. Money is not the answer to everything. And never doubt Graham Taylor.

Chamberlain, Bazeley, Kennedy, Palmer, Millen (Hazan 68), Yates, Smart (Daley 87), Hyde, Ngonge (Noel-Williams 78), Johnson, Robinson
Manager Graham Taylor
Scorers Johnson 8, 61, Yates 58, Hazan 79
Scorer Andersen 59
Attendance 13,063

So near, and yet so far

The Second Division was within touching distance, but having forced their way into a strong position on Good Friday, Watford collapsed over Easter and the dream of promotion would have to wait another five years.

Bill McGarry had built a good team, one that looked capable of making the step up. He had young Pat Jennings in goal and Charlie Livesey in attack.

The arrival of Duncan Welbourne from Grimsby added steel to the defence and when McGarry persuaded Jim McAnearney to join from Plymouth it was the firmest indication to date that the club was determined to push on.

Before McAnearney, Cliff Holton was the only player to cost Watford as much as £10,000.

A brilliant run of results since the turn of the year had thrust Watford into contention. They won 12 out of 15 and were suddenly being talked of as the most likely side out of Crystal Palace, Coventry City and Bournemouth to make it.

As it often does, Easter held the key. Watford hosted Colchester United at Vicarage Road on Good Friday. Colchester were frustrating opponents and would often go away having restricted Watford to a single point.

This wasn't a free-flowing display but it was just the sort of stubborn performance teams destined for promotion are adept at producing.

Ron Crisp gave Watford the lead after a neat move involving Ken Oliver, Livesey and McAnearney.

It was a controversial goal, perhaps foreshadowing the one that finally achieved promotion for the Hornets against Plymouth five years later.

Crisp's firm drive from 25 yards hit the bar and bounced down on the line.

Colchester equalised when the jitters in the Watford defence got the better of them. The visitors then spent ten minutes camped in Watford's penalty area, winning four corners in a row as a result.

But Watford dug in and then eased away. McAnearney was brought down in the area and George Harris smashed home the penalty. Late on Oliver rode two challenges to add the third.

Vicarage Road sensed that this was it. With two promotion places up for grabs, Watford had risen to second in the table at just the right time. They could almost smell Division Two.

Unfortunately it all unravelled with indecent haste. They were thumped 3-0 at Shrewsbury the following day, then won only one of their last seven games.

The dream was to be put on ice until Ken Furphy arrived.

Jennings, Bell, Jones, Crisp, Chung, Welbourne, Spelman, McAnearney, Livesey, Oliver, Harris
Manager Bill McGarry
Scorers Crisp 26, Harris pen 67, Oliver 78
Colchester scorer Grice 53
Attendance 18, 393

Division One, Monday May 5 1986

Try telling today's Chelsea fans, with their expectations of Champions League football and regular trophies, that only 25 years ago they lost 5-1 at home to Watford in a stadium that was crumbling around them.

Tell them that only 12,017 people turned up for their final league match of the season and they will probably deny it ever happened.

Tell them the cracked and broken terraces were so sparsely populated that the big electric fences installed by Ken Bates to keep hooligans in check looked like some kind of perverse joke.

At the time, Chelsea were symbolic of almost all that was wrong with the English game. Run-down, unfriendly, almost bankrupt. How times change...

There were no expensive foreign imports in this workmanlike Chelsea team, just Joey McLaughlin, Doug Rougvie, Nigel Spackman, Gordon Durie and David Speedie.

Watford had actually considered buying Durie when he was at Hibernian but, unlike Chelsea, didn't think he was worth a £400,000 punt.

Chelsea's young keeper Les Fridge, standing in for Eddie Niedzwiecki, had a nightmare. He just didn't warm up.

He had to pick the ball out of the net after a minute and 40 seconds when Worrell Sterling's deep cross was headed down by John Barnes for Brian Talbot to drill in. Talbot scored again just ahead of half-time before Watford ran amok in the second half. Taylor threw David Bardsley on in an advanced position, convinced that the full-back could thrive. The term 'wing back' hadn't been invented yet but that was the position Taylor had in mind.

Bardsley's first goal was a sweet free-kick. The second was a mazy run from his own half. Bardsley covered 50 yards and beat five Chelsea players before slotting the ball under the keeper.

Speedie got one back before Colin West made it five. That, perhaps, was the day's only downside. The Rangers manager, Graeme Souness, was there to watch West and a week later he signed him for the Scottish club.

Watford, meanwhile, rounded off their fourth season in Division One with an emphatic away win.

And yet there were doubts from some about the club's progress. They had finished 12th in the table and reached the FA Cup quarter-final. The fact some saw that as a disappointment demonstrated how far the club had come. Admittedly, Chelsea were not of the stature then that they are now but it was still an incredible result. It was proof that on their day, Watford could rip other First Division sides to pieces with the pace of their attacks.

Oh what we'd give for a 5-1 win at Stamford Bridge these days.

Coton, Gibbs, Sinnott (Bardsley 45), Talbot, Terry, McClelland, Sterling, Blissett, West, Jackett, Barnes.
Manager Graham Taylor
Scorers Talbot 2, 43, Bardsley 64, 77, West 85
Chelsea scorer Speedie 79
Attendance 12,017

FA Cup fifth round, Saturday February 15 2003

Smith puts Sunderland to the sword at the second attempt

'Someone was smiling on us that day,' says Ray Lewington. A twice-taken penalty by Tommy Smith was enough to give Watford victory and plunge the Stadium of Light into darkness.

Sunderland were on their way to a record low Premier League points total of 19 and had the look of a side that knew its number was up.

'We did feel they might be there for the taking,' says Lewington. 'We knew the crowd might not be too patient with them. They had some chances early on and if they had taken them, it would have been a completely different game.'

Kevin Phillips should have scored after just nine minutes but he managed to shoot wide after being sent clear by Tore Andre Flo.

That early miss seemed to shatter Sunderland's already fragile confidence. Watford didn't create many clear-cut chances but they did control possession, playing with the sort of poise you'd expect from the home team.

But if the Premiership experience had taught Watford anything, it's that possession is not nine tenths of the law. You can appear in command one moment yet be dumped on your backsides the next.

Even dreadful teams can conjure up one moment of invention. The longer it went on, the more the Watford fans feared Sunderland would shake themselves out of their trough of mediocrity and create a chance.

On the hour, Sunderland made a double substitution, replacing Julio Arca and Flo with Talal El Karkouri and David Bellion. It did little to lift the home team but it has to be said, Watford didn't look like scoring either.

Referee Mike Dean gave Watford a penalty. Heidar Helguson went down when he was sandwiched between Jody Craddock and Jason McAteer.

Smith's first penalty was weak and hit Thomas Sorensen's legs. Sunderland thought they had got away with it. But Dean ordered it to be re-taken because Sorensen had moved off his line before Smith had kicked the ball.

Smith's second shot was not much better but it squeezed into the corner off Sorensen's palm.

Alec Chamberlain had to rescue Watford a number of times in the last 20 minutes as Sunderland flooded forward in desperation. Howard Wilkinson blamed the referee for robbing his team but as Lewington said: 'Yes, we got the benefit of a decision, which you don't always get away from home, but you make your own luck.'

Chamberlain, Ardley, Cox, Gayle, Robinson, Nielsen, Vernazza, Hyde, Mahon, Helguson, Smith (Doyley 86)
Manager Ray Lewington
Scorer Smith pen 65
Attendance 29,916

Division One, Boxing Day 1986

Handing Watford a trip to Kenilworth Road on Boxing Day had to be someone's idea of a joke.

Luton Town's response to the problem of hooliganism was to ban all away fans from their ground and introduce an unpopular identity card scheme for their own fans.

And Luton had followed Queens Park Rangers by installing an artificial pitch. Watford and Luton were rivals but they had once had so much in common as small clubs punching above their weight.

In the mid-Eighties, Luton veered off in another direction. The Hornets were respected as the family club, while the Hatters banned away fans. The Kenilworth Road pitch was a carpet, while Vicarage Road was a sand-topped bog. Both were unplayable but at least Watford's was authentic.

The Hornets had a pop star chairman, the Hatters had a Tory MP, the Thatcherite David Evans. The clubs were now like chalk and cheese.

Hardly any Watford fans made the trip to Bedfordshire for the high noon kick-off. Instead of a fierce, festive atmosphere between two local rivals, it was cold and sterile.

Luton fundamentally missed the point that watching football should be an interactive experience.

There were some Watford fans who managed to get inside, perhaps about a hundred or so. Presumably some were friends with Luton members who had managed to get them a ticket.

Luton had an impressive record on their plastic surface, which was something Graham Taylor felt gave the team an unfair advantage. Combine that with the absence of any travelling support and the odds were stacked against most visiting teams.

Watford were 2-0 up after just 17 minutes. First Gary Porter bundled the ball in at the far post, beating the Luton defenders to the punch, after Wilf Rostron had floated in a free-kick.

Then Kevin Richardson grabbed a rare goal. Worrell Sterling's cross was nodded down by John Barnes for Mark Falco to gather.

The big striker was dispossessed by Mal Donaghy, who tried to dribble clear only to lose control. The ball squirmed away from him and Richardson strode forward and blasted it in off the underside of the bar.

Luton missed a penalty in the 59th minute but the rest of the game was as lifeless as the atmosphere. There was no raucous singing, no banter between two sets of supporters, just a nightmarish vision of what football might become if the forces of conservatism got hold of it. This was a great result but almost all Watford's supporters were denied the chance to witness it.

Instead they were at home, listening to the radio or watching Ceefax.

Coton, Bardsley, Rostron, Richardson, Sims, McClelland, Sterling, Barnes, Falco, Jackett, Porter
Manager Graham Taylor
Scorers Porter 7, Richardson 17
Attendance 11,140

WATFORD..........3 SOUTHAMPTON.................2

The Championship, Sunday September 16 2007

Darius Henderson nearly moved on when Nathan Ellington arrived from West Brom for a record £3.25m.

But he came off the bench to score twice as Watford came from 2-1 behind to beat Southampton.

The last-minute winner wasn't pretty, Henderson bundled it over the line from an Adam Johnson cross, but it sparked incredible celebrations.

'We've had to build bridges,' said Aidy Boothroyd. 'But Darius said to me "Gaffer, you never do learn, do you? When I play, we win." I can't argue with him now.'

Watford initially adapted well to life back in the Championship. The squad had more depth and the team looked more resilient than their rivals.

With Tommy Smith on one wing and Jobi McAnuff on the other, they stretched the Saints. Ellington looked so bright at times, as he had done on his debut against Ipswich, when he hit the post.

When the Saints equalised Danny Shittu's goal, Boothroyd had a couple of aces up his sleeve. He threw on Johnson and Henderson, only for the Saints to take the lead shortly afterwards.

It was a stark reminder of just how competitive the Championship could be. Although Watford had been in control, they suddenly faced the prospect of ending up with nothing.

That was until Henderson scored twice in the final ten minutes to send the Rookery end into raptures.

Poom, Stewart, Shittu, DeMerit, Doyley, McAnuff (Johnson 59), Mahon, Williamson (Mariappa 81), Smith, King, Ellington (Henderson 66)
Manager Aidy Boothroyd
Scorers Shittu 41, Henderson 80, 90
Southampton scorers Rasiak 45, Dyer 69
Attendance 15,915

A BLISTERING START

Just as they did in 2000, Watford started well on their return from the Premiership. They were eight points clear after 15 games before falling apart. They only just clung on to clinch a play-off place, before losing to Hull City.

August

Sat 11	Wolves	A	W	2-1
Sat 18	Sheffield United	H	W	1-0
Sat 25	Leicester City	A	L	1-4

September

Sat 1	Ipswich Town	H	W	2-0
Sun 16	Southampton	H	W	3-2
Wed 19	Cardiff City	A	W	2-1
Sat 22	QPR	A	D	1-1
Sat 29	Blackpool	H	D	1-1

October

Tue 2	Sheffield Wednesday	H	W	2-1
Sat 6	Scunthorpe United	A	W	3-1
Sat 20	Hull City	H	W	1-0
Tue 23	Coventry City	A	W	3-0
Mon 29	Crystal Palace	A	W	2-0

November

Sat 3	West Brom	H	L	0-3
Tue 6	Norwich City	A	W	3-1

The Championship, November 6 2007

		P	W	D	L	F	A	Pts
1	Watford	15	11	2	2	27	16	35
2	West Brom	15	8	3	4	31	16	27
3	Bristol City	15	7	6	2	21	14	27
4	Charlton	15	7	4	4	19	15	25
5	Coventry City	15	7	3	5	20	20	24
6	Wolves	15	6	5	4	22	21	23

Division One, Saturday April 27 1996

Forget for a moment the fact that Watford didn't manage to stay up. This was a day when everyone could be proud of their boys, even if they were wearing an unfamiliar, and some would say, ugly, burgundy and green kit.

Thousands of Watford fans made the trip to Norwich knowing that the afternoon could end in relegation and despair. Defeat would seal their fate.

Victory might – just might – give them a chance to wriggle out of trouble. They were out for the count at the beginning of April, now they at least had a chance.

And it felt like the impossible might be on the cards when David Connolly turned in the penalty area and was brought down by Rob Newman.

There weren't even two minutes on the clock when Watford were given a penalty. Connolly converted it and then they had to withstand a barrage of Norwich attacks to preserve their lead.

Kevin Miller was outstanding in the Watford goal. He pulled off a number of saves to keep the Canaries at bay.

Ten minutes into the second half, Miller was beaten by a fine, curling free-kick from Ian Crook.

Suddenly, a Watford team that had been so bold then so brave under fire looked deflated. The travelling fans knew a draw would not be enough if Portsmouth drew against Ipswich.

The revival, inspired by Taylor, Blissett and Jackett looked to have come just too late.

When Taylor returned in February,

he asked everyone in the squad to write down what they thought the team should be. 'We were in a bad position when Graham, Luther and Kenny came in,' says Gary Porter. 'And it took a while for things to turn around. It wasn't until quite late in the season when there was nothing else left but to go for it that we gave ourselves a chance.

'When you know you have to win or you're going down, you find strength and togetherness and we did that.'

In the 67th minute, Gary Porter got the ball outside the penalty area and hit a left-footed piledriver that deceived the Norwich goalkeeper, Bryan Gunn.

It was a sensational goal and it kept Watford alive.

'Graham said to me afterwards that he had hoped I wasn't going to shoot from so far out,' says Porter. 'I said "That's your fault for telling us that if you don't shoot, you don't score."

'We gave ourselves a chance but we were up against Martin O'Neill's Leicester team on the last day and they needed to win to get in the play-offs.'

Leicester won 1-0 and Watford went down. 'We gave it a good go,' says Porter. 'We turned it round but we left it perhaps a week or a fortnight too late.'

They didn't stay up but the win over Norwich gave so much hope and pride.

Miller, Bazeley, Barnes (Ludden 45), Hessenthaler, Page, White, Porter, Palmer, Ramage, Mooney, Connolly
Manager Graham Taylor
Scorers Connolly pen 2, Porter 66
Norwich scorer Crook 55
Attendance 14,118

WATFORD..........1 MANCHESTER UNITED.......0

FA Cup third round, Saturday, January 2 1982

In 1977, Ron Atkinson had been one of the names mentioned as Watford's possible new manager. The job went to Graham Taylor. In 1981, both men were on the shortlist as candidates to replace Dave Sexton at Manchester United.

United opted for Atkinson but you could say they might have been better off going for Taylor.

Perhaps Taylor wasn't flash enough for United. He didn't have Big Ron's penchant for champagne, jewellery or bespoke Italian leather shoes.

Watford were going well in Division Two when the draw for the FA Cup third round threw up an opportunity to test themselves against one of the best.

The pundits had already pencilled them in as one of the sides likely to go up. Now they could get a taste of what life in the top flight might be like.

Bad weather meant there had been a rash of postponements. Watford hadn't played since December 12. The team had a break from competitive matches but that didn't mean they had their feet up. Taylor decided to make the most of the opportunity and with the Christmas fixtures called off, he set about devising a game plan that would beat United.

He withdrew John Barnes into a deeper position to mark Bryan Robson and put the new arrival from Holland, Jan Lohman, on the left flank.

The night before the game, Taylor called all his staff together and they went for a meal at The Alpine in Bushey Heath. It started a cup tie tradition that would last a couple of years until the team reached the FA Cup final in 1984. Before every cup tie, the staff would have a meal and a few drinks. There would be songs and joke-telling.

The pitch at Vicarage Road was in a bit of a state and after a few months at United, Big Ron had obviously forgotten the joys of sitting on an uncovered bench. The pitch was boggy and he feared for his expensive shoes but, after a brief hesitation, he tiptoed his way across the mud.

His United players showed a similar reluctance to get dirty.

Watford were hungrier. Ross Jenkins gave Kevin Moran a hard time and Luther Blissett ran Martin Buchan's ageing legs into the ground.

What pleased Taylor most was that the goal came from a move they'd practiced over and over in training.

Les Taylor's corner was punched clear by Gary Bailey. Taylor then ran infield, anticipating where the clearance might land, so he was able to send an early cross deep into the box towards Lohman. The Dutchman's header was blocked by the United keeper but it fell straight to Lohman who scored at the second attempt.

For the second time in four years, Watford had knocked United out of a cup competition. Now it was less of an upset, more an indication of what was to come.

Sherwood, Rice (Armstrong), Pritchett, Taylor, Terry, Bolton, Callaghan, Blissett, Jenkins, Barnes, Lohman
Manager Graham Taylor
Scorer Lohman 44
Attendance 26,104

WATFORD..........1 NEWCASTLE UNITED 0

FA Cup third round third replay, January 18 1989

Roeder's own goal breaks Magpies after more than seven hours

In the days before penalty shoot-outs, FA Cup ties just went on and on until there was a winner.

After a third replay and 450 minutes of play, a Glenn Roeder own goal finally separated Watford and Newcastle.

This was the longest FA Cup tie Watford had ever been involved in and even in the decisive fourth match there was very little to divide the sides.

The two teams had already met in the Simod Cup before Christmas, when Watford beat the Magpies 2-1.

Jim Smith, the Newcastle manager, felt his team should have been given a penalty in the first match.

A marathon cup tie

Saturday, January 7
Newcastle United 0 Watford 0

Tuesday, January 10
Watford 2 Newcastle United 2 aet

Monday, January 16
Newcastle United 0 Watford 0 aet

Wednesday, January 18
Watford 1 Newcastle United 0 aet

Seven Watford men played all 450 minutes of the Newcastle marathon. They were Tony Coton, Nigel Gibbs, Willie Falconer, John McClelland, Rick Holden, Neil Redfearn and Tim Sherwood.

After that game, the two managers tossed a coin to determine the venue should the replay also end in a draw. Steve Harrison lost the toss.

At Vicarage Road, Neil Redfearn gave Watford the perfect start, scoring in the first minute. Kevin Brock equalised before the Brazilian striker Mirandinha gave Newcastle the lead with a penalty. Watford levelled when Redfearn scored again, also from a penalty.

So it was back up the A1 to the north-east, where Smith was again appealing for a penalty in another goalless draw.

The third replay was at Watford two days later. By now it had become a war of attrition between two tired sides who were too familiar with each other.

Yet again there was extra time as the tie threatened to become a stalemate.

With just seven minutes to go, Rick Holden fired in a speculative shot from 25 yards. It was flying wide until it deflected off Glenn Roeder and bounced in. Watford were through at last and beat Derby in the next round before losing to Nottingham Forest.

Coton, Gibbs, Jackett, Sherwood, Miller (David Holdsworth 45), McClelland, Redfearn, Wilkinson (Roberts 90), Thompson, Falconer, Holden
Manager Steve Harrison
Scorer Roeder og 113
Attendance 15,115

SHEFFIELD UNITED 1   WATFORD 4

The Championship, Tuesday February 6 2006

'Marlon, Marlon. Born is the King of Vicarage Road'

'When we got back to the dressing room after the game there was a real belief that we were going to do it,' says Jay DeMerit.

'I remember Aidy coming in and saying that everyone was looking at us now. That result was a huge marker in the sand for us.

'All over the pitch things were going well. There weren't many better striking partners than Marlon King and Darius Henderson. Ashley Young had matured from this skinny little kid and he could really do some damage. We had James Chambers and Jordan Stewart going forward. Matty Spring and Gavin Mahon hustled everyone.

'And at the back, Malky and I had got this thing going. He would take the big muscly guy and I'd look after the quicker guy. He had all the experience to organise us well and we were so solid.

'Sheffield had Ade Akinbiyi up front with Steve Kabba, who had been scoring a lot of goals, but we dominated them. There was this feeling that we were not going to lose too many games.'

The new year had got off to the best possible start, with a 2-1 win at Luton. 'I came on as a sub,' says DeMerit. 'And I was totally fresh behind the ears as far as rivalries were concerned. I didn't know what local derbies were like. It was fierce but when we won that we went on a run and nothing intimidated us.'

The Blades were second in the table, ten points behind Reading but 11 ahead of Leeds. Watford were third, lurking but unfancied.

Neil Warnock's side were in for a hammering. Chris Eagles scored early on. After 25 minutes United had David Unsworth sent off for pushing Eagles in the face. Even against 10 men, Watford came under heavy pressure but they defended well and administered stinging blows on the counter attack.

Marlon King beat Leigh Bromby to score the second goal before Paul Ifill got one back.

King smashed home his second on the turn and Hameur Bouazza seized on another Bromby mistake near the end to make it 4-1. The result may have been a touch flattering but it was a clear signal of intent from the Hornets.

'Hearing their fans boo them off was a big confidence-booster to us,' says DeMerit. 'Because we had gone there with a plan and we made that happen.'

Foster, Doyley, DeMerit, Mackay, Stewart, Eagles (Chambers 45), Spring (Bangura 53), Mahon, Young (Bouazza 77), King, Henderson
Manager Aidy Boothroyd
Scorers Eagles 6, King 47, 69, Bouazza 88
Sheffield United scorer Ifill 58
Attendance 20,791

WATFORD.........3 CHARLTON ATHLETIC.......2

Worthington Cup fourth round, November 27 2001

There was so much to like about this performance. The passing was crisp but purposeful. The goals were well-taken. There was a sense that everything was going to turn out okay.

With the score 1-1, Paul Robinson looked to have given Watford victory on the hour, when he finished off a brilliant passing move with a fine finish.

Tommy Smith wasted a chance to put the tie beyond doubt when his weak penalty was saved by Dean Kiely ten minutes from time.

And then Charlton equalised in the last minute. John Robinson ghosted in unmarked to head home Claus Jensen's cross. But Watford refused to be cowed. In extra time Heidar Helguson scored the winner when he hurled himself at the ball and the far post after Kiely had parried Smith's shot.

The manner of the victory made Vialli's next move all the more peculiar. In the last eight, Watford were drawn to face the only other team from outside the Premiership, Sheffield Wednesday.

Faced with a one-off tie that had to be settled on the night, Vialli decided to pack the midfield and play one striker. Despite a bright start at Hillsborough, Watford lost 4-0.

If Vialli had produced a few more displays like the one against Charlton, Watford would have been promoted. They had showed a rare understanding of how to beat teams with pace.

Chamberlain, Robinson, Cox, Issa, Vega, Doyley, Hyde, Vernazza, Gayle (Fisken 45), Noel-Williams (Helguson 90), Smith
Manager Gianluca Vialli
Scorers Vernazza 17, Robinson 60, Helguson 99
Charlton Athletic scorers Brown 43, Robinson 90
Attendance 12,621

...Vialli's misses

Huge signing-on fees and wages... the cost of Vialli's signings was punishing.
MISSES
Stephen Hughes
Had previously been transferred from Arsenal to Everton for £3m. Made just 13 starts for Watford and was emblematic of many of Vialli's shortcomings.
Ramon Vega
Swiss international who had played for Tottenham and Celtic. Rumoured to be the most expensive recruit of the lot in terms of wages.
Patrick Blondeau
Signed on a free transfer from Marseille. Played 27 times. Full-back who looked as if he felt the whole experience was beneath him. Joined French semi-pro team

Créteil after being released by Watford.
David Noble
Hailed as the next big thing, the young midfielder came on loan from Arsenal and offered promise. It was unfulfilled. Has spent most of his career since in the lower divisions.
Pierre Issa
The first wave of arrivals failed to spark immediate success so Vialli brought in some more. The South African international's most famous moment was when he was dropped off a stretcher during the Birmingham home match.
Paul Okon
Vialli's last roll of the dice. Joined on loan from Middlesbrough in January. Left before the season was over. Awful.

Division One, Sunday March 8 1987

Televised football was still a relative novelty in the late Eighties. There were perhaps a dozen matches screened each season and to have a game picked by either BBC or ITV was something of an honour.

Everton were in the hunt for their second league championship in three seasons and Watford were in the middle of an FA Cup run.

Adrian Heath gave the Toffees the lead in the first half and Watford looked like they were suffering stage fright.

The Hornets were a different side in the second half and goals from Mark Falco and Luther Blissett gave them a memorable win over the champions-elect. Of Watford's eight seasons in the top flight, this was one of only two occasions that they managed to beat the side that went on to win the title – the other time was against Liverpool in 1983.

Blissett's equaliser was an instinctive header. Somehow he connected with a vicious volley from Nigel Gibbs that was going well off target. Falco tapped in the winner five minutes from time.

Blissett's goal was his 157th for the club. He was chasing Tommy Barnett's record of 160, which had stood since 1939. He got his 161st goal in the 4-3 defeat at Charlton in April.

Coton, Bardsley, Rostron, Richardson, Sims, McClelland, Blissett, Barnes, Falco, Porter, Sinnott (Gibbs)
Manager Graham Taylor
Scorers Blissett, Falco
Everton scorer Heath
Attendance 14,014

ON THE BOX

Watford's first scheduled live match was at home to West Ham in October 1983 but a strike by BBC technicians meant it was not screened. Here are the first ten Watford games to be broadcast live on television in the UK.

Everton 2 Watford 0	FA Cup final	
May 19 1984	BBC/ITV	
Watford 2 Liverpool 3	Division One	
January 12 1986	BBC	
Watford 1 Chelsea 0	FA Cup 4th round	
February 1 1987	ITV	
Watford 2 Everton 1	Division One	
March 8 1987	BBC	
Watford 0 Nottm Forest 3	FA Cup 5th round	
February 19 1989	BBC	
Luton Town 2 Watford 0	Division One	
November 29 1992	ITV	
Watford 2 Middlesbrough 0	Division One	
October 10 1993	ITV	
Watford 1 Crystal Palace 3	Division One	
November 28 1993	ITV	
Crystal Palace 0 Watford 2	Division One	
May 8, 1994	ITV	
Luton Town 2 Watford 0	Division One	
November 29 1992	ITV	

Watford were on ITV twice in 1994-95, a 1-1 draw at Luton and a 1-0 home win over Millwall on Good Friday.

In 1995-96, the 2-0 home defeat to Norwich was screened by ITV, as was the final-day loss to Leicester City.

The first Watford game shown by Sky Sports was the 1-0 FA Cup win over Northampton Town in November 1996.

Division One, Tuesday August 31 1982

Determined to ensure that Watford were among the fittest, if not *the* fittest, in Division One, Graham Taylor took his team to Norway for an old-fashioned boot camp.

It was brutal. They got up early and ran a couple of miles from their lodgings (hotel would be too grand a word for the place) to the training ground. They did a couple of hours of work, then ran back for breakfast.

There would be another, longer, session later in the morning before they rested while the sun was at its hottest.

And most evenings they played a match, against some fired-up local side. The players were used to being pushed hard by Taylor but this was extreme.

But it was for a good reason. Taylor knew the players had to be fit enough to start matches at a high tempo and sustain it to the end. Established First Division teams with more accomplished players might wilt in the face of such a physical challenge.

Watford's first away game was at The Dell. Only two years ago, they had been humbled 4-0 in the first leg of a League Cup tie before that incredible comeback at Vicarage Road. Now the two teams met as equals.

Most of the First Division teams thought they knew what to expect. Plenty of long balls and lots of aggression. Taylor wanted to surprise them.

Shortly after Watford had won promotion, they went on tour to New Zealand. Southampton's Alan Ball happened to be on the same flight and

he encouraged the Watford players to have a drink, which didn't please Taylor too much.

When they got off the flight, the 1966 World Cup winner said: 'Wait until you get into the First Division, boys. We'll teach you how to play football.'

In fact, it was Lawrie McMenemy's Saints who were taught a lesson.

This was one-way traffic, even if David Armstrong managed to equalise after Nigel Callaghan's early goal.

Watford pulverised the Saints and created 26 attempts on goal. The home players were given barely a second to dwell on the ball.

Having led 2-1 at half-time, they might have expected Southampton to come at them in the second period but Watford kept their boots on their opponents' throats.

Gerry Armstrong scored the third and Ross Jenkins got the fourth near the end.

In only their second match in the top flight, Watford had put the ball past the England goalkeeper, Peter Shilton, four times.

As they came off the pitch, Graham Taylor waited for Alan Ball. 'Not bad for a side that can't play, are we?' he said.

'You'll shock a few if you play like that every week,' came the reply.

Sherwood, Rice, Rostron, Blissett, Bolton, Jackett, Callaghan, Armstrong, Jenkins, Lohman, Barnes
Manager Graham Taylor
Watford scorers Callaghan 12, 33, Armstrong 48, Jenkins 77
Southampton scorer Lawrence 16
Attendance 19,714

WATFORD............ 1 NEWCASTLE UNITED........ 0

Division One, Tuesday March 23 1993

Furlong and Waugh slow Keegan's charge to the Premier League

The Kevin Keegan revolution was well underway at St James' Park. Newcastle were top of Division One and were already preparing for life in the Premier League.

Keegan had just signed Scott Sellars from Leeds and Andy Cole for a club record £1.75million. They were five points clear at the top of the table and looking to take another step towards the championship trophy. Watford were struggling in the league and had lost five in a row before Newcastle's visit.

Keith Waugh, the 36-year-old reserve goalkeeper, came into the side because Perry Suckling had taken a knock. 'I felt I was fit and would have played,' says Suckling. 'In truth, I got the hook. Keith played magnificently. It was a first-class goalkeeping display. At times, he kept us in it.'

It was Waugh's night – the only time in seven appearances for Watford that he ended up on the winning side.

That night he was inspired, keeping Newcastle at bay when they looked like opening the scoring.

Early in the second half, Waugh made two incredible saves in the space of two minutes. First he filled the goal and blocked David Kelly's shot when Lee Clark had found him in space with just the keeper to beat. Then he pushed Cole's firm, swerving effort over the bar. Waugh's heroics stirred the Hornets and they began to attack with more purpose.

Furlong's goal came when Gary Porter's free-kick caused a melee in the penalty area. David Holdsworth headed it down, Ken Charlery poked it with his toe to Furlong and the striker smashed home his 22nd goal of the season.

Waugh kept the saves coming and Barry Ashby booted a Newcastle effort off the line in the last minute as Watford held on. Keegan took defeat relatively well, although he did moan about the bobbly pitch.

'It was a great result,' says Andy Hessenthaler. 'We grafted for it but we were good value for the points. They had spent a lot of money on players, millions, and already the gap was opening between the haves and the have-nots.

'After the game, I pulled up at the lights on my way home. I looked across and Kevin Keegan was sitting in the back seat of the car next to me. He had a chauffeur driving him but I was the one with a big grin on my face.'

Waugh, Solomon, Ashby, Dublin, Holdsworth, Lavin, Hessenthaler, Willis (Bazeley 79), Furlong, Charlery, Porter
Manager Steve Perryman
Watford scorer Furlong 58
Attendance 11,634

Chopra shows his eye for goal in turf war

BURNLEY.............. 4 WATFORD 7

Divsion One, Saturday April 5 2003

Seven days before an FA Cup semi-final against Southampton, Watford went goal crazy at Turf Moor.

They had only scored 12 times away from home all season but the arrival of Michael Chopra, a 19-year-old poacher with an eye for goal, gave them a huge boost before the cup tie.

'The reason I brought Michael in was purely his goalscoring,' says Ray Lewington. 'We'd been to see him play for Newcastle reserves quite a few times and I felt he was good enough. Bobby Robson was the Newcastle manager and he wasn't too keen to let him go out on loan but I said: "I tell you now, he will play in the semi-final." That's the only reason we got him.

'Our play up to the penalty box was usually so good but we were so wasteful. I felt that against Southampton we would have less of the ball and so we'd get fewer chances.'

Chopra certainly scored goals. He transformed a run-of-the-mill fixture at Turf Moor into a classic.

'I'm not so sure it was a classic,' says Lewington. 'It was an absolute freak. It was 5-4 at half-time and I remember turning to Terry Burton and shaking my head. We were leading but I wanted to have a go at the defence because they were struggling against Gareth Taylor.'

At times the game was more like a basketball match. Wayne Brown gave Watford the lead after 13 minutes, heading in from a Neal Ardley corner.

Two minutes later, Taylor equalised for Burnley. A minute after that Micah Hyde put Watford back in front.

Then there were ten minutes of relative calm before Neil Cox made it 3-1. Three minutes later Chopra got his first goal and suddenly Watford must have thought they had a comfortable lead. 'At 4-1 you are in control. Even away from home you shouldn't let them back into the match,' says Lewington. 'But we kept giving them chances.'

There were four more goals in the ten minutes before half-time. Steve Davis and Taylor cut Burnley's deficit to one goal. Chopra made it 5-3 and Taylor scored again.

'In 700-odd games I've never let in four before half-time and gone on to win,' says Alec Chamberlain. 'We were a bit embarrassed when we went in because every attack seemed to end with a goal. Ray was trying to calm us all

Michael Chopra fires the first of his four goals in an astonishing win over Burnley.

down and he said: "You've scored five but you're really only 1-0 up.

'They are all over the place at the back so the team that wins this is going to be the one that sorts out their defence in the second half.'

'Gareth Taylor was a strange player,' says Lewington. 'I worked with him at Palace and I never really worked him out. He could be unstoppable on his day but the rest of the time he could be lacklustre.

'He was having a lot of success from crosses so I told them that if we kept allowing the ball in the box, he'd have another hat-trick. We worked hard in wide areas to cut out crosses in the second half and it tightened things up.'

At the other end, Chopra got his second, third and fourth goals to become the first Watford player to score four in a league match since Luther Blissett in 1982.

It is not an exaggeration to say that

in the end it could have been 10-6.

'Michael was superb that day,' says Lewington. 'As a manager, it makes you look good when a lad you've got in on loan scores four but I was confident in his ability. You look at a striker and you ask whether they can do it. He scored four away from home in his second game for the team. There are plenty of good strikers who don't do it away from home too often.

'Today he's still a very good player at Championship level but I am a little surprised he hasn't gone a bit higher.

'And I suppose, if I was being picky, it's a shame he didn't save a couple of those goals for the semi-final but football doesn't work like that.'

....

Chamberlain, Cox, Brown, Mahon, Glass, Ardley, Vernazza, Hyde, Nielsen, Chopra, Smith
Manager Ray Lewington
Watford scorers Brown 13, Hyde 16, Cox 26, Chopra 29, 40, 61, 90
Burnley scorers Taylor 15, 39, 45, Davis 35
Attendance 10,208

WATFORD..................2 LIVERPOOL....................0

Division One, Saturday December 6 1986

This was the day John Barnes scored a magical goal, one that convinced Kenny Dalglish, the Liverpool manager, to take him to Anfield.

Watford produced a vintage display to defeat the league and cup holders fair and square.

Dalglish had retired and everyone knew Ian Rush was on his way to Juventus at the end of the season, so Liverpool needed new forwards.

There had already been speculation that Barnes, having turned down several new contract offers from Watford, might also move to Italy

But after a sensational 35-yard run through the Liverpool defence and stinging shot past Bruce Grobbelaar, Barnes went straight to the top of Dalglish's wish list.

John McClelland scored the first with a fine header. Watford dominated Liverpool in midfield, with Gary Porter and Kevin Richardson in superb form.

The direct edge had been taken off Watford's play a little bit in what was to turn out to be both Barnes and Graham Taylor's final season at the club.

Barnes' form had been patchy as speculation of his imminent departure grew. But he was back to his blistering best against the champions.

That season Watford beat all of the eventual top four at home but this was the most scintillating performance.

Coton, Bardsley, Rostron, Richardson, Terry, McClelland, Callaghan, Barnes, Falco, Jackett, Porter
Manager Graham Taylor
Scorers McClelland 25, Barnes 63
Attendance 23,934

RECORD TRANSFERS

A list of Watford's most significant transfer fees paid and received (source Watford Observer). Barnes moved for a bargain £900,000 because Watford's hands were tied by the transfer tribunal system, which was based on the size of the fee paid for the player in the first place. Barnes had cost a set of kit from Sudbury.

IN

Luther Blissett	Milan	1984	£500,000
Nordin Wooter	Real Zaragoza	1999	£950,000
Heidar Helguson	Lillestrom	2000	£1.5m
Allan Nielsen	Tottenham	2000	£2.25m
Espen Baardsen	Tottenham	2000	£1.25m
Marcus Gayle	Rangers	2001	£900,000
Damien Francis	Wigan	2006	£1.5m
Danny Shittu	QPR	2006	£1.6m
Jobi McAnuff	C Palace	2007	£1.75m
Nathan Ellington	WBA	2007	£3.25m

OUT

Luther Blissett	Milan	1983	£1m
John Barnes	Liverpool	1987	£900,000
Tony Coton	Man City	1990	£1m
David James	Liverpool	1992	£1m
Bruce Dyer	C Palace	1994	£1.25m
Paul Furlong	Chelsea	1994	£2.3m
Kevin Miller	C Palace	1997	£1.55m
Heidar Helguson	Fulham	2005	£1.3m
Ashley Young	Aston Villa	2007	£9.65m
Hameur Bouazza	Fulham	2007	£3m
Marlon King	Wigan	2008	£3m
Danny Shittu	Bolton	2008	£2m
Darius Henderson	Sheff Utd	2008	£2,
Tamas Priskin	Ipswich	2009	£1.7m
Tommy Smith	Portsmouth	2009	£1.8m
Mike Williamson	Portsmouth	2009	£3m
Danny Graham	Swansea	2010	£3.5m

CRYSTAL PALACE............0 WATFORD............2

The Championship, Monday October 29 2007

When Aidy Boothroyd talked to Sky television after as comfortable an away win as you'll ever see, he was in bullish mood. By the time he spoke to the written press a little later, he had toned things down a bit. Perhaps he realised his mistake.

'You ain't seen nothing yet,' he said at first. 'We are nowhere near our best. There's a lot more to come.'

Shortly afterwards he said: 'It's a very open league. There are plenty of teams who can stop us. But it's great to win when you're not playing well.'

Goals from Tommy Smith and Marlon King gave Watford their fifth win in a row and moved them six points clear at the top of the table.

Adam Johnson, the winger on loan from Middlesbrough, was in sensational form. He terrified the Palace defence every time he got the ball and created King's goal with a brilliant run and cross. But the warning signs were there that perhaps Watford were relying on Johnson too much.

It had been a brilliant start and Watford looked well set to challenge for an immediate return to the Premiership. The victory over Palace was their tenth in their opening 13 matches.

But they were about to be brought crashing down to earth. The following Saturday they lost 3-0 at home to West Bromwich Albion. That kicked off a run of four wins in 16 matches that saw the team slip out of the automatic promotion places. It wasn't just that the wheels fell off. They rolled into a ravine and exploded into flames.

Johnson went back to Boro so the creative edge was lost. Crucially, Boothroyd's assistant, Keith Burkinshaw, left because his wife was seriously ill.

Jay DeMerit says losing Burkinshaw had a big effect. 'Keith was Aidy's voice of reason,' he says. 'Aidy was a fiery guy who took a lot of risks. He wore his heart on his sleeve. Keith reeled him in a bit. There's something to be said for being over-confident.

'The goals dried up, then we started leaking silly goals. We had a bigger squad and you need nine or ten guys to be on the same page driving it forward. If you have a few who are questioning the leadership, it's a problem. Suddenly, instead of working together, people are blaming each other. The manager then starts to question the players and he thinks we're not listening.

'It's hard to put your finger on one thing, but I think we lost what got us to the Premiership in the first place. All that togetherness wasn't there. We started to rely on just one guy.'

At Selhurst Park there was no hint of the deflating run to come. On the surface, everything looked fantastic as Watford sliced Palace into pieces. But appearances can be deceptive.

Lee, Stewart, Shittu, DeMerit, Doyley, Mahon, O'Toole, Johnson, Smith (McAnuff 68), King (Ellington 75), Henderson (Priskin 75)
Manager Aidy Boothroyd
Scorers Smith 32, King 67
Attendance 13,986

And so, the story begins at Edgeley Park

STOCKPORT COUNTY...... 1   WATFORD 3

Division Four, Saturday August 20 1977

If anyone had told you that this was to be the start of a journey that would take the club to the First Division, the FA Cup final and into Europe, you would have questioned their sanity.

But this is where it all began. At Edgeley Park in Stockport, in front of three thousand people.

The match was no classic. One of Stockport's directors described Watford afterwards as 'not a bad rugby team'.

Graham Taylor was determined not to hang around in the Fourth Division for a moment longer than necessary and he wanted his team to combine physical strength with an attacking approach.

He knew that getting out of the basement division required guts as well as guile. The players he signed in that first year, such as Sam Ellis and Ian Bolton, offered plenty of both.

Taylor said that 90 per cent of the matches would be like this and that the team with the sharper cutting edge would prevail.

In the final third, Watford were far better than County. Ross Jenkins scored the first when he beat the Stockport goalkeeper in a race to meet Keith Pritchett's flighted free-kick and headed over him and into the net.

Stockport levelled a minute later only for Watford to win a penalty when Alan Mayes was hauled down. There was some debate whether the foul had taken place inside or outside the box but Mayes made sure he fell well inside to persuade the referee.

Sam Ellis thumped home the kick and Watford grafted and battled to keep Stockport at bay. In the end, Watford's superior fitness told and they created a number of chances near the end, with Jenkins putting one away.

Taylor refused to get carried away. 'We are going to have to play a lot better than that,' he said. He was not wrong, because the following week, they lost 3-1 at home to York City.

After that, they were superb. They won 14 and lost three of their first 17 matches and were beaten only five times all season. They hit the top of the table in late September and never looked back.

Watford picked up a lot of fans on their remarkable journey but very few can say they were there when it all started back in August 1977.

Sherwood, Geidmintis, Ellis, Garner, Pritchett, Bond (Downes 74), Joslyn, Bolton, Jenkins, Mercer, Mayes
Manager Graham Taylor
Scorers Jenkins 15, 84, Ellis 18 pen
Stockport scorer Proudham 16
Attendance 3,056

MILLWALL .... 0 WATFORD 4

Division Two, Boxing Day 1991

Hornets make Christmas turkeys out of the Lions

Was there ever a football ground with less festive spirit than The Den? Cold Blow Lane, the road leading down to an unwelcoming stadium, could not have been more aptly named.

The prospect of a Boxing Day visit to Millwall was about as inviting as reaching into the bottom of your Christmas stocking and finding something damp and unpleasant.

But if Millwall's fans could be menacing towards visiting teams and supporters, they could be absolutely savage to their own players.

Watford were having trouble of their own at home. With the crowd quick to grumble, confidence was low.

Here, they played with fluidity and verve. The first goal came after half an hour when Lee Nogan was pulled down as he tried to make a run into the area. Gary Porter curled the free-kick into the net. Shortly afterwards, David James produced a sensational save. John McGinlay hit a dipping volley from 30 yards and James flung himself at full stretch to tip the ball round the post.

It was the sort of acrobatics that impressed Liverpool, who signed James, still only 21, for £1.25million the following summer.

Steve Butler, who was only in the team because Luther Blissett had complained of chest pains during training on Christmas Day, scored the second with a neatly placed lob.

Jason Drysdale added the third after Watford carved through the Millwall defence. Darren Bazeley got to the byline, paused for the perfect pass and then found Drysdale unmarked in the area.

Millwall's fans then turned on their team. As the Watford supporters cheered every one of their team's passes, the Millwall supporters booed their own players.

When their goalkeeper, Keith Branagan, rushed out of his area and hauled down Andy Hessenthaler, the Millwall fans joined in with Watford's chants of 'off, off, off'. They booed when the referee showed only a yellow card.

While there was not much Christmas cheer on the terraces, there was plenty of generosity on the pitch. The Lions allowed Butler to score his second towards the end of the game.

James, Gibbs, Drysdale, Dublin, Holdsworth, Solomon, Hessenthaler, Nogan (Bazeley 50), Butler, Porter, Nicholas (Putney 85)
Manager Steve Perryman
Scorers Porter 31, Butler 35, 83, Drysdale 57
Attendance 9,237

Premiership, Saturday November 4 2006

Aidy Boothroyd was finding out the hard way that self-belief doesn't get you too far in the Premiership.

It was November and the Hornets had not won any of their 10 league games. They weren't in the bottom three because they had scraped together a few draws but they desperately needed a win. The Premiership season didn't do Boothroyd too many favours. Marlon King sustained a long-term injury.

Before the Middlesbrough match Ben Foster, the goalkeeper, was ruled out with a knee injury. Watford's luck didn't look like changing.

That was until the sixth minute when Hameur Bouazza's off-target shot hit Jonathan Woodgate and bounced in.

Suddenly, Watford felt like the world, though firmly against them, was not an entirely unjust place. And they began to play with real verve, subjecting Middlesbrough to the sort of runaround they'd been on the receiving end of themselves at the Arsenal a few weeks earlier.

Admittedly, Boro were

awful and barely created a chance, while Ashley Young, Tommy Smith, Jordan Stewart and Bouazza all went close.

If the Watford fans were fearing a cruel equaliser out of the blue, Young eased their worries when he pounced on a poor George Boateng clearance and steered it home.

That was enough to secure three deserved points and give Boothroyd something to build on.

It was a victory that offered so much hope and encouragement that this Premiership season might turn out differently to the previous one.

Premiership wins are a rarity. There can be weeks, months, between them. We were already learning to savour them.

'I genuinely believe there are three teams worse than us,' said Boothroyd afterwards. Sadly, Watford would not win in the league again until January 23.

Lee, Doyley, Shittu, DeMerit, Stewart, Smith, Francis, Mahon, Bouazza, Young, Henderson
Manager Aidy Boothroyd
Scorers Woodgate og 6, Young 60
Attendance 18,951

WATFORD'S PREMIER LEAGUE WINS

1999-2000						2006-07			
Aug 14	Liverpool	A	1-0		Nov 4	Middlesbrough	H	2-0
Aug 21	Bradford City	A	1-0		Jan 23	Blackburn Rovers	H	2-1
Sept 18	Chelsea	H	1-0		Feb 10	West Ham United	A	1-0
Dec 28	Southampton	H	3-2		Apr 9	Portsmouth	H	4-2
Mar 18	Sheffield Wednesday	H	1-0		May 5	Reading	A	2-0
May 14	Coventry City	H	1-0					

Premier League finishing position

		P	W	D	L	F	A	Pts
20	Watford	38	6	6	26	35	77	24

Premier League finishing position

		P	W	D	L	F	A	Pts
20	Watford	38	5	13	20	29	59	28

WATFORD................4 LUTON TOWN................3

FA Cup third round replay, January 10 1984

The famous four give Hornets the edge in a compelling cup classic

Even the Hatters manager, David Pleat, had to admit that although he didn't like the outcome, he had enjoyed all 210 minutes of an enthralling and dramatic FA Cup tie.

Before the third round draw had been made, Graham Taylor suggested that Watford had a 'better than one in eleven' chance of reaching Wembley.

And then the balls came out of the velvet bag, sending Watford to the worst possible place. Kenilworth Road.

Twenty-six minutes into the tie, and Watford's dreams of a cup run were hanging by a thread. They were 2-0 down to a pair of deflected goals. Watford needed to respond quickly, and they did.

John Barnes got one back within a minute and Maurice Johnston equalised from the penalty spot. The second half was a real blood and thunder affair but there were no further goals, so it was back to Vicarage Road.

This time, Watford led 2-0 inside half an hour. Nigel Callaghan gave them the lead and George Reilly doubled it.

Luton scored at a crucial time when Mal Donaghy got one back just before half-time.

When John Barnes scored a superb individual goal five minutes into the second half, it looked as if Watford had done enough to shrug off their fierce rivals. Of course, they should have known better.

Two goals in five minutes from Paul Walsh got Luton back on terms. The pace of the game was frantic but the skill levels were high.

The final 20 minutes were blistering. There were two teams intent on defeating each other. Credit must go to Luton for refusing to settle for a draw.

Taylor later said he knew his team would come out on top in extra time. 'As long as we did nothing silly, we'd got them.'

Extra time was tense. Both teams continued to go for the throat and there were some heart-stopping moments at both ends. Three minutes into the second period, Johnston popped up to score the winner. It meant all of Watford's forwards were on the scoresheet.

Taylor called it the match of the season and in terms of carefree attack play, it was. Watford and Luton shared a similar mentality but they played the game in very different ways.

Knocking that mob in white and orange out of the cup tasted almost as sweet as reaching the final itself.

Sherwood, Bardsley, Rostron, Taylor, Sims, Franklin, Callaghan, Johnston, Reilly, Jackett, Barnes
Manager Graham Taylor
Scorers Callaghan 4, Reilly 28, Barnes 50, Johnston 108
Luton scorers Donaghy 44, Walsh 65, 69
Attendance 20,586

PORT VALE .... 1 WATFORD 2

The tension was unbearable. At times, Watford's fans could simply not watch – and not just because the setting sun behind the Vale Park was blinding.

A week earlier, the game had been postponed after heavy rain during the afternoon. Now it was on, Watford knew victory would take them into the play-off zone with just two games left.

The Hornets had won five in a row to force themselves into contention when all hope looked to have been lost.

Terry Challis, the *Watford Observer* cartoonist, summed up the situation beautifully. He depicted a Hornet rapidly gaining ground on a nervous-looking pig (Bolton are the Trotters) and a terrified wolf (Wolves) with the caption 'The marathon is over, now it's time for the sprint finish.'

Watford lost the toss and had to kick into the sun in the first half. It made things very awkward for the defenders. 'Kenny Jackett said to me before the game that if I was in doubt I should just head the sun,' says Steve Palmer.

Allan Smart, sent off against Tranmere, was suspended so sat in the stand among the Watford supporters and remembers the night he willed the team on with the fervour of a lifelong fan.

This was not a dead, end-of-season fixture for Port Vale. They were fending off relegation and couldn't afford to lose their game in hand at home.

It was an edgy match from the start and Watford's nerves didn't really settle after Tommy Mooney had given them the lead because Vale were level four minutes later. Palmer and Alan Lee clashed off the ball and Tommy Widdrington scored the resulting penalty.

A minute later, Paul Robinson was lucky to avoid a red card when he lunged late and hard at Stewart Talbot after the whistle had been blown and the ball had gone. It was a horrible challenge that left Talbot with a broken leg.

Mooney scored Watford's second goal on the hour mark and then there was the agony of waiting for the final whistle for the supporters.

The celebrations at the end were epic, as if the belief coursed from the supporters to the team and back again.

Six wins had hauled Watford up to fifth in the table. Now they had one foot in the play-offs, Graham Taylor had to work his magic and keep the players focused. 'Every game was a big game but it was all about winning by then,' says Mooney. 'We knew we had to win every game. Normally you concentrate on the performances and hope that the results follow but this was different.

'After beating Port Vale you could tell everyone was thinking we were going to do it. No one dared say it but in the Port Vale dressing room we knew we were going to Wembley.'

Chamberlain, Bazeley, Kennedy, Page, Palmer, Robinson, Ngonge, Hyde, Mooney, Johnson, Wright (Hazan 80)
Manager Graham Taylor
Scorer Mooney 24, 60
Port Vale scorer Widdrington 28 pen
Attendance 7,126

WEST HAM UNITED........... 0 WATFORD............. 1

FA Cup fourth round, Saturday January 27 2007

McNamee lands the first blow as Hornets do the Upton Park double

Over the years, there have been a number of fine young players who have not quite fulfilled their early potential. It is a myth that a promising young player must mature into a John Barnes or an Ashley Young.

For every Barnes and Young there have been a handful of Rod Thomases or Anthony McNamees.

Having seen off Stockport County in the FA Cup third round, Watford had to travel to Upton Park to face fellow Premiership strugglers West Ham.

Bobby Zamora hit the bar in the first minute for West Ham and the hosts had another couple of great chances before Watford got the only goal of the game.

Roy Carroll came off his line to deal with a long ball but mistimed his jump and the ball fell near McNamee.

The diminutive winger threw himself in the air to pull off a great bicycle kick. Moments of brilliance like this that made McNamee a favourite with the fans, despite his inconsistency.

McNamee had asthma, which meant his endurance was badly compromised. However, in short bursts he promised so much. He could run at defenders, turning them inside and then out. But he could also contort himself so much that he'd run into a cul-de-sac and find he had nowhere left to turn.

In that respect he was more like Rod Thomas, the prodigious winger who emerged in the late Eighties but had faded by the early Nineties, than John Barnes.

McNamee's goal – one of only two he scored for Watford – set up a tense second half.

West Ham dominated and put the Hornets' defence under immense pressure. The Hammers created chance after chance but a combination of good luck and heroic defending somehow kept Zamora, Luis Boa Morte and Carlton Cole at bay. Ben Foster made a number of great saves too.

It kept the cup run going, which diverted attention away from the slog of trying to preserve their Premiership status. In the fifth round, Watford beat Ipswich Town to set up a quarter-final clash with Plymouth.

A fortnight later, Watford were back at Upton Park for a league match. Guess what? They did it again. A goal from Darius Henderson and another brilliant performance from Foster and Malky Mackay gave Watford a 1-0 win. As Foster, the former chef said: 'It beats stirring duck soup at Café Rouge.'

Foster, Mariappa, Mackay, DeMerit, Stewart, McNamee (Powell 72), Bangura, Francis, Bouazza, Smith, Henderson
Manager Aidy Boothroyd
Scorer McNamee 42
Attendance 31,168

Cup thrashing adds coppers to the coffers for cash-strapped Hornets

WATFORD...............5 SOUTHAMPTON...........2

Carling Cup fourth round, Tuesday November 9 2004

Almost 19 months had passed since the teams had met in the FA Cup semi-final at Villa Park. How things had changed.

Only four of Watford's semi-final line-up survived the constant rounds of cost-cutting. Southampton were a club in decline. Their new manager, Steve Wigley, was under fire, having gone 10 Premiership games without a win. The Saints were there for the taking.

Watford had proved themselves difficult to beat but were struggling to turn draws into wins.

This was precisely the sort of game they needed. 'I knew Steve because we played together at Sheffield United,' says the Watford manager Ray Lewington.

'He's still a good friend but he was having a bad time there and I felt that if we could get at them, they might not be up for it.

'The last thing a team that is doing badly in the Premiership wants is a League Cup tie.

'Win it and no one gives you any credit and you don't get any points. Lose it and confidence takes another dive.'

Southampton had to call on their third choice goalkeeper, Alan Blayney, because of injuries and Watford made it a miserable night for him.

Bruce Dyer headed the first from a Neal Ardley free-kick after 39 minutes. 'We played really well in the first half,' Dyer says. 'We ran at them and we could tell they didn't like it at all. It took a while for us to get the goal but at half-time, the manager told us to really go for them because they were wobbling.'

They certainly were. James Chambers got the next two, the first a volley from Ardley's corner, the second a firm shot from Dyer's neat pull-back.

Ardley's wicked deliveries, Dyer's unpredictable running and Helguson's raw aggression were giving the Saints nightmares.

By now, the visitors were falling apart. Heidar Helguson got the fourth. A typical goal from the Icelandic striker, scored with the glorious, emphatic power and subtlety of a shot from a blunderbuss.

'We dismantled Southampton,' says Lewington. 'Okay, so they were very low on confidence but it was a great performance from our players. When you play

Hameur time: Bouazza slams Watford's fifth past the Southampton keeper Alan Blayney.

a struggling team from the Premiership it can go one of two ways. Fortunately for us, they collapsed when we put the pressure on them.

'I felt sorry for Steve because when we were three up the fans were giving him a lot of abuse. He didn't last there much longer after that.

'He was a good friend but we needed that result for ourselves. It meant money for the club, which was absolutely vital. We had lost all the high earners but we were still a good team.

'The one thing I was grateful for was that Helguson stayed. He is one of my favourite players of all the ones I've ever coached. He was adamant he didn't want to leave and I was delighted he didn't. If he'd gone, we would have lost so much and it would have upset me.'

Dexter Blackstock pulled one back but within 30 seconds one of the young subs, Hameur Bouazza, got Watford's fifth. Southampton did get another one back right at the end but there was no hiding the fact this was a drubbing.

For Lewington the emergence of Bouazza and Ashley Young, who also came on, proved Watford could survive the budget cuts.

'Ashley was a talent but the question was would he make it? He was so painfully thin back then,' says Lewington.

'I remember our academy coach Davie Dodds telling me then that he'd play for England one day. He had so much quality but I was frightened people would snap him in half. I knew he had a chance with his ability and the fact he wasn't intimidated.

'He was durable. We had Anthony McNamee but I don't think people realised how serious his asthma was. He had genuine ability but he could hardly run 200 yards and was never fully fit.'

Lee, Ardley, Gunnarsson, Cox (DeMerit 85), Dyche, Dyer (Bouazza 75), Mahon, Darlington, Helguson, Chambers (Young 71), Doyley
Manager Ray Lewington
Scorers Dyer 39, Chambers 52, 62, Helguson 66, Bouazza 84
Southampton scorers Blackstock 84, Ormerod 88
Attendance 13,008

FA Cup sixth round, Sunday March 9 2003

....

The draw for the quarter-finals had given Watford a chance. They were drawn at home and they had avoided Arsenal and Chelsea.

They had to wait to see who won the fifth round replay between Burnley and Premiership side Fulham, knowing that the Lancashire team would provide a better chance of reaching the semi-finals. 'The home draw was absolutely crucial to us,' says Ray Lewington. 'We knew we had a chance against most teams at home. Maybe not the top sides from the Premiership but anyone else.

'We also knew that this was likely to be our only chance to get through. Turf Moor, when it's full, is a difficult place to go, so we wanted to get the job done at home.'

Watford's preparations were hit when striker Tommy Smith suffered minor injuries in a car crash a fortnight before the game.

The cup run was vital to Watford's financial future. Having narrowly avoided administration in the autumn, the books still made grim reading.

Nine players had been told they were to be released at the end of the season and another nine were waiting on tenterhooks to see what the club could afford to offer.

Two weeks before the Burnley match, Stephen Glass, who was brought in from Newcastle United on one of Gianluca Vialli's handsome contracts, was told that he would not be offered a new deal. Even on drastically reduced terms, Watford could not afford him.

Although high on tension, the first hour or so of this contest was low on quality. The two Division One teams were engaged in a desperate scrap to gain the upper hand but neither appeared to have the wit or guile to gain it.

And then, suddenly, everything clicked into place for Watford. Passes that had been misplaced began to find their men. The Hornets started to put a few useful moves together and chances started to appear.

After an hour, Heidar Helguson missed from five yards after Marcus Gayle had crossed beautifully from the left. Then Smith should have scored when he met Gavin Mahon's centre.

Burnley tried to hold them at bay but Watford kept going. They got the breakthrough after Helguson's fine shot was tipped over by Marlon Beresford.

From Neal Ardley's corner, the ball fell to Mahon, who tapped it to Smith to scramble over the line.

If that wasn't a beautiful goal, the one six minutes later was. Stephen Glass lined up to score a fantastic free-kick that flew over the wall and into the net.

It bagged the Hornets a semi-final place and a million pounds, if not a new contract for the scorer.

....

Chamberlain, Ardley, Cox, Gayle, Robinson, Mahon, Vernazza (Hand 65), Hyde, Glass, Helguson, Smith (Noel-Williams 77)
Manager Ray Lewington
Scorers Smith 74, Glass 80
Attendance 20,336

WATFORD................3 ARSENAL........................0

Division One, Tuesday April 1 1986

The night after the day before

Considering how many managers complain about fixture congestion and the demands placed on players today, how would Arsène Wenger react if he was told his side had to play on consecutive days?

And imagine the furore there would be if the mighty Gunners were beaten not once, but twice, by unfashionable opponents. That's what happened when, in the space of 30 hours, Watford beat Arsenal 5-0 on aggregate to pile the misery on the managerless club.

'When I tell young players today that we once beat Arsenal two days in a row, they don't believe me,' says Nigel Gibbs.

Watford had been due to face Arsenal at Vicarage Road on Boxing Day but the game was postponed because the pitch was frozen.

The match was re-arranged for April 1, to kick off just 27 hours after the two sides were due to meet at Highbury.

Until about a decade ago, it wasn't that unusual for teams to occasionally be required to play two days in a row, particularly at Christmas.

Arsenal were in disarray and two meetings with Watford were the last thing they needed. Their manager, Don Howe, had recently quit the job because of rumours the board were about to make an approach for Terry Venables.

Watford showed no mercy, despite being without half a dozen first team players. At Highbury, as the home fans protested against the board, Watford won 2-0.

The Hornets' teenage Welsh striker, Malcolm Allen, scored his first goal for the club and John Barnes got the other.

If Arsenal's fans thought it was a fluke they were in for more of the same the next day. Rumour has it the Arsenal's players drowned their sorrows that evening and some of them were still a little worse for wear when they faced Watford again the following night.

The first goal came when Barnes crossed and Neil Smillie's header was blocked by John Lukic only for Smillie to react smartly to stab the ball home.

Five minutes later, Martin Keown pulled down Barnes right on the edge of the box.

The referee gave Watford the benefit of the doubt and pointed to the spot. Kenny Jackett scored the penalty.

In the second half Allen scored his second goal in as many days when he finished off a fine passing move involving Barnes and Brian Talbot with a flourish.

The press focused on Arsenal's humiliation, of course, but there was no doubt that Watford had been far the better side.

Coton, Gibbs, Rostron, Talbot, Terry, McClelland, Smillie, Bardsley, Allen, Jackett, Barnes
Manager Graham Taylor
Scorers Smillie, Jackett pen, Allen
Attendance 18,635

CHELSEA.............1 WATFORD.....................3

Division Two, September 12 1981

The discovery of a superstar

Two years earlier, Graham Taylor had seen his Watford team lose 2-0 at Stamford Bridge and decided he had to make some serious changes if they were to cope with the Second Division.

Since then, Watford's progress had been steady, rather than spectacular. Having survived relegation during their first season in Division Two, they had hauled themselves up to mid-table with a strong finish to their second.

But Taylor's view was they had to make a strong challenge for promotion in the 1981-82 season or momentum might be lost.

It was another match at Chelsea that suggested to him that he had discovered the final piece of his jigsaw and that Watford were ready to push on.

Once in a while a young player comes along who everyone agrees has something special that sets them apart from the rest.

After winning 3-1 at Chelsea, Taylor thought to himself: 'We may have found a jewel here.'

The 17-year-old winger John Barnes had handled the racist abuse from the unenlightened on the terraces and the rough challenges from the Chelsea defenders with the sort of strength and maturity that belied his years.

Barnes had been quietly impressive ever since he first played for the junior and reserve teams but it wasn't until he spent the summer training with the first team that he began to demonstrate the full range of his skills and ability.

Often, the club captain and right back, Pat Rice, would have to mark Barnes in training. It wasn't an experience he particularly enjoyed. In fact, when Barnes gave him a particularly hard time one day, he feared his own career might be drawing to a close.

'The thing about Barnes was he had this easy confidence,' says Rice. 'And the nightmare for defenders was that he rarely did the same thing twice in a match. He wasn't a one-trick pony like a lot of wingers. He had pace, he could pass, he could make space for himself, he could beat you by going outside and by cutting inside.'

Bertie Mee, Watford's assistant manager, gave Rice a lift home from training one day and asked him whether he thought Barnes would be ready to make his first team debut in the coming season. 'He's ready now,' was Rice's unequivocal reply.

Although Barnes was quiet during his brief appearance as a substitute against Oldham Athletic he got into the team against Chelsea because Luther Blissett was suspended following his dismissal at Newcastle on the opening day of the season.

Barnes was the star of the show at Stamford Bridge. Watford welcomed back Ross Jenkins, who had spent the summer playing in the United States to help him recover from injury.

Nigel Callaghan gave Watford the lead before half-time only for Clive Walker to equalise shortly afterwards.

In the second half, the two teenage wingers, Barnes on the left, Callaghan on the right, began to stretch Chelsea.

With Jenkins winning everything in the air, Watford bombarded them.

Wilf Rostron, who was to be converted into an attacking left-back in the home match against Chelsea later in the season, scored the second after bursting forward from midfield.

Gerry Armstrong got the third to seal a comfortable win that meant the Hornets would be marked down as early contenders for promotion.

But it was the discovery of Barnes that excited Taylor. 'It gave the whole team an extra dimension,' he says.

'We had a balance to our attack and he was a very different style of winger to Nigel on the other side. Suddenly we had two very potent attacking options, which was very hard for teams to cope with. When you look for key moments, finding John Barnes was one of them.'

Sherwood, Rice, Jackett, Taylor, Sims, Bolton, Callaghan, Armstrong, Jenkins, Rostron, Barnes
Manager Graham Taylor
Scorers Callaghan 39, Rostron 62, Armstrong 81
Chelsea scorer Walker 42
Attendance 20,036

WHO'S THE GREATEST?

Is this the greatest ever Watford XI? If you had to pick players based on just their performances for Watford, could you do better than this?

Tony Coton
Steve Sims   John McClelland
Nigel Gibbs   Wilf Rostron

Richard Johnson   Kenny Jackett

Nigel Callaghan   John Barnes
Luther Blissett   Cliff Holton

What about picking a team based on the achievements of Watford players throughout their careers?

1 Pat Jennings
Played for Watford in 1963-64., then Spurs and Arsenal and in two World Cups. 119 caps.
2 Pat Rice
Won league and FA Cup double with Arsenal in 1971. Capped 49 times by Northern Ireland.
3 Gary Williams
Won the league and European Cup for Aston Villa. Played for Watford from 1990 to 1991.
4 Kevin Richardson
Was in Everton's 1984 FA Cup-winning team. Won league with Arsenal after leaving Watford.
5 Filippo Galli
Member of Milan's legendary team managed by Capello. Won the European Cup three times.
6 John McClelland
Captained Glasgow Rangers won the league with Leeds and played in the World Cup twice.
7 Ashley Young
Still early days at Old Trafford but has the making of a Manchester United hero.
8 Luther Blissett
Played for Milan. Won 14 England caps and scored a hat-trick against Luxembourg.
9 Tony Currie
Idolised at Sheffield United, Leeds and QPR. Played for England 17 times.
10 Kevin Phillips
Has scored over 250 goals, including 30 during his first Premiership season with Sunderland
11 John Barnes
Two league championships and two FA Cups at Liverpool and 79 caps for England.

The Championship, Friday December 10 2010

Danny Graham and Queens Park Rangers were both bound for the Premier League.

Jingle bells, jingle bells, jingle all the way. Oh what fun it is to see the Hornets win away.

With Christmas just around the corner, Watford delivered an early present for their fans by outplaying the league leaders at Loftus Road.

Queens Park Rangers had not lost in the league all season but Watford ripped them apart with a deft display of counter-attacking football.

This was Malky Mackay's team at its best. With John Eustace holding the midfield securely, Don Cowie, Will Buckley, Stephen McGinn and Jordon Mutch were able to take turns breaking forward to support Danny Graham.

Graham's two goals were of such sublime quality it was becoming clear that the task of keeping him at Vicarage

Road might prove beyond Watford.

They were two ahead at half-time, and Graham's second soon after the break put the game out of QPR's reach. It wasn't until the last minute that Tommy Smith scored a consolation.

The match was shown live by the BBC and any Watford supporters who recorded the match had a half-time treat to look forward to – a glorious musical montage of the Elton John and Graham Taylor era. That crisp December night it felt as if Mackay was building something similar.

Loach, A Taylor, M Taylor, Mariappa, Doyley, Eustace, Cowie, Buckley (Deeney 80), McGinn (Sordell 75), Mutch, Graham
Manager Malky Mackay
Scorers Graham 26, 48, Mutch 30
QPR scorer Smith 89
Attendance 14,079

PLYMOUTH ARGYLE .....0 WATFORD..............1

FA Cup sixth round, Sunday March 11 2007

It's rarely a good sign when your manager starts seeing a conspiracy theory in the kick-off time.

Watford's sixth round tie at Home Park was moved to Sunday teatime so it could be shown live by BBC and Aidy Boothroyd said, 'They have done their best to make sure there is an upset. The pitch is not the best and it's a long way down there. Everything's against us.'

It has to be said, Watford were ripe for an upset. Second from bottom in the Premiership, the FA Cup had at least provided some light relief from what had become a grim slog.

After victory over Ipswich Town in the fifth round, Watford got a slice of luck in the draw that wouldn't have gone amiss in the league – they were paired with the only non-Premiership side left in the competition.

The press seized on it as a re-run of the 1984 semi-final and billed it the Battle of George Reilly's ear.

The goalscorer in that Villa Park clash 23 years earlier had been attacked while working on a building site in 2003. His assailant bit a chunk out of his earlobe and said: 'That's for Plymouth.'

Despite Boothroyd's fears, Watford were thoroughly professional and got the job done.

'We knew we had to work hard to get ourselves up for that game,' says Jay DeMerit. 'We'd been playing in the Premiership where every week you face a huge challenge. You go to impressive grounds and you're playing against some of the best players in the world.

It's pretty easy to get motivated, because you know that if you're not on top of your game you can get embarrassed.

'There's always a risk that people relax a little bit, mentally, when they then go and play a team from a lower division. We didn't do that. We went there and we were solid.'

Before the match, Plymouth re-enacted a strange 77-year-old ritual that they claimed had helped them win promotion from the Third Division. They placed a giant pasty behind the goal at the Davenport Road end.

Hameur Bouazza's superb first-time shot from Steven Kabba's pass knocked the stuffing out of Plymouth and their pasty.

But Argyle laid siege to Watford's goal in the second half and Ben Foster and his defence had a couple of lucky escapes.

Plymouth's manager Ian Holloway was frustrated but full of admiration for Foster's display.

'To be honest, I used to like that fella,' he said of the Watford keeper. 'But in the second half he stopped us reaching a cup semi-final.'

Boothroyd acknowledged Watford had ridden their luck. 'We have lost games where we've had spells like they had, so we know what it's like to give it everything and not get the breaks.'

Foster, Mariappa, Shittu, DeMerit, Powell, Smith, Francis, Mahon, Bouazza, Kabba (Chambers 59), Priskin (Henderson 73)
Manager Aidy Boothroyd
Scorer Bouazza 21
Attendance 20,652

WATFORD.......... 1 MANCHESTER UNITED.......0

Division One, Tuesday September 16 1986

The comic book story of a teenage striker who stunned Manchester United

The story of a teenage striker coming off the bench to score the winner against Manchester United is the stuff of schoolboy dreams.

Iwan Roberts was 18 years old, six feet three, but still feeling his way, hoping he had what it took to become a professional. As a lad from north Wales, he was one of Tom Walley's boys, which meant that life was all about hard work and discipline.

'I was doing okay for the reserves but the great thing about Graham Taylor was that he was not scared to put young players into the first team if he had to. We didn't have a big squad and even as a teenager, you were made to feel part of things. If you were the reserve team centre forward, you knew that if anything happened to the first team number nine, you would get the call.'

Roberts had made his debut against Ipswich Town in the pouring rain in March. Colin West got injured against QPR but Taylor hoped he would be fit, so left the decision as late as he could.

'On the Friday, Graham called me into the office and told me to ring my parents and tell them to come down from Wales because I was definitely going to be on the bench,' says Roberts. 'The club paid to put them up in the Hilton hotel on the A41 and they sat in the family enclosure. It was a

proud day for them. He didn't tell me I was in the team until Saturday morning but I had a sleepless night anyway.'

The Ipswich game was goalless and few chances fell his way. 'I was up against the England centre half, Terry Butcher, who was a tremendous player.'

Despite holding his own against Butcher, Roberts made only three more substitute appearances that season.

West moved to Glasgow Rangers in the summer and Taylor started the season with John Barnes and Luther Blissett playing through the middle.

Then Barnes got injured so the manager put Nigel Callaghan up front at Norwich and it worked well. Watford won 3-1 and Callaghan impressed in a central role. The next visitors to Vicarage Road were Manchester United. They had not started well and Ron Atkinson was under increasing pressure.

Taylor persisted with Callaghan as a striker but put Roberts on the bench.

'In those days, with only one sub, you knew that if the manager wanted to make a change, you'd be going on,' says Roberts. 'But Graham wasn't one to make substitutions for the sake of it. I was just hoping I'd get to come on near the end.'

Although United were struggling in the league, having won just one of their first five games, they still had plenty

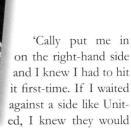

of quality, although goalie Chris Turner, the man who had let in eight at Vicarage Road playing for Sunderland probably still had nightmares about the place.

United dominated the first half. They had more possession and more chances, eight to Watford's one, a Steve Terry header that went straight into Turner's arms.

Brian Talbot was doing a sterling man-marking job on Bryan Robson but it was the equivalent of the little boy using his finger to plug the dam. You sensed that eventually it was going to burst and Watford were going to get washed away.

At half time Roberts didn't get long to dwell on what he was ahead of him.

'Graham put me on at half-time because I think he felt I could win a bit more in the air against Moran and McGrath, who were excellent defenders but they weren't the tallest,' he says. 'Graham told me to just play my normal game, forget the opposition, forget the surroundings, just do what I always did.

'I remember winning my first header and it settled me down a bit but United were a very good team in a false position and it was hard to get into the game.'

United continued to create chances while Watford's impact in the final third was minimal. And then Roberts got a chance, only the second clear-cut opportunity Watford had in the game.

'Cally put me in on the right-hand side and I knew I had to hit it first-time. If I waited against a side like United, I knew they would shut me down. I just wanted to hit it as sweetly as I could.'

Roberts timed his shot perfectly. The ball flew low, skimming across the turf, into the corner, just out of Turner's reach.

'I was still concentrating on the game but your head is swimming,' he says. 'I was a Liverpool fan as a kid, I'd come on as a sub and I'd scored against United. As much as it's selfish to say so, I was desperate for us to hold on because to say you've scored the winner means so much more.

'As long as I live I will remember two goals, my 200th, at Gigg Lane, Bury, when I was on loan for Cambridge, and my first against United.

'A TV crew from Wales had been filming Malcolm Allen and me all week. I can picture them interviewing Tom Walley afterwards. Tom said exactly the right thing. "Yeah, he's done okay. He's scored the winner against Manchester United but it's only one goal. He hasn't done nothing yet." That was the best thing Tom could have said.'

Coton, Talbot, Rostron, Richardson, Terry, McClelland, Bardsley, Blissett, Callaghan, Jackett, Sterling (Roberts 46)
Manager Graham Taylor
Scorer Roberts
Attendance 21,650

BLACKBURN ROVERS......3 WATFORD 4

Division One, Tuesday September 12 2000

Hornets survive crisis to leave Rovers running on empty

Britain was in the grip of a fuel crisis. Farmers and lorry drivers had blockaded oil depots in protest at the soaring cost of diesel. Queues formed on the forecourts, then the petrol pumps ran dry.

There was an away game to get to. Watford laid on an extra coach for the supporters as many opted to leave their cars at home. Fewer than 200 Watford fans managed to make the journey but they witnessed a thriller.

With Robert Page injured, Tommy Mooney was made captain for the night. 'We got to the hotel before the match and the gaffer gave me the news,' says Mooney. 'I had been captain before but it's always special to lead out the side. It's a very proud day.

'Graham gave me the complimentary tickets to pass round to the lads but most of them were not given out. Few of the families could make it because of the petrol crisis.'

Watford's season had got off to a fantastic start with four wins from their opening five league games. Only a draw against Wimbledon, who had also been relegated from the Premiership, blotted a perfect record.

Mooney went to the pre-match meeting in the referee's room and if he needed any further motivation for the game, Blackburn's manager provided it.

'Graeme Souness was not the most likeable chap,' he says. 'He was being derogatory about how direct we were, trying to make jokes to the ref that the ball was going to be shelled into the box. He was having a go and trying to get onside with the ref at the same time. I thought, if he'd said some of those things to me in a shopping centre I'd have knocked him out.'

But it was Watford who were on their knees after little more than quarter of an hour. With Page absent from the defence and Matt Jansen running amok, the Hornets were two down and the small band of hardy souls who'd made the journey to Lancashire must have wondered why they'd bothered.

David Dunn scored the first after six minutes, then Nathan Blake scrambled the second over the line after his initial header had rebounded off the bar and fallen at his feet.

Two minutes later, Micah Hyde pulled one back when he struck a fine shot from the edge of the area after Allan Nielsen's corner.

The turning point came after 20 minutes when Jansen, who was integral to everything Rovers did in attack, was badly injured in a collision with Espen Baardsen and had to go off.

In midfield, Hyde began to run the show. This was one of his finest games for Watford. He dropped deep, he went forward, he linked the defence and the attack and he spread the ball wide. It was one of those days when he seemed to have the ball on a string like a yo-yo and could send it out and gather it back at will.

Watford were level when Heidar Helguson stooped to head in from a Paul Robinson cross and then Hyde gave them the lead with a beautifully placed shot from long range. He found the only available space between the post and Alan Kelly's outreached palm.

They went from 2-0 down to 3-2 up in the space of 20 minutes thanks to fine attacking play. Mooney made it 4-2 with a thumping header that said 'Take that, Souness' before Blake set up a nervy final few minutes with Rovers' third.

'It was an amazing game but very surreal to go over to the Watford fans at the end,' says Mooney. 'There can't have been more than a hundred of them there and you could pick out individual faces. It felt like we'd done it for them.

'Souness kicked off in the press conference, complaining about the way we played. I didn't care about that but I do remember getting back to Vicarage Road at one in the morning and worrying if I had enough fuel to get home.'

Baardsen, Cox, Robinson, Palmer, Ward, Hyde, Mooney, Noel-Williams, Smith, Helguson (Gibbs 82), Nielsen
Manager Graham Taylor
Scorers Hyde 18, 37, Helguson 35, Mooney 65
Blackburn scorers Dunn 6, Blake 16, 87
Attendance 17,258

Watford's best start to a league campaign promised an instant return to the Premiership.

They were unbeaten for 15 games and, together with Fulham, were well clear at the top. Towards the end of that run, they lost 3-0 at home to a young Manchester United team in the League Cup, which was a harsh reminder of how tough the top division could be.

Then the wheels fell off. Seven defeats in the next eight matches, including a 5-0 thrashing at Fulham on Boxing Day, saw them slip out of the play-off places when automatic promotion had looked within their grasp. They eventually finished ninth. What went wrong? 'If I knew what it was, we'd have gone up,' says Mooney. 'It can go either way. We were on a great run at the start and couldn't stop winning, even when we weren't playing well. Then we couldn't win, even when we were playing well. Finally the confidence just deserts you.'

August				
Sat 12	Huddersfield Town	A	W	2-1
Sat 19	Barnsley	H	W	1-0
Sat 26	Wimbledon	A	D	0-0
Mon 28	Sheffield United	H	W	4-1
September				
Sat 9	Portsmouth	A	W	3-1
Tue 12	Blackburn Rovers	A	W	4-3
Sat 16	Crewe Alexandra	H	W	3-0
Sat 23	Stockport County	A	W	3-2
October				
Sun 1	Birmingham City	H	W	2-0
Sat 14	QPR	H	W	3-1
Tue 17	Gillingham	H	D	0-0
Sat 21	Nottingham Forest	A	W	2-0
Tue 24	Bolton Wanderers	H	W	1-0
Sat 28	Wolves	A	D	2-2
November				
Sat 4	Grimsby Town	H	W	4-0

DIVISION ONE

November 4, 2000

		P	W	D	L	F	A	Pts
1	Watford	15	12	3	0	34	11	39
2	Fulham	15	12	2	1	37	10	38
3	Birmingham	16	9	4	3	25	13	31
4	Bolton	17	8	6	3	27	19	30
5	Burnley	16	8	5	3	17	17	29
6	Preston	16	8	4	4	19	14	28

WATFORD.............2 SUNDERLAND.............1

Division One, Saturday January 30 1999

S underland were well on their way to the Premiership, propelled there by Niall Quinn and Kevin Phillips.

They were top of the league and went on to win the title by a distance but they came up against a Watford team that embodied all the qualities that typified a Graham Taylor side.

The Hornets produced a result and performance that they could store in the memory banks and summon as inspiration later in the season.

Watford had been dipping, having failed to score a goal in the league for three matches, but there was a positive feeling in the air before this one.

Nick Wright played at centre forward alongside Gifton Noel-Williams and they were every bit as dangerous as Quinn and Phillips.

'Tony Daley was out on the right wing,' says Wright. 'He wasn't as quick as in his Aston Villa days but he still had the ability to go past a player and put in a cross.'

Daley ran at Sunderland from the start and it was clear the visitors didn't fancy that too much.

It was Daley who set up the first goal. 'My objective was to move the defender away and then make some space for myself just before the ball came over,' says Wright. 'It was a great delivery and I managed to get a good contact on it.'

Spurred on by a loud, passionate crowd that matched the fervour of the visiting hordes from the north east, Watford kept going forward.

Once a Hornet, always a Hornet. When the crowd chanted 'Kevin, what's the score, Kevin, Kevin, what's the score,' Phillips turned and held his hands up to answer. One-nil. The Vicarage Road end roared its approval.

It was one apiece soon enough. Quinn levelled towards the end of a breathtaking first half.

Remarkably, Watford found they were able to step it up a gear after the break. The winning goal was a thing of beauty. Ben Iroha took a long throw that Noel-Williams controlled on his chest with grace and care.

In one smooth movement he lashed a looping half-volley on the turn. The ball pinged off his foot and flew past Thomas Sorensen. It was the finest goal he had scored for Watford. For such a strapping, powerful man, Noel-Williams was capable of surprising suppleness.

Soon after, his entire career was jeopardised when he was crunched by a terrible challenge from Paul Butler. The resulting knee injury kept him out for a year and he was never the same again.

Watford had beaten the best team in the division and Butler had exacted his revenge. Although Watford spluttered through the first part of spring, the win over Sunderland was always there as a reminder of what they could achieve.

Chamberlain, Bazeley, Kennedy, Page, Palmer, Iroha, Wright, Hyde, Noel-Williams (Mooney 67), Johnson, Daley (Hazan 81)
Manager Graham Taylor
Scorers Wright 18, Noel-Williams 53
Sunderland scorer Quinn 36
Attendance 20,188

WATFORD.................3 SOUTHPORT.................2

Division Four, Saturday April 29 1978

Watford were already champions, crowned after a win at Scunthorpe earlier in the month.

This was their final match of a triumphant season and it brought their 30th league win, making it the most successful season in the club's history.

In his first season, Graham Taylor had delivered a trophy, the Fourth Division championship, to sit alongside the Third Division title won in 1969.

The players went on a lap of honour after the game. After three seasons in the bottom division, the supporters were just relieved the team had hauled themselves up a rung.

Taylor, of course, was already looking ahead. He had told Elton John he wanted to sign three players to add to a squad he felt was already good enough to finish in the top six in Division Three.

Elton, struck by his manager's drive and ambition, said after the match: 'Graham is an incredible motivator. He can turn ordinary people into those with a superhuman work-rate. I am absolutely convinced he will be England's manager one day.'

The game itself was emblematic of the rise Watford were about to enjoy. They were saying goodbye to places that had been all too familiar over the past 20 years. They would no longer have to go to Halifax, Hartlepool or Darlington on a regular basis.

And they certainly wouldn't have to go to Southport. The two clubs were headed in very different directions.

DIVISION FOUR

End of the season

		P	W	D	L	F	A	Pts
1	Watford	46	30	11	5	85	38	71
2	Southend Utd	46	25	10	11	66	39	60
3	Swansea City	46	23	10	13	87	47	56
4	Brentford	46	21	14	11	86	54	56
5	Aldershot	46	19	16	11	67	47	54
6	Grimsby Town	46	21	11	14	57	51	53

While Watford were upwardly mobile, their opponents were about to be voted out of the league.

Having finished second from bottom for a third consecutive season, the other Football League clubs cast a cross against them when they were forced to apply for re-election.

They didn't know it at the time but this turned out to be Southport's final Football League fixture.

The referee, Ronald Crabb, was also saying farewell to the league, for he was retiring. He was determined to go out on a high, as the centre of attention.

Mr Crabb awarded three penalties. Keith Pritchett converted both of Watford's in the opening quarter of an hour before O'Neill pulled one back, also from the spot. Blissett made it 3-1 before half-time and although Southport pulled another back, Elton's rocket men had achieved lift off. It was to be quite a journey.

Rankin, McClenaghan, Garner, Bolton, Pritchett, Booth, Bond, Downes, Pollard, Mayes, Blissett
Manager Graham Taylor
Scorers Pritchett 6 pen, 13 pen, Blissett 44
Southport scorers O'Neill 37 pen, Cooper 70
Attendance 10,089

MIDDLESBROUGH 1   WATFORD 2

Division Two, Saturday March 23 1991

David Byrne scored the winning goal with what turned out to be his final touch in a Watford shirt.

His left-footed shot won the goal of the season award and was the catalyst for the most unlikely escape act in the club's history. It is remarkable to think he never played for the first team again.

The Hornets were six points adrift at the bottom of the table having not won for almost three months.

A 3-0 defeat at home to Blackburn in midweek seemed to have confirmed Watford's fate. A trip to high-flying Middlesbrough offered little hope of an upturn in fortunes and another defeat would surely make relegation a reality.

Boro had a string of chances but neither side had managed to break the deadlock. With 15 minutes to go, Steve Perryman told David Byrne to warm up. He was going on.

'Steve and I had fallen out. Colin Lee signed me earlier in the season but he got the sack and it was clear I wasn't Steve's type of player,' says Byrne.

'Steve told me to go on and do something special. I replied that he wasn't giving me very long to do it.'

Within a minute of Byrne getting on the pitch, Ian Baird put Boro ahead, beating Glenn Roeder to the ball and applying a composed finish.

It is not overstating matters to say that Watford now needed a miracle.

Ten minutes from the end, they were thrown a lifeline. Gary Porter curled a free-kick from the edge of the penalty area around the wall and just inside Andy Dibble's right-hand post. Suddenly there was a glimmer of hope.

Time was running out and the game was into the final minute. 'They had a corner that David James came out to catch,' says Byrne. 'I made a run into a bit of space and he threw it out. He had a huge throw so I picked it up on the halfway line.

'Every step forward I took, their defenders took a step back, so I kept going. It got caught under my feet so to get it free I took it onto my left, which was never my strongest side. I only used to stand on my left foot but they had all backed off instead of closing me down so I thought it was shit or bust.

'I hit it and as soon as it left my foot I knew the lad Dibble wasn't going to get to it.' Byrne pulled off a somersault in celebration and seconds later the referee blew the full-time whistle.

Watford went on to win six of their final ten games to avoid relegation but Byrne didn't play a part in any of those matches.

He was sent out on loan a few times and eventually joined St Johnstone.

Has a player's final touch of the ball for a club ever been more influential? Without that goal it is probable that Watford's incredible revival would not have got off the ground.

James, Gibbs, Drysdale (Denton 83), Dublin, Ashby, Roeder, Callaghan (Byrne 75), Nicholas, Wilkinson, Porter, Falconer
Manager Steve Perryman
Scorers Porter 81, Byrne 89
Middlesbrough scorer Baird 76
Attendance 14,583

WATFORD..............3 PORTSMOUTH..........0

Carling Cup fifth round, November 30 2004

Twenty one days after the slaughter of Southampton, Watford put paid to Portsmouth's Carling Cup hopes. Both south coast clubs were in utter disarray as autumn turned to winter and the Hornets made sure they took full advantage.

Pompey had just lost their manager, Harry Redknapp, who resigned unhappy at Milan Mandaric's decision to appoint Velimir Zajec as director of football.

Watford were also reeling. Three days earlier, they had led 2-0 after 21 minutes at Upton Park only for West Ham to come back and win 3-2.

Ray Lewington sensed Portsmouth might be vulnerable but there was no doubting that, even without their talismanic and charismatic manager, they were far better opposition than their neighbours had been.

However, when Lewington saw the visiting side's team sheet before the game, he was puzzled. 'They had been playing 4-4-2 but when I saw their team sheet I wondered how he was going to get that formation out of the players he'd picked,' he says.

'When the game kicked off, it was clear they were going with three at the back, which suited us down to the ground because we had wide players who could get behind them.'

After surviving an early scare, when Linvoy Primus caught the Watford defence cold only to send the ball over the bar from six yards, Watford began to stretch Pompey.

From a Neil Cox free-kick, Heidar

Bruce Dyer scored Watford's third and Portsmouth were down and out.

Helguson leapt with his customary desire and defiance. He outjumped the goalkeeper, Jamie Ashdown, who had, perhaps unwisely, decided to come out to the edge of his area to get the ball.

Helguson's header sent the ball looping in the air. There was a pregnant pause as Watford's fans held their breath hoping it had enough power to get over the line. Desperate lunges by a couple of defenders couldn't stop it.

At half-time, the occasion took a bizarre and slightly pantomime sinister turn. With a Watford scarf round his neck and over his long black leather trenchcoat the Black Sabbath singer Ozzy Osbourne, together with his wife Sharon, walked onto the pitch to a surprisingly rapturous reception. They were there to film a piece for the ITV show *X-Factor*. Was it an omen?

Surely, with the Prince of Darkness on their side, Watford couldn't fail.

In the second half, Portsmouth changed their formation to try to cope with Watford's wide play but it didn't do them much good. If anything, Watford played even better.

Jermaine Darlington sent over yet another cross for Helguson to slot his second of the game. Four minutes later, Bruce Dyer capped what was probably his finest performance in a Watford shirt when he scored from close range after Ashdown had blocked a shot from James Chambers.

Three-nil and it could have been more. Neal Ardley hit the underside of the bar and Paul Devlin was also denied late on. The Premiership side had been well and truly stuffed.

Just as the cheers were beginning to fade, the victorious Hornets came out of the tunnel for an encore and the supporters nearly lifted the roof off.

For the second season in a row, and on a budget of little more than buttons and pocket fluff, Ray Lewington had taken Watford to a major semi-final. No wonder it felt so good.

Lee, Darlington, Dyche, Cox, Doyley, Ardley, Mahon, Gunnarsson (Blizzard 45), Chambers, Dyer (Devlin 79), Helguson (Fitzgerald 88)
Manager Ray Lewington
Scorers Helguson 24, 57, Dyer 61
Attendance 18,887

WALKING AMONG GIANTS

The four teams that went into the hat for the semi-finals of the Carling Cup were Chelsea, Manchester United, Liverpool and Watford.

So what if there was very little realistic chance of actually reaching the final? This is what the cups used to be all about. A chance to rub shoulders with the greats.

Watford were drawn against Liverpool and had to travel to Anfield first. 'I thought, over the two legs, we could have won,' says Lewington. 'It was very close. We went up there and played 4-5-1 to try to get around Steven Gerrard. He had that free role in midfield and, as we saw, it only took a moment for him to hurt you. He scored a very scrappy goal. We had a couple of good chances – Gunnarsson with a diving header and H [Helguson] hit the bar at the end. We had a real go and a few of the Liverpool players said we'd been the better side.'

Trailing 1-0, Watford now had a real chance but Lewington knew that Liverpool would be very dangerous. 'Premiership sides love it if you come onto them because they can pick you off with their quality. We decided not to go all out. We couldn't be gung-ho, we had to be cagey and keep it tight. The longer it went on, the better our chance of getting a goal.'

Thirteen minutes from time Gerrard conjured another decisive moment to send the Reds to Cardiff. 'Top players can be anonymous for much of a game but they can create something special to knock you out,' says Dyer.

One evening, less than two months after Watford had lost to Liverpool in the Carling Cup semi-final, Ray Lewington took a call from Oliver Phillips of the *Watford Observer*.

'Oli said to me "I hope I'm wrong but my sources tell me you're getting the sack in the morning." At ten past seven the next day, the phone rang. I knew as it was ringing who it would be.'

It was Graham Simpson, the club's chairman, who wanted Lewington to meet him at the stadium.

'I knew what was coming but there hadn't been the normal signs. Usually there's a build-up to a manager getting sacked. The crowd are getting edgy and people look away when they see you in the corridor. Of course some fans were frustrated but I don't think everyone fully appreciated the restrictions we were working under.

'The disappointing thing was that I wanted to say goodbye to the players but I was told I was barred from the training ground. I didn't think I deserved that.'

A few days later, one of the players got in touch and said they'd like to meet Lewington in a pub near the training ground in London Colney so they could say their farewells 'That was nice of them. We had a drink and I wished them all the best,' says Lewington, who went on to work for Fulham in a range of coaching capacities.

Only in retrospect did Lewington piece together the changes that had been happening behind the scenes at Vicarage Road.

'We hadn't paid any agents a penny for two years and then we took James Chambers from West Brom. The chief executive [Mark Ashton] had worked at West Brom and he said he could get him. We paid money for him and I later found out that an agent had been involved too. Slowly the penny drops.

'A couple of weeks before I left, there were a few things happening that made me wonder. I heard that the chief executive had a meeting with a player from another club, offering him a place and telling him he'd be captain. As it turned out, the player didn't join, but it was clear that things were being talked about that I wasn't party to.'

The Hornets replaced Lewington with Aidy Boothroyd, who had been a youth development offer at The Hawthorns when Ashton was there.

Lewington says: 'The worst thing was seeing that suddenly there was money available for players. I had done what I had set out to do. We brought the wage bill down from ten million to £2.3m. We couldn't sign players unless we had money from elsewhere.'

Lewington was only able to take Paul Devlin because Elton John paid the wages.

'I looked at who they were now signing and I knew what the wages would be. These were people I'd have had no chance of getting because there simply wasn't the money.

'The one thing you know as a manager, one day you'll get the sack. I don't have any regrets. I loved it at Watford. Graham Simpson was great for the first two years but he seemed to have a change of personality in the third year.'

The supporters may have been frustrated with the lack of progress in the league but given the budget cuts, it was an achievement just to keep the team in the division.

And Lewington is the only manager other than Graham Taylor to take the club to two major cup semi-finals.

Photograph: Press Association

Cliff Holton and Dennis Uphill (number nine) causing chaos in the Birmingham area.

40   WATFORD............2 BIRMINGHAM CITY............1

FA Cup third round, Saturday January 9 1960

Watford prepared to take on First Division Birmingham City with a three-day trip to Margate, where they worked on stopping the threat posed by winger Harry Hooper.

They spent a lot of time running at the full-back Bobby Bell, preparing him for the potential onslaught from the fast and direct winger.

The team's pre-match meal was steak and chips at the One Crown pub in the town. It obviously worked because after 20 minutes they were 2-0 up.

Seven minutes in, Holton bullied the Blues keeper Johnny Schofield, forcing him to fumble Micky Benning's cross. The ball fell to Dennis Uphill who only had to force it across the line from a yard. Holton got the second himself, turning on a knock-down from Hartle

to blast home one of finest goals for Watford. Although Hooper pulled one back from long-range six minutes from time, Watford reached the fourth round for the first time since 1950.

'We had everything to gain and very little to lose,' said Uphill. 'We knew we had a good chance if we could get the early goal. And when we did, it proved that these First Division teams are just flesh and blood like us.'

'I have played for the big fellows when they have been knocked out by the little clubs,' said Holton. 'It's nice to be on the side of the underdogs now.'

Linton, Bell, Nicholas, Catleugh, McNeice, Chung, Benning, Holton, Uphill, Hartle, Bunce
Manager Ron Burgess
Scorers Uphill 7, Holton 19
Birmingham scorer Hooper 84
Attendance 31,314

ARSENAL .... 2 WATFORD 4

Division One, Saturday November 27 1982

Graham Taylor did well to keep a straight face when he told the press after the game that the Highbury crowd must be unused to such rip-roaring entertainment. 'When was the last time they saw six goals in a game here?' he asked, rhetorically.

It did little to defuse the growing storm surrounding Watford's style.

Victory at Tottenham Hotspur at the start of the month had shaken up English football's establishment.

The new kids on the block and their take-no-prisoners approach was the big talking point, with the purists fretting that Watford's style was going to mean the end of English football as we knew it. Even Don Howe, Arsenal's assistant manager, suggested that if everyone adopted Watford's way, the game would be set back 20 years.

And that is why Taylor's comment was loaded with sarcasm. The Highbury crowd was used to seeing defenders putting their arms and up appealing for offside. They were used to seeing more backpasses than crosses into the box. One-nil to the Arsenal was not just a terrace chant. It was a mantra.

GUNNERS' BOGEY TEAM

Watford won eight of the 12 Division One games against Arsenal. They also won the 1987 FA Cup quarter-final. The Hornets even did the double in 1987-88, the season they were relegated from the top flight.

Season	H	A	Season	H	A
82-83	2-1	4-2	85-86	3-0	2-0
83-84	2-1	1-3	86-87	2-0	1-3
84-85	3-4	1-1	87-88	2-0	1-0

Stewart Robson drove in a fine goal to open the scoring but Watford's pace, commitment and refusal to lie down completely unsettled the hosts.

The press complained about the long ball that led to Watford's equaliser just before half-time. A big punt upfield from Steve Sherwood was flicked on by Ross Jenkins, then Luther Blissett found John Barnes in space in the area. Barnes drilled a low shot that George Wood could not keep out of the net.

But they ignored the beauty and simplicity of a goal that started in one penalty box and ended in the other, taking just six touches from four players.

Shortly after half-time Kenny Jackett put Watford ahead when Arsenal failed to cope with a long Steve Sims throw.

Barnes made it 3-1 when he got in behind a flat-footed Arsenal defence. Brian Talbot pulled one back before Watford got a fourth. Barnes thought he had a hat-trick but the last touch came from Robson on the line so it was officially an own goal. It was harsh on Barnes because the ball was going in anyway.

Taylor prevented Pat Rice, the former Arsenal captain, from talking to the press afterwards but it did little to quell the controversy. However, they could talk all they liked. One thing was clear: Watford were here to stay.

Sherwood, Rice, Rostron, Taylor, Sims, Bolton, Callaghan, Blissett, Jenkins, Jackett, Barnes
Manager Graham Taylor
Scorers Barnes 43, 58, Jackett 50, Robson og 76
Arsenal scorers Robson 39, Talbot 72
Attendance 34,287

Not for the faint-hearted

PETERBOROUGH UNITED ...... 3 WATFORD 4

Division One, Tuesday April 5 1994

The moment of ecstasy and relief was short-lived. Watford's fans had barely recovered their breath after celebrating Gerard Lavin's incredible long-distance strike when they were brought crashing down to earth by Peterborough's equaliser.

Watford managed to hold on for less than a minute. A calamitous error by Perry Digweed gifted Tony Adcock his second goal.

The battle to avoid relegation was difficult and tense enough without their fingers hovering permanently over the self-destruct button.

Glenn Roeder's side went to London Road knowing that defeat would make their chances of survival much

BEFORE THE GAME

Bottom of Division One

		P	W	D	L	F	A	Pts
19	Barnsley	38	13	7	18	48	55	46
20	West Brom	39	11	11	17	51	56	44
21	Oxford United	39	11	8	20	44	64	41
22	Watford	39	10	8	21	53	74	38
23	Birmingham	40	9	10	21	38	62	37
24	Peterborough	39	8	12	19	38	53	36

slimmer. The night before the game, Oxford had beaten Wolves 4-0 to land Watford in the bottom three again.

If ever there was a definition of a relegation six-pointer, this was it. Posh were bottom of the table.

Watford were fighting hard though, thrashing about like a drowning man. Dennis Bailey rescued a point against Leicester four days earlier with a last-minute diving header. But there comes a moment in every relegation battle when hard-earned draws are not enough. And this was that moment.

The London Road pitch was rutted and hard. Neither team was flush with confidence. It wasn't an aesthetically pleasing match, it was all about heart and determination.

What followed was an incredible see-saw battle that offered the hand of safety to both teams. In the end, it was Watford who grabbed on for dear life.

The fans had responded, travelling in huge numbers, cramming themselves into every inch of the little terrace. And they were in full voice too. No one was under any illusions about how much this game mattered. Defeat would probably spell disaster.

Roeder's pre-match team talk was still ringing in their ears when Watford went a goal behind. Colin Foster, the colossus who had gone some way to plugging the leakiest defence in the division, was injured.

Roeder fielded three centre halves, Keith Millen, Keith Dublin and Robert Page and implored them to keep it tight early on. But with just two minutes on the clock, John McGlashan cut through the gap that Watford generously left open for him to give Posh the lead.

'Sometimes as a manager you do wonder if you've wasted your breath,' says Roeder. 'You never want to give away goals but in a match when there's so much at stake, you want to start well.'

Watford battled back to equalise after 18 minutes when Paul Furlong found the net. The rest of the half was cagey, error-strewn stuff.

In the first minute of the second half, Andy Hessenthaler missed an open goal and five minutes later Watford were behind again when Tony Adcock scored from the penalty spot. The terrace housing the away fans writhed with despair and desperation.

Watford were using up all their bullets shooting themselves in the foot. Peterborough were playing just as poorly but were getting the breaks.

For quarter of an hour, all appeared to be lost. Then Keith Dublin bundled the ball into the net and the lifeline was within reach again.

Lavin's goal seven minutes later was a rare moment of clarity in a drawing room comedy of a match. At times you wouldn't have been surprised had a player's shorts fallen down as he attempted a clearance in the penalty box. The full-back's shot from 30 yards barely achieved lift-off. It skimmed across the ground, cutting the few remaining blades of grass on the pitch on its way into the bottom corner.

The relief was unbelievable. The away fans celebrated with everything they had. For a moment it felt as good as winning the league championship.

All hope appeared gone within sixty seconds. From the highest of highs to the lowest of lows in the blink of an eye. Some Watford fans were still celebrating as Adcock put the ball in the net at the other end after Digweed's mistake. But this was no time to wallow in self-pity. Roared on by their fans, Watford rallied and ten minutes from time Bailey's hooked shot deflected off a defender's head and bounced, bobbled and rolled into the net.

And this time, thank goodness, they did hold on because not many Watford hearts could have withstood another Peterborough goal.

Digweed, Lavin, Drysdale, Page, Dublin, Millen, Hessenthaler, Ramage (Johnson 61), Furlong, Porter, Mooney (Bailey 75)
Manager Glenn Roeder
Scorers Furlong 18, Dublin 65, Lavin 72, Bailey 80
Peterborough scorers McGlashan 2, Adcock 50 pen, 73
Attendance 7,734

Division One play-off semi-final first leg
Sunday May 16 1999

'We came into the dressing room and Graham asked us if we were disappointed it was only 1-0. Everyone said they were. Graham told us to forget it, because there was no way we could change it. All we could do was finish the job in the second leg' – *Steve Palmer*

For half an hour, Watford absolutely battered Birmingham. On a warm, bright Sunday afternoon the Hornets threw themselves forward and had the ball in the net after just five minutes.

A Peter Kennedy corner was headed in by Michel Ngonge. Yes. The first blow had been landed. Now for another. Come on, let's get another.

Watford gave everything they had but wave after wave of attack fell just short. They had a string of chances but that second goal simply didn't come. Nick Wright lobbed the keeper and watched as the ball skimmed the bar. In the second half, Tommy Mooney hit the post with a header.

There was a sense of anxiety among the crowd. A fear that one-nil might not be enough.

'We played so well and dominated for long periods,' says Nick Wright. 'We were very pleased because we'd come up with a plan and it worked well. We played with a front three; Michel in the middle, Tommy and me out wide. They had Gary Rowett, Martin Grainger and Michael Johnson at the back. We knew

that of the three, Johnson was the least comfortable on the ball, so the plan was to press Grainger and Rowett but allow Johnson time to be the one to play the ball out. This worked well for us because it meant we won a lot of the ball, often in areas high up the pitch.'

After 19 minutes, Paul Robinson was booked for throwing the ball away – a rush of blood to the head the 20-year-old would come to regret.

In the second half, as Birmingham sought to get themselves off the hook. Trevor Francis threw on Peter Ndlovu.

Quarter of an hour from the end, Ndlovu broke clear and Robinson ran across to challenge him. The tackle was late and rash and Ndlovu made the most of it. The referee showed Robinson a second yellow card and the distraught youngster trudged off knowing he would miss the second leg.

The Blues did come close to getting an equaliser when Alec Chamberlain dropped a cross and had to scramble to stop either Dele Adebola or Paul Furlong from putting it into the net.

When the final whistle went, there

Graham Taylor knew all about unearthing gems and polishing rough diamonds.

If his achievements in the late Seventies and early Eighties were impressive, the team he built in the late Nineties was assembled in an even thriftier fashion.

Of the 14 players who took part in the play-offs, Taylor inherited eight when he returned to the manager's hotseat in the summer of 1997. Taylor's most expensive signing was Micah Hyde, who cost £250,000 from Cambridge. He also spent £200,000 on Jason Lee from Nottingham Forest and, later, Alon Hazan from an Israeli club.

The team that reached the Premiership cost just £25,000 more than Bristol City had paid Fulham for Tony Thorpe in summer 1998.

Five of the 14 players who secured promotion had been products of Watford's youth system.

Player	Fee	Club	Year
Alec Chamberlain	£40,000	Sunderland	1996
Darren Bazeley	£0	youth team	1991
Peter Kennedy	£130,000	Notts Co	1997
Robert Page	£0	youth team	1993
Steve Palmer	£135,000	Ipswich	1995
Paul Robinson	£0	youth team	1996
Michel Ngonge	£0	Samsunspor	1998
Micah Hyde	£250,000	Cambridge	1997
Tommy Mooney	£95,000	Southend	1994
Richard Johnson	£0	youth team	1992
Nick Wright	joint fee	Carlisle	1998
Allan Smart	£175,000	Carlisle	1998
Alon Hazan	£200,000	Ironi Ashdod	1998
Nigel Gibbs	£0	youth team	1983

was a sense of immense relief but also frustration. The score should have been far more convincing.

In the dressing room, the players sat, slightly deflated, knowing that another goal would have put them in a far, far stronger position.

But on the other hand, they had seen out the match with ten men and kept a clean sheet, which might prove vital in the second leg.

'We were disappointed because we over-ran them at times,' says Mooney. 'Michel and I beat up the centre halves. We were stereotypical, I suppose, but people couldn't cope with us. We were organised and single-minded, good at set-pieces. It wasn't rocket science but we focused on what we were good at.'

Taylor told them to forget the game and move on. They had won the game. Now all they had to do was travel to St Andrew's and see it through...

Chamberlain, Bazeley, Kennedy, Page, Palmer, Robinson, Ngonge (Hazan 81), Hyde, Mooney, Johnson, Wright (Smart 67)
Manager Graham Taylor
Scorers Ngonge 5
Attendance 18,535

A NIGHT CAMPING IN OCCUPATION ROAD

Did you spend the night in Occupation Road, waiting for the ticket office to open so you could ensure you'd be at the second leg in Birmingham?

I did, together with some friends. We took a tent, some food and a tape player (more of that later) and headed to the stadium.

At just after eight o'clock one May night – 13 hours before tickets were due to go on sale – we joined an already growing queue.

We had a couple of pints in the Red Lion on Vicarage Road and then settled down for the evening. Thank goodness it wasn't raining.

There was a spirit of camaraderie tinged ever-so-slightly with a sense that we were taking things a bit too far. No one dared ask the question 'What are we doing here?' But, equally, no one wanted to risk having to stay at home and watch the match on television.

What about the tape player? Well, every hour, on the hour, to mark the passing of time, we played a crackly recording of Z-Cars.

The sun was shining by the time we had the tickets in our hot little hands. Four hours after the ticket office opened they had still not sold out and people were able to stroll up to the window and buy a ticket without queuing. But so what? Those of us who camped out had a story to tell. – **Lionel Birnie**

WATFORD........3 QUEENS PARK RANGERS.......1

The Championship, December 7 2009

Were you there when Doyley scored?

After eight years and 269 games, Lloyd Doyley finally scored a goal. What a goal it was too. A diving header that rocketed past the QPR goalkeeper Radek Cerny.

Doyley's long wait for a goal had become something of a standing joke. He was ribbed by his team-mates about it and the fans urged him to shoot as soon as he crossed the halfway line.

The goal led to a chant 'We were there when Doyley scored' and a t-shirt. And it spurred Watford to come from behind to beat QPR.

Rangers had taken the lead through Patrick Agyemang and it looked as if they were going to reach the break with their lead intact.

Just before half-time, Watford had a spell of pressure. The ball was played from the left flank to Don Cowie, who was in space on the right-hand side of the penalty area. The Scot lifted the ball back across the goal with a beautifully-judged first time cross.

Doyley, who had been involved earlier in the move, had continued his run to the edge of the six-yard box, and threw himself at the ball.

It was the perfect Superman-style diving header. 'I kept going forward and no one really picked me up,' he says. 'Don sent over a cross-shot and it was coming straight at me.

'My first thought was to make good contact with it. I threw myself at it and after I'd headed it, I kept my eyes open so I could watch where it went.

'It went straight into the net and as I landed on the ground I looked across to make sure I wasn't offside.

'Then I heard the cheers. The goal was at the Vicarage Road end, the opposite end to where most of the Watford supporters were, so there was a split-second before they realised it was in. Then another split-second before they realised it was me who'd scored.'

Jay DeMerit was coming back from injury so was on the substitutes' bench. 'I saw someone dive in at the far post and it went in,' he says.

'Then the crowd went absolutely crazy. It was louder than for a regular goal. We were looking at each other and going "Was that Lloyd? Did Lloyd just score?" I have to admit, I didn't believe it until they called out his name because I swear, I had never seen Lloyd score in training.'

Doyley confirms that it was the first goal he had ever scored for Watford. 'I've never scored for the junior or reserve teams,' he says. 'I've scored a few in training,' he adds, grinning, before qualifying the statement when we say we'll check up on him.

'I've always been a defender. Even in youth and schools football I was a defender and my job is to stop goals.

'I used to get some stick for it from the other lads and someone suggested I should take a penalty but they never let me.'

In the dressing room at half-time, everyone slapped him on the back and congratulated him but Doyley says the players soon turned their thoughts to winning the game.

'It was only 1-1. Scoring a goal was great but I wanted my goal to be in a match we won rather than a draw or a defeat. Everyone was really up for the second half and we played very well.'

Cowie scored Watford's second but they had to wait until deep into injury time to put the match to bed. The brilliant young midfielder Tom Cleverley, who had dominated Rangers for large spells of the game, found himself with plenty of time and space.

But the game is remembered for being the night Doyley finally broke his duck.

....

Loach, Mariappa, Doyley, Harley (Severin 82), Cathcart (DeMerit 46), Hodson, Cowie, Cleverley, Eustace, Graham, Ellington (Henderson 57)
Manager Malky Mackay
Scorers Doyley 43, Cowie 56, Cleverley 90
QPR scorer Agyemang 33
Attendance 15,058

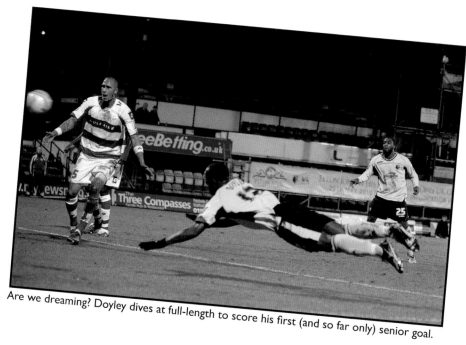

Are we dreaming? Doyley dives at full-length to score his first (and so far only) senior goal.

RECORD APPEARANCES FOR THE GOLDEN BOYS

At the end of the 2010-11 season, Lloyd Doyley moved up to 15th in the list of all-time Watford appearances, with a place in the top 10 well within reach.

Apps	Name	Years	Goals
503	Luther Blissett	1976-92	186
491	Nigel Gibbs	1983-02	7
472	Gary Porter	1984-97	56
457	Duncan Welbourne	1963-74	25
431	Tommy Barnett	1928-44	160
428	Kenny Jackett	1980-90	34
420	Arthur Woodward	1926-39	18
419	Johnny Williams	1964-75	2
404	Wilf Rostron	1979-89	30
398	Ross Jenkins	1972-83	142
372	Charlie White	1909-25	86
348	Stewart Scullion	1966-76	55
341	Skilly Williams	1913-26	0
341	Frank Smith	1921-31	31
334	**Lloyd Doyley**	**2001-**	**1**
333	Fred Gregory	1911-26	17
329	Andy Rankin	1971-79	0
318	George Catleugh	1954-64	16
312	Taffy Davies	1931-50	72
306	Tommy Smith	1997-09	64
303	David Holdsworth	1988-96	14
301	Dennis Bond	1964-77	42
300	Bobby Bell	1957-64	2
298	Nigel Callaghan	1980-91	52
296	John Barnes	1981-87	85
291	Tony Coton	1984-90	0
288	Alec Chamberlain	1996-07	0
287	Ian Bolton	1977-83	36
287	Tommy Mooney	1994-01	64
286	Micah Hyde	1997-04	44
280	Darren Bazeley	1990-99	27
277	Richard Johnson	1991-03	22
274	Keith Eddy	1966-72	31
272	Steve Palmer	1995-01	9
269	Steve Sherwood	1977-87	1
259	Vince McNeice	1957-64	1
253	Walter Lees	1968-76	11
252	Robert Page	1993-01	3
252	Paul Robinson	1996-03	9

Statistics include Southern League, Football League and Premier League, FA Cup, League Cup, Uefa Cup, Football League Trophy, Full Members Cup and Anglo-Italian Cup games only. Appearances include starts and as a substitute up to May 2011.

Premiership, Saturday September 18 1999

Smart Hornets bring Vialli's Blues down to earth

The Premiership and its hype and self-importance could be irritating at times but this was one of those rare days when all the pundits had to sit in their armchairs and accept that sometimes might doesn't mean right.

Even in these pre-Abramovich days, Chelsea spent enough money to keep a small country going. They had two World Cup winners, Marcel Desailly and Didier Deschamps, and an exciting Italian manager.

And three days earlier, they had drawn 0-0 with Milan in the Champions League and they had a visit to Hertha Berlin to look forward to the following week. A trip to Vicarage Road was treated like an unpleasant inconvenience, like having to complete your tax return between two foreign holidays.

On the other hand, Watford had just beaten Wigan Athletic – they were in Division Two in those days – in the Worthington Cup.

Watford were trying to compete with the big spenders. A week before Chelsea were due in town, Graham Taylor signed Nordin Wooter from Real Zaragoza in Spain or £950,000, which was then a record fee.

Wooter was a 23-year-old Dutch winger who had played in a Champions League final, having come on to play ex-

tra-time in Ajax's defeat to Juventus in 1996. His career had stalled and the fact most of his appearances at both Ajax and Zaragoza had been as a substitute should have tempered the excitement.

On his debut he was magnificent. He ran with short, rapid strides and could twist this way and that. We weren't to know then that many of his journeys ended up in dead-ends.

From the start, Watford wanted it more than Chelsea. Perhaps the Londoners thought playing in the Champions League meant they had earned the right to dictate games like this.

Watford refused to go along with that. Steve Palmer was a more effective, more willing 'water-carrier' than Didier Deschamps. Robert Page and Mark Williams allowed Tore Andre Flo and Chris Sutton to get on with their Premiership histrionics when things didn't go their way, nicking the ball from under their feet or getting a head to it first.

Wooter added another dimension to the attack. Everything he did was bold, new and exciting. We didn't realise that the end product he promised would rarely come.

Watford were simply a better and more motivated team than Chelsea in all areas of the pitch and as the first half drew to a close the Blues' frustration was becoming apparent. But there was the doubt in Premiership matches that no matter how well you played, disaster lurked around the corner. A lapse of concentration or a moment of brilliance can smack you under the ribs and leave you winded.

In the second half, Watford were even better. When Wooter ran at Chelsea they looked terrified. He found the right pass, to Paul Robinson, who laid it off to Allan Smart.

Smart hit a first-time shot early enough to catch Ed de Goey cold.

It was an astonishing goal, every bit as impressive as the one at Wembley that helped Watford to the Premiership in the first place. And it came with a new, slightly embarrassing celebration that paid homage to the kilted shot-putter on the Scott's Porage Oats box. You could almost hear the pundits. 'A Scotsman, scoring in the Premiership. How quaint.'

'It was incredible to get my first goal in the Premiership. Talking to *Match of the Day* afterwards I kind of played it down,' says Smart. 'I didn't want to big ourselves up and I was trying to be respectful to Chelsea but I don't think the gaffer was impressed.

'It was a real high but seven days later I was in hospital. How I didn't get a penalty for what Alex Manninger did to me at Highbury... I pushed the ball past and he came out at me, in the air. My studs caught in the turf and tore my ankle cartilage and ligaments. That was the season over for me.'

Gianluca Vialli's response to going a goal down was to bring on a couple of handy substitutes, Gianfranco Zola and Dan Petrescu.

As much as Zola's trickery could be mesmerising, he was not hurting Watford. In fact, the home side went closest to scoring again. There was a glorious moment when Palmer dispossessed Deschamps, strolled forward and smacked a low shot just wide. It thumped against the advertising hoarding as if to say: 'We're warning you.'

Towards the end, Chelsea's discipline deserted them. Tommy Mooney, the hero at Anfield, came on. 'We had a corner and Desailly tried to put his finger in my eye, so I hit him in the ribs,' he says. 'Then I was running down the left and he took me out. I tried to carry on but my kneecap was round the back of my knee.'

Watford saw out the rest of the game comfortably. The pundits didn't give them the credit they deserved, of course. They focused on Chelsea's shortcomings and the size of the task ahead of them in Europe.

But you have to wonder what it was about Chelsea's performance that prompted the Watford directors to think: 'Their manager could do a job for us in a couple of years.'

Chamberlain, Gibbs, Robinson, Page, Williams, Hyde, Easton, Palmer, Kennedy, Wooter (Wright 65), Smart (Mooney 80, Ngonge 86)
Manager Graham Taylor
Scorer Smart 57
Attendance 21,244

Division Two, Tuesday April 28 1998

Promotion had been secured but the championship was still up for grabs and Graham Taylor really wanted that trophy. Watford had to win this, their game in hand, to have any chance of overhauling the leaders, Bristol City, on the final day.

It could have been a tense day but for a light-hearted move to enable Steve Palmer to become a record-breaker. In those days before squad numbers were ubiquitous, Palmer had the honour of becoming the only player to wear each of the numbers one to 14 in a season.

All he needed to do was line up in goal, wearing the number one.

'It was a strange one but it was nice to set a record. For it to count, I had to go on the teamsheet as number one,' says Palmer. 'So I went out in Alec's top and did the warm-up as the goalkeeper.

'We'd agreed with Bournemouth that whoever won the toss, we'd have the kick-off. So we were relying on Richard Johnson kicking the ball out to allow Alec and I to swap jerseys.'

Chamberlain says: 'I had won player of the season but I was photographed with the trophy wearing an outfield shirt, which was odd. I didn't know what to do in the warm-up and it did affect my routine.

'I had to line up at centre-half. My biggest concern was if Johnno had fallen over, Bournemouth could have attacked and I'd have had to make a tackle on the edge of the box.'

'When we went 1-0 down early on I thought we'd jinxed ourselves.'

Watford recovered in the second half to win 2-1 and a championship showdown on the Thames was all set.

Chamberlain, Bazeley, Kennedy, Palmer, Millen, Mooney, Noel-Williams (Robinson 81), Hyde, Lee, Johnson, Hazan (Slater 45)
Manager Graham Taylor
Scorers Lee 47, Noel-Williams 69
Bournemouth scorer Stein 14
Attendance 12,834

STEVE PALMER'S SHIRT COLLECTION

Before every club in the league had squad numbers, players wore shirts from one to eleven. Broadly-speaking, each number related to a position on the pitch. Number one was the goalkeeper, of course, two and three the left and right backs and nine the centre forward.

As the 1997-98 season drew to a close, someone noticed that Steve Palmer had worn almost all the different numbers.

In the final matches, Graham Taylor fixed it so that Palmer could wear No.1 and No.9 and complete the full set from one to 14.

Here is when he first wore each shirt and how often he pulled them on that season.

No.	First worn	Games
1	Bournemouth H (April 28)	1
2	Bristol Rovers A (October 14)	2
3	Chesterfield A (January 31)	3
4	Burnley A (January 10)	3
5	Preston A (August 30)	8
6	Bristol City H (December 13)	1
7	Wigan Athletic A (April 4)	1
8	Luton Town A (October 4)	6
9	Fulham A (May 2)	1
10	Carlisle United H (March 17)	3
11	Brentford A (January 24)	3
12	Brentford H (August 23)	7
13	Millwall H (October 18)	1
14	Carlisle United A (August 16)	1

FIRST SPURS...

DIVISION ONE - Saturday May 11 1985

33 **TOTTENHAM HOTSPUR.......1 WATFORD.........5**

1-5

May 1985 was the bleakest month in the history of English football and so it was particularly poignant that Watford, a club that symbolised everything that could be good, positive and fun about the game, were having a great time.

Watford won 5-1 at White Hart Lane playing bold, exciting football.

Their achievement was completely overshadowed by a tragedy at Bradford City. An old wooden stand caught fire and 56 people died. Later that month was the Heysel disaster.

Watford, the family club, who took pride in trying to entertain people in a safe, friendly environment, were trying to buck the trend.

As Steve Perryman, who played in the Spurs defence that was given such raw treatment that afternoon, said: 'Watford were really making an effort to win people over. I lived in Ickenham and the leaflets used to come through my door. They said that Watford scored the most goals and were the most attacking team in the First Division.

'They weren't a Tottenham or an Arsenal who could rely on 30,000 fans turning up, they had to make themselves attractive. In lots of ways, they were leading the way for other clubs.'

Nigel Callaghan, Luther Blissett and John Barnes put Watford 3-0 up inside half an hour. 'The last team you wanted to face if you were having an off-day was Watford,' says Perryman. 'If you weren't careful, they could tear you to pieces.'

Glenn Hoddle pulled one back from the penalty spot in the second half but a Danny Thomas own goal and a fifth from Colin West completed the most comprehensive hammering Tottenham had endured on their home ground for years. 'To lose 5-1 at home, my God, that was unacceptable,' says Perryman. 'When we played away at Watford, we used to work hard on what they were going to throw at us, but at home I think we felt it was our ground and we'd dictate the play. Well, we didn't that day.'

The fact that the national papers were reluctant to give Watford the credit they were due irritated Graham Taylor. 'I've only read about how badly they played rather than how well we played, so very little has changed.'

Coton, Gibbs, Rostron, Taylor, Terry, McClelland, Callaghan, Blissett, West, Jackett, Barnes
Manager Graham Taylor
Scorers Callaghan 14, Blissett 17 pen, Barnes 28, Thomas og 79, West 83
Tottenham scorer Hoddle 67 pen
Attendance 23,167

THEN UNITED

32   WATFORD........5   MANCHESTER UNITED........1

5-1

Lightning never strikes twice, they say. Well, two days after thrashing Spurs, Watford beat another of the giants 5-1.

Manchester United had the perfect excuse for having an off-day. They were five days away from an FA Cup final against the league champions, Everton.

But take nothing away from the Hornets. They dismantled United every bit as impressively as they had Spurs.

Again, Nigel Callaghan gave Watford a flying start. The winger scored twice in the opening quarter of an hour.

Callaghan's second was a curling free kick that flew over the heads of both Steve Terry and John Barnes, who were running in to meet it, and beat United keeper Gary Bailey at the far post.

Colin West grabbed the third and

Luther Blissett and Kenny Jackett piled on the misery in the second half before Kevin Moran got one for United in the last minute.

Blissett got badly injured after about an hour. He collided with Bailey's knee when he went for the ball and fractured his skull. When he had recovered, Les Simmons, the groundsman, presented him with the patch of blood-soaked turf from where the collision had happened.

At the end of an extraordinary week, Watford travelled to Anfield and led Liverpool 2-0 before finally going down 4-3 in another remarkable game.

Watford scored 13 goals in the space of a week against the teams that finished second, third and fourth in the league. 'We were still being Watford,' says Graham Taylor. 'We looked to attack, no matter who the opposition was. People assumed that the big teams had an off-day.' In fairness to United's manager Ron Atkinson, he didn't make any excuses. 'We weren't taking it easy. We were hammered, plain and simple.'

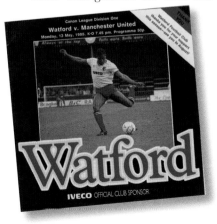

....

Coton, Sinnott, Rostron, Taylor, Terry, McClelland, Callaghan, Blissett (Porter 68), West, Jackett, Barnes
Manager Graham Taylor
Scorers Callaghan 10, 14, West 33, Blissett 66, Jackett 80
Manchester United scorer Moran 90
Attendance 20,047

Division One, Saturday September 28 2002

Lewington's proudest day after players agree to take a pay cut

The phone rang in Ray Lewington's office at the training ground in London Colney. It was Tim Shaw, the chief executive, saying that he and the chairman, Graham Simpson, were on their way to see him. They urgently needed to talk.

Within 15 minutes of sitting down, Lewington knew what a parlous state the club's finances were in.

They were days away from being placed in administration unless they could show the bank that they were able to repay some of the debt.

The extravagance of the Vialli era, the reckless spending, expensive long-term contracts and the collapse of the broadcaster, ITV Digital, had pushed the club to the brink.

It was reported the club needed to claw back around £9million to avoid administration. 'Tim Shaw was very honest,' says Lewington. 'He said that unless everyone at the club took a pay cut, including the players, we would be in administration and decisions would be taken above our heads.

'The banks wanted some of their money back and they wanted it back now. It really was as simple as that.

'I felt we had no option but the tricky thing was that it had to be voluntary because the club couldn't touch the wages if the players refused.

And in order to do it, there had to be 100 per cent agreement.'

Shaw spelled out the situation to the players in the gym at the training ground in London Colney. He said that if they agreed, everyone at the club would defer 12 per cent of their wages indefinitely and with no guarantee they would ever get it back. The players listened and then held a meeting.

Meanwhile, against this backdrop of turmoil, Lewington had to prepare his team for a trip to Bramall Lane.

'The players consulted the PFA and I think the PFA advised them not to do anything,' says Lewington. 'I know there were some dissenting voices but we let them have their meetings and tried to concentrate on the football.'

It wasn't easy. The issue loomed over the whole club like a dark cloud. The players held the club's future in their hands.

'We were walking on eggshells for three or four days,' says Lewington. 'The players had a few meetings but they couldn't agree. They were all in different positions. Some had big mortgages and families and as much as people have their opinions on footballers' wages, it was still a considerable sacrifice the players were being asked to make.

'We tried to keep things as smooth as possible but good training sessions need that competitive element at times. It's a physical game and everyone was on edge so you had to try to avoid situations where tempers might get frayed. We, the management and coaching staff, also avoided talking about it because we didn't know which way they were going to go.'

In the end, the players agreed to defer, rather than waive, 12 per cent of their wages. Although there were no guarantees, the players were told they would be repaid what they were due if the club could afford it, but that survival was the priority. If the team had a good cup run, for example, the players might get some of their money.

'Not everyone was happy about it but I think they all realised it was the right thing to do,' says Lewington, who thought he might face a battle to hold the team together.

'It was, potentially, a very awkward situation. As a manager you have to be able to criticise when it's needed as well as praise. The thing was, once they'd agreed to do it, they became really tight as a group,' he says. 'They had made this decision and they were all in the same boat. They didn't bring it up. They didn't use it as an excuse. They were much stronger.'

The club rallied, the new supporters' trust came into its own and it was rumoured comedian Jim Davidson had donated £2,500.

But Sheffield United are never an easy team to face, particularly at the end of a turbulent week when training took a back seat. 'I had to be careful too,' says Lewington. 'There was no way I would use the wage cut as some kind of motivator. It wouldn't have been at all appropriate. But in the dressing room before the game you could see it in their eyes. They were determined and they were together.'

Watford's resolve was put to the test after ten minutes. Wayne Allison put the Blades in front. The Hornets could have crumbled but they didn't. They were up against it for long spells but they kept fighting and they got a little bit of luck.

In the space of 60 seconds towards the end of the first half, the match was turned on its head. Phil Jagielka bumped Heidar Helguson over in the area and the referee Chris Foy gave a penalty and sent off the United defender.

Neil Cox smashed home the kick with so much power it was as if he was releasing the week's tensions on behalf of the whole club.

A minute later, Helguson touched home from a low Paul Robinson cross.

Micah Hyde was sent off for a second bookable offence late on but Watford held firm.

'Players always go over to the supporters at the end of a game to thank them but this time there was genuine warmth,' says Lewington. 'Given all we'd been through it was one of the proudest days of my career.'

Chamberlain, Doyley, Cox, Gayle, Robinson, Ardley, Hyde, Hand, Nielsen (Glass 84), Helguson, Webber (Johnson 90)
Manager Ray Lewington
Scorers Cox 36 pen, Helguson 37
Sheffield United scorer Allison 10
Attendance 16,301

FA Cup sixth round, Saturday March 10 1984

Who can forget the moment of genius from John Barnes that opened the scoring and silenced the big, hostile St Andrew's crowd?

A long kick from Steve Sherwood reached the edge of Birmingham's area and forced an awkward header from Noel Blake.

The ball fell to Barnes on the left-hand corner of the box. He controlled it with his back to goal, turned quickly then jinked between Peter McCarrick and Martin Kuhl with two deft touches of his left foot. Now he had space he hit a hard, dipping shot with the outside of his left foot that dived like a remote-controlled missile under the bar but above the desperate reach of City keeper Tony Coton.

Barnes admitted the ball bobbled as he prepared to hit it, meaning it sat up nicely for him to achieve the power and swerve. Coton called it 'a flukey one' but it was a goal fit to win any cup tie.

There was still a long way to go, and this bruising Blues side was difficult to grind down even if they created few clear-cut chances.

GOAL OF THE SEASON

The top five goals in the *Watford Observer*'s poll in 1983-84 would have been worthy winners.
1. John Barnes' first at Birmingham in the cup
2. Nigel Callaghan's 25-yarder at Levski Spartak
3. Les Taylor's drive at Birmingham in the cup
4. Barnes' mazy run at home to Luton in the cup
5. Nigel Callaghan's second at Notts County

Nigel Callaghan had a goal disallowed eight minutes later and although Watford were well on top, they knew City would come at them.

The start of the second half was brutal. City seemed to want to turn the pitch into a battleground and Watford were happy to fight fire with fire.

Birmingham equalised on the hour when a low, driven cross flew at Steve Terry and the defender was unable to get his body out of the way. The ball bounced off him into the net.

In the end, it was Watford's fitness that saw them through. As City paid for the physical nature of the game, Watford came into their own and began to find space.

Les Taylor fired in an unstoppable shot, then Barnes stabbed one in at the far post to clinch a semi-final place. 'When we beat Birmingham, there was a feeling in the team that we were going to make it to Wembley,' says Kenny Jackett. 'It was one of the most impressive team performances I played a part in and John's goal was special. Not many players can do that.'

Sherwood, Bardsley, Rostron, Taylor, Terry, Franklin, Callaghan, Johnston, Reilly, Jackett, Barnes
Manager Graham Taylor
Scorers Barnes 23, 80, Taylor 78
Birmingham scorer Terry og 60
Attendance 40,220

Division One, Saturday October 23 1993

Three-nil down with twenty minutes to go... Step forward Gary Porter

Watford won a penalty in the 90th minute. Gary Porter had the chance to score the most unlikely winner and complete his first senior hat-trick. He didn't turn down the chance.

Only 7,492 supporters turned up to see Watford take on Bolton Wanderers. With 25 minutes still to play and their team 3-0 down, some of the home supporters voted with their feet. The ground was emptying fast.

It had been a terrible performance and the Hornets showed no sign of making it respectable, let alone mounting the most remarkable comeback Vicarage Road has ever seen.

There must have been fewer than 7,000 in the ground when Gary Porter got his first goal, meaning the number of fans who can say 'I was there' is pretty small.

Watford fielded the youngest line-up in their Football League history, with an average age of just 22 and a half.

The first half was abysmal. Watford's defence was all over the place. The centre half partnership was Barry Ashby, who was 22, and Julian Alsford, who was just 20. Behind them was another 20-year-old, Simon Sheppard, who was making only his 23rd first-team appearance between the posts.

Bolton were ahead after 16 minutes when David Lee went past Gerard Lavin and crossed. The ball hit Ashby and fell straight to Jason McAteer whose shot went through Jason Solomon's legs and past Sheppard.

Although Watford rallied a little, their goal was living a charmed life. Six minutes before half-time, Lee picked up the ball and strode past three Watford defenders. Instead of beating Lavin, this time he crossed early. Lee's looping ball completely deceived Sheppard. The goalkeeper was caught between the devil and the deep blue sea and he turned to watch it fly over his head and dip under the bar.

Glenn Roeder couldn't wait to get his players into the dressing room at half-time to sort things out.

'We were struggling like mad out there,' he says. 'There's only so much you can do from the touchline but when I got the chance, I let them have it. I am a calm person when I talk but people don't realise that I could lose my temper like the best of them in the dressing room. I can be very vocal. I didn't like to do it all the time because players can switch off if you're always ranting and raving. It has to be rare, it has to be swift and it has to be harsh and on that occasion it was.'

When the match resumed, Roeder must have wondered if he'd been talking to himself. Six minutes into the second half, Bolton scored their third. Mark Patterson had plenty of time to cross to the far post. No one challenged John McGinlay, who was allowed to head across goal. Alan Thompson was unmarked in the six-yard box. All he had to do was slide the ball home. Game over.

Roeder decided to put Ken Charlery on in place of young Alex Inglethorpe, who had not caused the Bolton defence too many problems.

Charlery did have an impact but Watford were all huff and puff and very little inspiration. Some of the fans were heading for the exit, Gary Porter, the captain, couldn't blame them.

'No one wants to hear booing, and seeing your own fans going home with more than 20 minutes to go is even worse,' he says. 'But we had been poor. Nothing went right for us at all. Sometimes that just happens. I can assure you, no one goes out to play badly but you get days when you simply don't get anything right.

'I saw people leaving. We hadn't given any sign that we were going to score, let alone get back into the game.'

So what changed? Charlery won a couple of headers and had a half-chance. 'We had nothing to lose,' says Porter. 'Maybe Bolton relaxed a bit and thought they had the game won but we were just trying to contribute something to the game.'

With 70 minutes gone, it was still 3-0. What followed was an astonishing turn-around. Porter played a one-two with Charlery, and Porter shot from the edge of the penalty area. 'The first one was just a relief,' he says. 'You've been awful, you're 3-0 down and then you get a goal so at least you've managed to do something. I remember running straight back to our half to get on with it.

'There weren't any celebrations because all you're doing is saving a bit of face. We'd got to 3-1 and you think "If we can get another, maybe we can make it a game." It was unlikely but you're just trying to make it difficult for them. I don't think I believed we were going to get back into it.'

Three minutes later, Porter got a second goal. This time Charlery nodded it down, Lee Nogan laid it back and Porter wriggled between a couple of Bolton defenders before scoring with his right foot. 'Now this was different. I ran into the back of the net to get the ball and sprinted back to the centre spot with it,' says Porter. 'There were still 15 minutes to go and suddenly you think you can get a draw. You feel that confidence go through the team. And for the opposition, the opposite is true. Their shoulders dropped and there wasn't the same zip in their step. Five minutes earlier they had the game won, now they have a fight on their hands. That's a very difficult position to be in. The fans who stayed suddenly think it's on. Maybe we can get a draw here.'

Watford had to wait but with a couple of minutes remaining, Charlery controlled a long clearance from Sheppard beautifully. With a couple of touches he made a shooting opportunity and he fired home from outside the box. The ball was perfectly placed and flew into the bottom corner, just out of Aidan Davison's reach.

The home side didn't stop there. They won a corner, which Porter took. The ball was flicked on and Bolton's Mark Seagraves handled it. The referee pointed to the spot.

Porter placed the ball on the spot. 'I was very confident,' he says. 'I knew this was a chance to score my first senior hat-trick and to win the game having been 3-0 down. I was very confident even though I knew a lot was on it. Imagine missing that penalty, it would have been horrible.'

Within seconds of Porter scoring, the referee blew the whistle. Roeder, though delighted, was not getting carried away. 'We were celebrating in the dressing room and Glenn was very happy but at some point, when it had all calmed down, he reminded us to look at the game as a whole. We had been dead and buried at 3-0.'

Roeder bumped into Jack Petchey, the club's owner, in the corridor. 'I thoroughly enjoyed that Glenn,' Petchey said. 'Couldn't we arrange for that to happen more often?'

Sheppard, Dublin, Lavin, Hessenthaler, Alsford, Ashby, Dyer, Solomon, Inglethorpe (Charlery 56), Porter, Nogan
Manager Glenn Roeder
Scorers Porter 71, 74, 90 pen, Charlery 88
Bolton scorers McAteer 16, Lee 39, Thompson 51
Attendance 7,492

Danny Graham piles on the misery for Millwall, scoring the fifth of Watford's six goals.

MILLWALL .... 1 WATFORD 6

The Championship, Saturday September 18 2010

Kenny Jackett won't forget his first match as a manager against his old club in a hurry.

Watford handed Millwall a good old-fashioned hammering. It was one of those magical performances that leaves supporters wondering where it came from and why it doesn't happen every week.

From the start, the Hornets were rampant, attacking with the sort of pace that suggested they wanted to score as many as possible and get the match over and done with.

John Eustace started the ball rolling, bundling in Don Cowie's corner. Six minutes later Jordon Mutch struck a searing shot and in injury time at the end of the first half Marvin Sordell tapped in the third.

Watford didn't stop there. Adrian Mariappa headed another Cowie corner before the Lions grabbed what was already a mere consolation goal.

Danny Graham got his goal before Martin Taylor rounded off the rout and sent the away fans to heaven.

There were six different scorers – the first time that had happened since the win over Bradford in 1989 – but all 14 Hornets were heroes at the New Den.

Loach, A Taylor (Hodson 70), M Taylor, Mariappa, Doyley, Eustace, Cowie, Buckley (McGinn 60), Mutch, Graham, Sordell (Deeney 68)
Manager Malky Mackay
Scorers Eustace 7, Mutch 13, Sordell 45, Mariappa 54, Graham 77, M Taylor 90
Millwall scorer Trotter 56
Attendance 12,562

Division Three, Monday May 14 1979

There were nine agonising days between Watford's gripping 3-2 win at Sheffield Wednesday and the final game of the season against Hull City.

In that time, Watford could only watch and wait for Swansea, Swindon, Shrewsbury and Gillingham to play their matches.

By the time Hull arrived, Watford lay third in the table and knew that a win would be enough to secure a second successive promotion.

It had been a close fight between half a dozen teams but they held their destiny in their own hands. Graham Taylor trusted his men to get it done.

Roared on by the biggest crowd to watch a league match at Vicarage Road since 1969, Watford started well.

Roger Joslyn put them ahead after just ten minutes, which went a little way to settling the nerves and stoked the carnival atmosphere.

There was to be a nervous wait for confirmation, though. Watford played well but they couldn't quite see off the Tigers until the hour mark.

Ross Jenkins scored his 29th league goal of the season to give the home side some breathing space.

Luther Blissett earned a penalty when he was chopped down in the box. Ian Bolton shaped like he was going to opt for power and then coolly slotted the kick past the keeper to make it 3-0.

That, surely, would be enough.

Bolton turned to all four sides of the ground, thumping his fist on his chest to mimic his beating heart.

There had been some sticky moments, not least a 3-0 defeat at home to Colchester on Good Friday, but nothing could stop Watford now.

Blissett rounded off a comprehensive win towards the end and the fans celebrated and sang for the remaining ten minutes. The team did a victorious lap of honour for the second May in a row and the fans headed to the town centre for the inaugural party in the pond. Although the council reported sternly that two pike had died during the celebrations, it was to become a local tradition.

Watford topped the table that night and although Shrewsbury pipped them to the title by winning their last match, the Hornets were going up.

TOP LEAGUE CROWDS

The biggest attendances for league matches played at Vicarage Road.

27,968 QPR	0-1	Div 2	Aug 1969
27,632 Luton Town	1-3	Div 3 South	Feb 1937
27,373 Tottenham	0-1	Div 1	Mar 1983
27,173 Liverpool	2-1	Div 1	May 1983
26,347 Hull City	4-0	Div 3	May 1979

Sherwood, Stirk, Harrison, Booth, Bolton, Garner, Blissett, Train, Jenkins, Joslyn, Downes.
Manager Graham Taylor
Scorers Joslyn 10, Jenkins 61, Bolton pen 70, Blissett 78
Attendance 26,347

No need for drama or nerves after first leg drubbing

Two-nil was a good lead but Matt Spring's third goal put the tie beyond Palace's reach.

Divsion One play-off semi-final first leg
Saturday, May 6 2006

Selhurst Park. There's nothing to like about the place. Admit it, who among the Watford faithful wasn't thinking: let's just go down there, keep it tight and get away with a draw. Give ourselves a chance in the second leg.

Aidy Boothroyd wasn't. Thirteen months before this match, he was picking up bibs and arranging cones for Kevin Blackwell at Leeds. Now he had led the Hornets into the play-offs at the first attempt and he was in no mood to be cautious.

His self-belief bordered on the megalomaniacal at times. Despite losing home and away to Palace in the league, he felt Watford would win.

Unlike in 1999, there was no last-minute charge into the play-offs. Watford made certain of their place with a 1-1 draw against Luton with four games to spare. There was time to think and Boothroyd made the most of it.

After the 2-1 win over Ipswich, he asked the crowd to stay behind and boo as his players staged a practice penalty shoot-out.

It was an idea he'd had after talking to Sir Clive Woodward, the England World Cup-winning rugby coach, who was working at Southampton.

Graham Taylor had done the same thing behind closed doors seven years earlier but the fact Boothroyd was prepared to risk ridicule doing it publicly increased the sense of belief people had in the team. Perhaps we were going to do this.

Palace were stubborn opponents in the first half. Watford created just one half-chance, for Marlon King. Palace should have scored when Andy Johnson shaped to shoot, only for Jordan Stewart to somehow get his leg in the way to block it.

A deep breath. Forty-five minutes to survive, then get them back to Vicarage Road. It seemed Boothroyd had the same idea because he replaced Darius Henderson with Al Bangura at half time. That's it. Don't give anything away, don't do anything stupid and leave ourselves a mountain to climb.

And then, a minute or so into the second half, Marlon King scored. It was superb shot after a smart turn.

Then Ashley Young whipped a free-kick over the wall and in. Two-nil. Are we dreaming? But there was more. Matt Spring fired in the third near the end. It was difficult not to get carried away.

Three-nil would be enough, wouldn't it? At the end, the announcer on the public address system implored the Palace fans to believe. 'It's not over yet,' he said. But it was over and everyone knew it.

The second leg was a dour, tetchy goalless draw featuring a touchline brawl. However, it wasn't even that nerve-wracking. Brilliant.

Foster, Stewart, Mackay, DeMerit, Doyley, Chambers (Eagles 83), Mahon, Young, Spring, Henderson (Bangura 45), King
Manager Aidy Boothroyd
Scorers King 46, Young 67, Spring 85
Attendance 22,880

'We were runners-up. The second best team in the country. No one can ever take that away from us'

Graham Taylor

WATFORD...........2 LIVERPOOL...........................1

Division One, Saturday May 14 1983

When the fixtures for Watford's debut season in Division One were published no doubt many supporters scanned them, noted the final match and thought: 'I hope we don't need to beat Liverpool to stay up.'

After an incredible nine months, Watford faced the champions with a European place already in the bag. The season had exceeded the wildest dreams of the most optimistic Hornet.

The front cover of the programme for the final game of the season was a celebration of the club's status, showing all the international players in their shirts.

Liverpool proved to be the best team by a distance, wrapping up the championship in April and then free-wheeling to the end of the season with a string of draws and defeats. While it is true they did not come to Vicarage Road in full swing, neither did they want to surrender.

This was the last game of Bob Paisley's incredible managerial reign before he handed over to the next man in the boot room pecking order, Joe Fagan.

Paisley had won six league titles, three European Cups, the Uefa Cup and three League Cups in nine years.

Elton John presented him with a cine camera as a retirement gift.

There were changes at Watford too. On the morning of the match, Ross Jenkins was told he was going to be released, bringing to an end an 11-year spell at Vicarage Road.

Jenkins had celebrated with his testimonial match against Luton Town earlier in the week.

Paul Franklin, the young central defender, was told that if he performed well against Luton, he would make his league debut the

following Saturday. The job for Franklin was a simple one: you're marking Kenny Dalglish.

Martin Patching, whose time at the club had been wrecked by a knee injury, was brought into the team. Patching scored the opening goal, which earned him another contract, although not a happy ending. He was released early the following season but a goal against Liverpool was a wonderful way to go.

The 2-1 win was Watford's 22nd of the season – only Liverpool won more. And when the results filtered through there was some astonishing news.

Manchester United, second in the table before the game and 2-1 up with five minutes to go at Notts County, had conceded two very late goals.

Remarkably, Watford were runners-up at the first attempt. The second best team in the country.

There is some debate whether the Watford fans really cheered when they heard Luton had won at Manchester City to save their First Division skin but really, who cared?

Watford's rise from the bottom of the league almost to the very top was completed with a victory over the champions. Runners-up. It can never happen again. Well, not without someone spending hundreds of millions.

....
Sherwood, Rice, Rostron, Patching, Sims (Lohman 62), Franklin, Callaghan, Blissett, Barnes, Jackett, Sterling
Manager Graham Taylor
Scorers Patching 39, Blissett 49
Liverpool scorer Johnston 62
Attendance 27,173

The story of a season. An essential read for every Watford supporter.

DIVISION ONE 1982-83
....

		P	W	D	L	F	A	Pts
1	Liverpool	42	24	10	8	87	37	82
2	**Watford**	**42**	**22**	**5**	**15**	**74**	**57**	**71**
3	Man United	42	19	13	10	56	38	70
4	Tottenham	42	20	9	13	65	50	69
5	Nottm Forest	42	20	9	13	62	50	69
6	Aston Villa	42	21	5	16	62	50	68
7	Everton	42	18	10	14	66	48	64
8	West Ham	42	20	4	18	68	62	64
9	Ipswich Town	42	15	13	14	64	50	58
10	Arsenal	42	16	10	16	58	56	58

Watford's highest ever finishing position in the league earned them a place in the Uefa Cup. In those days, only the champions qualified for the European Cup. The next five teams played in the Uefa Cup, which was a difficult and prestigious competition, unlike the modern day equivalent, the Europa League, which is seen by some as a sort of European booby prize. Luther Blissett topped the goalscoring chart too, with 27 league goals. At the other end of the table, Luton Town escaped relegation with a dramatic victory at Maine Road that sent Manchester City down. Who can forget David Pleat galloping across the pitch in celebration? Some swear that the Vicarage Road crowd cheered when news of Luton's survival was announced over the public address system. Even taking into account the spirit of friendship between the two clubs at Ross Jenkins' testimonial a few days earlier, it seems unlikely many Watford supporters would have been pleased to hear Luton had stayed up.

Seven shots from twelve yards put Hornets one step from heaven

The agony and ecstasy of a penalty shoot-out

24 | **BIRMINGHAM CITY..........1 WATFORD 0**

1-1 on aggregrate, Watford win 7-6 on penalties
Thursday May 20 1999

The eagle-eyed will have spotted that this is the only one of the 100 greatest wins that wasn't, technically, a win

The noise was almost suffocating. You had to hand it to the Blues' supporters, they had created a fierce atmosphere. When they sang their anthem *Keep Right On to the End of the Road*, instinct made you put your hands over your ears. The Watford fans tried to fight back, to sing with every ounce of effort they could muster. But you could barely hear yourself think.

The players had to block out all that noise and focus on the job in hand. That wasn't going to be easy. It was like trying to run into a force ten gale.

Within two minutes, the ball was in the net and Watford's defenders were on their knees.

The stadium erupted. The Hornets' hard-earned 1-0 lead had been wiped out before they'd even managed to settle. It was going to be a long, long night.

Watford left nothing to chance in their preparations for the second leg. For a few weeks, they had ended each training session with a full-scale penalty shoot-out. Just in case.

'Between the two games, I had this unbelievable feeling it was going to go to penalties,' says Allan Smart. 'We had practiced a lot. We knew our penalties. There were some days when I'd taken 20 or 30 penalties. I had developed my routine. All the players had. We knew exactly what we were going to do. Of course, in training, all our kicks were being saved, because the goalies knew where they were going.'

Their preparations for the game were not ideal. 'We stayed at a different hotel to normal,' says Mooney. 'For league games in Birmingham we stayed in the New Hall but it was booked up so the gaffer took us to The Belfry. As a creature of habit, I didn't like that.'

The team bus left the hotel in plenty of time but got caught in traffic. 'That added to the anxiety. We were rushing around and there wasn't a lot of time. Because there was some building work at the stadium, the changing room was a portacabin.' says Alec Chamberlain.

'We got there with about 45 minutes to kick off,' says Smart. 'Chambo was going absolutely ballistic because he didn't get to do his proper warm-up.'

The stadium filled up very early and the atmosphere was as hostile as it was intense. 'We did our warm-up, running back and forwards across the width of the pitch and some of the abuse we got when we were near the touchline was really nasty,' says Nick Wright.

By the time the game kicked off, the place was really rocking. 'I've been to Ibrox and Celtic Park but the buzz in St Andrew's that night topped them,' says Smart, who was on the substitute's bench. 'When the goal went in, you could feel the ground shaking. I was sat there, on the bench, thinking we were going to get pasted.'

Perhaps the lack of warm-up did affect the way Chamberlain started the game. 'I was disappointed with the goal,' he says. 'It was a corner that didn't get cleared properly. It was played back in and it was really hard to judge the trajectory. I tried to deal with it but didn't do one thing or the other and it bounced loose.'

Dele Adebola bundled the ball over the line and all hell broke loose.

Birmingham City 1 Watford 0

Now Watford had to stand up to the onslaught and hope they were strong enough. 'For the next ten minutes it was just a case of standing with our backs to the wall,' says Chamberlain.

'The noise when they scored that goal was what made me decide to join Birmingham a few years later,' says Mooney. 'You couldn't hear yourself think. I was shouting to Peter Kennedy, who was only about ten yards away, and he couldn't hear me.'

Watford threatened so little but while the aggregate score was level, the onus was on Birmingham to attack.

'Our ball retention wasn't great and we didn't attack much but everyone worked so, so hard to stop them,' says Chamberlain. 'I had quite a lot to do and I would say it was my best game in a Watford shirt. There was some heroic defending too.'

None more so than from Nigel Gibbs, who was standing in at left-back for the suspended Paul Robinson.

David Holdsworth was sent off for Birmingham early in the second half which meant the pressure on Watford eased a little bit.

Extra time meant another half-hour of tension. A goal now would probably settle it but penalties seemed inevitable.

Kennedy volunteered to take the first one, and scored it. 'I was careful not to react,' he says. 'We were taking them in front of the Birmingham fans and I didn't want to get carried away and make it harder for my team-mates.'

Paul Furlong, a former Hornet, was up next. Kenny Jackett gave Chamberlain a tip. 'Kenny knew Furs well,' says Mooney. 'He knew he'd change his normal penalty because he was playing against us, so he told Alec which way he'd go. And he was right.'

'Kenny told me Furlong would go to my right and I thought, that's good enough for me.' Chamberlain stopped it and Watford had the upper hand. For a minute, at least.

Steve Palmer missed his shot. He couldn't get the ball to sit neatly on the spot. 'It bobbled as I hit it,' he says. 'I almost got away with it because it hit the outside of the post. No one wants to miss one but it was early in the shoot-out so it wasn't disastrous.'

The penalties kept flying in and for Watford, the practice was paying off. 'I've never felt so nervous, yet so in control,' says Mooney.

In the end, someone had to miss. 'I was so disappointed I wasn't getting near them,' says Chamberlain. 'But poor old Chris Holland's kick wasn't the best. I think you can see I'm smiling before I've actually stopped it.'

Watford had done it. They had stood firm in the face of overwhelming odds and could now look forward to playing at Wembley.

And amid all the joy there was also a sense of relief for Steve Palmer. 'You'll see from the photos and the video that I'm the first person to get to Alec,' he says. 'That wasn't a coincidence. I was so happy he'd stopped that one.'

Chamberlain, Bazeley, Kennedy, Page, Palmer, Gibbs, Ngonge (Hazan 87), Hyde, Mooney, Johnson, Wright (Smart 87)
Manager Graham Taylor
Birmingham scorer Adebola 2
Attendance 29,100

Watford

Birmingham City

✓ 1-0
Peter Kennedy hits a shot left-footed with power. Kevin Poole gets a hand to it but the ball has enough pace on it to squeeze in off the post.

✗ 1-0
Former Hornet **Paul Furlong** pays for a casual run-up. His weak, placed effort is too close to Chamberlain, who goes the right way and stops it neatly.

✗ 1-0
Steve Palmer was unhappy with how the ball was sitting on the penalty spot. His connection is not the sweetest and his shot clips the outside of the post.

✓ 1-1
Although Chamberlain again goes the right way, the Blues left-back **Martin Grainger** thumps a powerful shot low into the bottom corner.

✓ 2-1
Australian **Richard Johnson** blasts his effort down the centre. The ball is rising all the way but fortunately the underside of the bar intervenes and it goes in.

✓ 2-2
Another who opts for power. Defender **Gary Rowett** put his foot through the ball and blasts it high into the corner, leaving the Watford keeper with no chance.

✓ 3-2
A short run-up from the flying full-back **Darren Bazeley.** Poole guesses the right way but he is nowhere near the ball, which flies into the top-left corner.

✓ 3-3
A calm, collected side-foot shot from the sub **Lee Bradbury** skids across the turf and finds the bottom left corner as Chamberlain falls to the right.

✓ 4-3
Tommy Mooney looks nervous as he takes ages to place the ball on the spot. There's a deep breath from our hero before he fires down the middle.

✓ 4-4
The strain is showing on the faces of the managers. **Bryan Hughes** puts the ball down, walks back, turns and runs up to despatch a perfect shot.

✓ 5-4
Into sudden death. As the skipper walks up, the Blues fans increase the volume. and the boos ring out. **Robert Page** hammers it, off the bar and in.

✓ 5-5
Another centre half, **Darren Purse**, follows Page, knowing he has to score or Birmingham are out. It's a cool penalty in the circumstances, neatly placed.

✓ 6-5
The striker **Allan Smart** is next. Taylor later admitted he feared for the Scot. But Smart had picked his spot, low to Poole's right, and slots home left-footed.

✓ 6-6
The pressure is back on City. The goalkeeper **Kevin Poole** steps up. He smashes it hard and high into the roof of the net. Then he has to face a kick...

✓ 7-6
As the tension reaches fever pitch, the Israeli **Alon Hazan** steps up. And what a cool customer he is. He sends Poole the wrong way and caresses the ball home.

✗ 7-6
Nine-and-a-half minutes feels like a lifetime. The stadium is on edge. **Chris Holland** has to score. No one deserves to miss but his shot is poor and Chamberlain stops it. It's over!

Division One, Saturday November 6 1982

Mad dogs upset the culture club and Fleet Street's finest

Rarely had the self-appointed guardians of the game had their noses put so firmly out of joint. And they didn't pull their punches when they filed their articles for the Sunday newspapers.

After frustrating Spurs for 90 minutes and then knocking them out cold at the death, Watford were in danger of offending their illustrious hosts.

During the early weeks of their first season in the top flight, Watford had been a refreshing curio. They had scored goals and created headlines.

Thrashing the likes of Southampton or Sunderland was one thing. When they ran into one of the big boys they were expected to know their place.

Tottenham were the darlings of Fleet Street, even though they had not won the championship since 1961. Spurs played the game the way it was supposed to be played.

Few journalists would admit they went to White Hart Lane to admire the passing, but devoid of any emotional investment in the outcome of a match, they were free to enjoy a style that was,

admittedly, easy on the eye. Watford were the ugly ducklings to Tottenham's graceful swans and many of the gentlemen of the press failed to appreciate that Graham Taylor's team were supremely fit and played to their strengths.

After an impressive start, Watford had slipped to eighth in the table after draws against Birmingham, Norwich and Coventry and defeats to Aston Villa and Notts County.

They had gone five matches without a win and had yet to meet any of the big four. The bubble was about to burst and the sophisticated Spurs looked like being the ones to provide the prick.

Far from being their comeuppance, the Hornets' visit to north London was proof that even the most famous and fashionable teams were simply flesh and blood. They could be beaten to the ball and tackled just like everyone else.

Watford accepted that they didn't have players capable of the same level of artistry as Glenn Hoddle or Ricky Villa. But they knew that if they were to allow Tottenham's best players time on the ball and space to operate they would be punished. So Les Taylor and Kenny Jackett, Watford's midfield duo, did the work of four men. They chased and harried. They closed people down and tackled with a ferocity that was fair but unequivocal.

Watford showed they were nobody's patsies. Suddenly, when put under such pressure, Hoddle's passes looked less like perfectly placed pennies from heaven but great lumpen hoofs forward.

It was a frustrating experience for a team that was used to expressing itself.

With time running out, Watford were on the verge of a hard-earned point and the journalists were preparing to dip their quills in bilious ink.

They were ready to castigate the First Division new boys for their approach. They painted Watford as a team that relied on booting the ball upfield and running after it with all the grace of a lumbering rugby pack.

And then, to add insult to injury, Watford scored.

Three minutes from the end, they won a throw-in. Luther Blissett ran over to take it quickly and Les Taylor surged forward.

Usually he took up a position outside the box but he decided to make a run, leaving Hoddle unmarked. Taylor says: 'I can still hear the gaffer now, yelling "No, Les, no." It's probably the only time I've ever disobeyed him. Luther took the throw, the ball fell to me and I just poked it in.'

There's nothing a football reporter likes less than having to rewrite their copy at short notice. As Graham Taylor, the son of a local sports journalist, later said: 'I have a good relationship with most journalists. There are one or two exceptions. They talk about the game but when there's been a late goal I do like to wind them up a bit. "Now you're feeling the pressure, aren't you boys?"'

The following day, Jeff Powell of the *Mail on Sunday* described Watford as a 'pack of wild dogs'.

Powell was not the only critic. Most of the papers had someone available to wring their hands and fret over the moral future of the game should every team play with the pace and controlled aggression of Watford.

'It was mathematical and it took the creativity and artistry out of the game,' says Powell. 'The pressing game was not an issue but it was the regimented style that grated. It was formulaic.

'Even John Barnes will tell you that he could only play with freedom in the final third. And the idea that football couldn't be played neatly, in triangles, through the midfield, has been confounded these days.'

Has it? Hasn't football always been a simple game? You put the ball in one net and try to keep it out of the other. Watford may not have been fancy but they were often better than Spurs.

Sherwood, Rice, Rostron, Taylor, Sims, Bolton, Callaghan, Blissett, Jenkins, Jackett, Barnes
Manager Graham Taylor
Scorer Taylor 87
Attendance 42,214

The beginning

WATFORD..............2 TRANMERE ROVERS 1

Division One, Saturday April 3 1999

What had looked at one stage so promising had fizzled out and faded away. After an extraordinary 18 months, Watford had finally run out of steam. It was bound to happen. The progress had been so rapid. The group of players assembled in the Second Division would probably need to be strengthened for a full-on push for the Premiership. Still, it was fun while it lasted.

Having been third in the table on Boxing Day, Watford's gallop had slowed to a canter. Now they were struggling to trot.

February and March had been little short of disastrous. Just one win in eight games, at QPR, had seen them slip to eighth in the table. They were now seven points adrift of the play-offs. The lights weren't out, quite, but they had dimmed considerably.

A goalless draw at Oxford had been poor but the one at home to Bury a week before Tranmere's visit was abject. It wasn't that they weren't trying. They were simply lacking inspiration. Goals had dried up and Graham Taylor had juggled his team around searching for something that would kick-start things.

It was starting to look like he was trying to complete a jigsaw puzzle knowing one of the key pieces was missing. The injury to Gifton Noel-Williams was beginning to cost the Hornets. Taylor brought in Guy Whittingham on loan but it was very quickly apparent he was not going to be the catalyst.

Watford needed something to spark them back into life. All was not lost just yet. Taylor hired a sports psychologist called Ciaran Cosgrave, who had worked in rugby and other sports, working his magic like some travelling shaman.

Cosgrave wore a bright pink shirt and talked about people seizing their opportunities in life. He talked about seeing the positive in every situation.

Equally important, according to Taylor, was that the players got to hear a different voice.

But Taylor had a trick up his sleeve too. A couple of days before the game against Tranmere Rovers, he pinned something on the noticeboard for the players to read.

It read: 'If you believe what I believe then you'll believe that anything is possible if you work hard enough.

'There are eight games to go. Eight wins will give us 79 points.

'79 points will give us a place in the play-offs.

'Two more wins means Wembley.'

# of a fairytale

It's slipping away. One-nil down and the frustration is etched on Graham Taylor's face.

The notice struck a chord with many of the players, including Steve Palmer. 'I suppose it is quite strange, looking back,' he says. 'I don't think anyone really thought we were going to do it but things snowballed.'

The notice was replaced with a new, updated one after each match as Watford's incredible run continued. Palmer managed to keep the original and still has it at home to this day.

But a notice pinned to the wall and positive vibes from a psychologist cannot account for a run of seven wins and a draw in eight games.

Watford still needed someone to

light the fuse. The first half against Tranmere was dire. As bad as anything Watford had served up all season.

Passes went astray, shoulders slumped. Partnerships that had looked so seamless earlier in the season now looked disjointed. Nothing was going right.

At half-time, Taylor let rip. This was the last chance. Were Watford going to let the season slip meekly from their grasp or were they going to scrap and battle to keep it on the rails?

Seven minutes after the restart, Taylor had his answer. David Kelly scored for Tranmere.

Taylor decided he needed to take drastic action. He was going to make a triple substitution, which was a symbol of his irritation as much as it was a final throw of the dice.

In the 64th minute he chucked on Alex Bonnot, Tommy Mooney and Michel Ngonge for Micah Hyde, Johann Gudmundsson and Guy Whittingham.

'Graham wanted me and Michel to go up front with Smarty and cause havoc, which we did,' says Mooney.

Watford desperately needed a wake-up call. Three minutes later, they scored, against the run of play.

Mooney, playing like a tornado on the left, fired the ball over to Peter Kennedy, who sent a shot skidding past the Tranmere goalkeeper.

The goal perhaps should have given Watford renewed hope but once the game restarted it soon settled into the same frustrating pattern. All sweat, little inspiration.

Watford kept attacking but without guile or cunning. It was like watching someone throw themselves repeatedly against a locked steel door. All they were getting was bruises.

Something dramatic needed to happen, something to lift the atmosphere created by just 8,682 supporters above the mundane.

Ten minutes from time, someone lit the torchpaper. Allan Smart and Clint Hill clashed off the ball while at the same time Richard Johnson lunged horribly at Kenny Irons. Suddenly tempers flared, hands were raised, chests were bumped and the adrenaline was, at last, pumping.

Tranmere's manager John Aldridge marched onto the pitch to talk to the referee, who then showed Johnson the red card.

The Aussie refused to go quietly and suddenly a tame, deflating occasion was on a knife-edge. Taylor was livid and the players were animated.

There was something to fight for and everyone wanted to get involved.

Aldridge argued angrily with the supporters in the main stand. Some of the tackles on the pitch were x-rated.

The referee, Graham Frankland, had lost all control. This was no longer football, it was a grudge match.

The crowd, small but fervent by now, roared Watford on.

No one was thinking about the play-offs, or Wembley or the Premiership. They just wanted to see their team win.

And now the team was fighting by fair means and, occasionally, foul, they had the supporters right behind them.

Watford won a corner. Allan Smart, taking his instruction to be a nuisance to heart, was causing chaos in the box. He was lively and aggressive. He stood right in front of the Rovers keeper, John Achterberg. He stood on his toes, or tried to hold his hands by his side.

The ball came into the box. There was a scramble. It was messy. Everyone was holding everyone else. The Watford players protested and the referee, by now so bemused and lacking authority, blew his whistle and went to talk to his linesman. There'd been a foul in the box, certainly, but who was the worst offender?

Mr Frankland pointed to the spot. Achterberg had held Smart and some-one else had pulled back Ngonge as he went to challenge for the ball.

Kennedy missed the penalty but Ngonge followed it up. Half the team celebrated wildly, the other half were involved in a scrap that started between Smart and Kelly, who were whacking each other.

'I had followed the penalty in and I'd trodden on the Tranmere player as we went in. It wasn't deliberate, but I didn't exactly get out of his way either. It was just handbags, really,' says Smart. 'He swung at me, I swung at him. The ref sent me off.'

As Smart left the pitch, Aldridge couldn't resist having another go.

'There were only about three minutes to go but there was a lot of in-jury time because of all the hold-ups,' says Smart. 'I was pacing up and down the dressing room praying that Tran-mere didn't equalise because I'd get it if they did.'

Watford held on and the supporters celebrated as if they'd won the league.

Now there were seven games to go and Watford's players were determined to play every one as if it was their last.

They would probably fall short but they were going to give it everything.

Two days later, on Easter Monday, Watford played at Birmingham City. With Smart suspended, Taylor put Mooney in at centre forward and recalled the former Aston Villa winger Tony Daley.

Mooney and Daley scored the goals in a fine 2-1 win. Watford were more cohesive than they had been against Tranmere but they still had the fire in their bellies.

'As I have learned, Birmingham fans forget nothing,' says Mooney. 'I was an ex-Villa man but Tony Daley took the pressure off me because he got all the stick.' By this stage, Mooney was playing to prove a point to Taylor. He had come within a whisker of leaving the club.

'I'd played very well at centre-half the previous season but I think there were doubts whether I'd handle the step up in that position,' he says. 'In pre-sea-son I played up front and in defence. On the opening day I played at the back against Portsmouth but it was the last game I played there. I was used very sparingly and I almost left the club.

'I spoke to Alex McLeish at Hibs and to several other clubs in Division One. I didn't want to leave Watford but it wasn't difficult for me to make the decision to leave because I wasn't play-ing. I was coming on as sub and I was very angry at that time.

'GT and I had some discussions, which usually he won, but I won a few that season. I was very close to going to Hibs and, in fact, after that Birmingham

AN INCREDIBLE RUN-IN

BEFORE THE GAME

Before the game against Tranmere Rovers, Watford's play-off hopes were virtually dead. They had slipped out of the top six but had also lost all their earlier momentum. It would need an extraordinary run to make it.

		P	W	D	L	F	A	Pts
1	Sunderland	38	25	10	3	74	23	85
2	Ipswich Town	38	22	7	9	54	25	73
3	Bradford City	38	21	7	10	66	39	70
4	Birmingham	38	19	12	8	59	31	69
5	Bolton	37	17	13	7	68	50	64
6	Wolves	38	17	11	10	56	37	62
7	Sheffield Utd	38	15	11	12	61	56	56
8	Huddersfield	39	14	13	12	55	61	55
9	**Watford**	**38**	**14**	**13**	**11**	**51**	**50**	**55**
10	West Brom	38	15	8	15	61	59	53

April 3
Watford 2 Tranmere Rovers 1
Up to seventh place but still seven points behind the play-off places after a tumultuous finale against Tranmere.

April 5
Birmingham City 1 Watford 2
The gap is now just four points after Tommy Mooney and Tony Daley score the goals at St Andrew's.

April 10
Watford 2 Bolton Wanderers 0
Micah Hyde and Mooney score in a dominant display. Hornets now just one point adrift of sixth place.

April 17
Crewe Alexandra 0 Watford 1
Mooney's first half goal is enough to win tense clash. Rivals' games in hand means gap is three points again.

April 24
Watford 2 Crystal Palace 1
Hyde's early strike sets up another vital victory. Now Hornets are level on points with sixth-placed Wolves.

April 27
Port Vale 1 Watford 2
Two Mooney goals on an unforgettable night in the Potteries put Watford into fifth place.

May 1
Barnsley 2 Watford 2
Bolton draw with Wolves on the Friday night meaning a point is enough to keep Watford fifth.

May 9
Watford 1 Grimsby 0
Hornets go into the final game knowing a win will guarantee a play-off place. Kennedy's goal seals it.

END OF THE SEASON

		P	W	D	L	F	A	Pts
1	Sunderland	46	31	12	3	91	28	105
2	Bradford City	46	26	9	11	82	47	87
3	Ipswich Town	46	26	8	12	69	32	86
4	Birmingham	46	23	12	11	66	37	81
5	**Watford**	**46**	**21**	**14**	**11**	**65**	**56**	**77**
6	Bolton	46	20	16	10	78	59	76
7	Wolves	46	19	16	11	64	43	73

Spring 1999 was one of the most magical times to be a Watford supporter. Over the course of seven weeks grew a sense of invincibility. The manager believed. The players believed. And the fans believed. One win followed another, followed another. From nowhere, Watford entered the play-offs as the in-form team.

MOONEY!

Mooney was a bit-part player through the season but he hit form at precisely the right time, scoring seven in six games to fire Watford into the play-offs.

Birmingham A 2-1 **Mooney**, Daley
Bolton H 2-0 Hyde, **Mooney**
Crewe A 1-0 **Mooney**
Palace H 2-1 Hyde, **Mooney**
Port Vale A 2-1 **Mooney 2**
Barnsley A 2-2 Ngonge, **Mooney**

game, I had messages on my phone asking if I was going to join.'

As the games went on, Mooney made himself a hero all over again. The goals kept flowing and Watford kept winning.

How much of it was down to the input from Mr Pink Shirt, Ciaran Cosgrave? 'Graham knew that he liked to talk,' says Mooney. 'He would have meetings about meetings and perhaps he could feel he was becoming a bit monotonous. Ciaran came in and he took the football out of the situation. He asked us what we wanted to achieve for ourselves, our families, our children. It's strange to think you needed to hear that from a different voice but I think it worked.

'Richard Johnson, Robert Page, Alec Chamberlain and myself had more meetings with him than the other lads and I think we all bought into it.'

Nick Wright says: 'Ciaran got us visualising things a lot more. It got us spending a lot more time together as a group and we began to think as a group.'

Steve Palmer agrees that Cosgrave's influence was important but that it could only be effective for so long.

'The techniques worked, for sure,' he says. 'But once we got into the Premiership I think they were less effective. A lot of it was about confidence, about showing that we were confident and being in people's faces. I remember when we played Arsenal at Highbury he wanted us to go out into the tunnel early and wait for them and stand up to them and look them in the eye.

'Now, the Arsenal side were massive. The likes of Martin Keown, Tony Adams, Patrick Vieira, even Thierry Henry and Dennis Bergkamp are six foot plus and weren't going to be intimidated by that, so I think it ran its course.'

But in the spring of 1999, one win became two and as the games flew by, Watford were suddenly the team everyone was getting worried about.

'The mental side of the game is massive,' says Peter Kennedy. 'People perhaps don't get how much it matters. The difference between going on a run of six wins or a run of six losses is tiny. We didn't know why we hit a sticky patch and, if truth be told, we don't know why it all came good. It was lots of little factors. The manager worked on everything and it all came together at just the right time. It was a helluva ride to be on and for those two months we thought we could beat anybody.'

Chamberlain, Bazeley, Kennedy, Page, Palmer, Robinson, Smart, Hyde (Bonnot 64), Whittingham (Mooney 64), Johnson, Gudmundsson (Ngonge 64)
Manager Graham Taylor
Scorers Kennedy 67, Ngonge 87
Tranmere scorer Kelly 53
Attendance 8,652

ARSENAL.................... 1   WATFORD................... 3

FA Cup sixth round, Saturday March 14 1987

Watford surf the wave of controversy to reach semi-final

The prologue to the explosive and controversial closing few minutes at Highbury had been written five months earlier.

The league game between Arsenal and Watford descended into farce when the referee, Brian Stevens, sent the goalkeeper, Tony Coton off.

Stevens awarded Arsenal a dubious penalty and Coton made his displeasure clear. 'I called the linesman a cheat,' he says. As Coton went off the pitch, handing his gloves and goalkeeper's jersey to winger Nigel Callaghan, Graham Taylor asked him what he'd said.

Taylor knew Coton could have few complaints about the dismissal but it did make a mockery of the game. 'It's the only time in my managerial career when I seriously considered calling the players off the pitch. There was just no point after that,' he said.

Watford lost the match 3-1 and Taylor fumed.

In the FA Cup, the Hornets had made heavy weather of the fifth round tie against Third Division Walsall.

After a goalless draw at Fellows Park they then shared eight goals in a fantastic replay at Vicarage Road before finally getting through when Walsall conceded an unfortunate own goal in the second replay.

The quarter-final draw was not kind to Watford. George Graham's Arsenal team had been top of the First Division for two months. They had hit a sticky patch but were still well in the hunt for the title.

More significant than that was their formidable record at home. They had lost just twice at Highbury all season.

Extra spice was added to the showdown when the FA announced that the referee would be none other than Brian Stevens..

Taylor lodged an official complaint with the FA. There was no chance of the authorities changing the referee but if Taylor could apply pressure without overstepping the mark it might work in the Hornets' favour.

Watford started the match well but fell behind when John McClelland and Coton got in a tangle. McClelland called for the ball and took it just away from the goalkeeper, who was mid-stoop trying to gather it. The ball ran loose for Ian Allinson to poke into the net.

Watford lived dangerously for a while but got themselves level when David Bardsley crossed for Luther Blissett to steer home at the near post.

Bardsley was have a great game in his new role as a winger. His pace and the directness of his runs was causing

Arsenal's players swarm around John Barnes, who was instrumental in this cup win.

Kenny Sansom, who was the England left-back, all sorts of problems.

At times, Bardsley made Sansom look like a statue as he ran past him and supplied yet another cross.

In the second half, Kevin Richardson broke through the midfield and played the ball wide to Bardsley, who skinned Sansom and crossed before Steve Williams could close him down. John Barnes met the cross with a fine glancing header that flew past John Lukic and in off the bar.

Arsenal were rattled and began to throw everything at Watford's defence. Steve Sims and McClelland coped well with the aerial threat of Niall Quinn.

As time ticked by, Arsenal's appeals for a penalty became desperate. 'They were messing the ref around,' says Sims. 'I was telling the ref "They're trying to get a penalty." They were trying to run the game themselves.'

A couple of minutes from time, Steve Williams lofted a free kick into the box. Quinn and Sims jumped for the ball. 'I got up early and headed it,' says Sims. 'He jumped under me and tried to claim I had leaned on him.'

The linesman flagged. The Arsenal players stopped and hollered for a foul. Watford played on.

'Steve Williams was trying to stop the ref running. The ref didn't blow and, as we all know, it's play on until the whistle goes,' says Sims.

Watford broke quickly. Gary Porter lifted the ball upfield to Blissett who ran at the Arsenal defenders, who were still appealing for the penalty. Blissett's shot hit Lukic but he followed up to score the rebound.

The stadium erupted. The Arsenal players surrounded the referee. George Graham harangued the linesman. But the goal stood. After the final whistle, the argument continued in the tunnel.

Arsenal were left with only their sense of entitlement and their anger.

For Watford's fans it was one of the most dramatic and exciting victories of the Eighties, even if the less said about the semi-final against Spurs the better.

....

Coton, Gibbs, Rostron, Richardson, Sims, McClelland, Bardsley, Blissett, Falco, Porter, Barnes
Manager Graham Taylor
Scorers Blissett 23, 88, Barnes 52
Arsenal scorer Allinson 12
Attendance 43,276

THE GREAT ESCAPE

Rock bottom, eight points adrift of safety with eleven games to go. It was all over....

'We weren't drowning, we had drowned. But somehow, we came back to life.'

Glenn Roeder

OXFORD UNITED 0   WATFORD 1

Division Two, Saturday May 4 1991

'The feeling of relief was immense,' says Steve Perryman, architect of Watford's most unlikely relegation escape.

'While the games were going on, I don't think I realised what it was taking out of me but when it was all over, I slept for three days solid. I took the odd phone call, including one from Elton John saying congratulations. I had my meals and then I would go back to sleep. I was mentally exhausted.'

Watford had been dead and buried for most of the season. Few were in any doubt they were on their way back to the lower divisions for the first time since 1979.

The season began badly under Colin Lee. They took just two points from the opening nine matches. Lee was sacked after a 1-0 defeat at Newcastle in late November. Gary Porter missed a pen-

alty in that game. 'It wasn't a nice feeling missing the penalty and then finding out the manager had got the sack,' he says.

But the arrival of Perryman and his assistant Peter Shreeves perked things up on the training ground, even if the initial fillip on the pitch proved to be only temporary.

'The training seemed to pick up,' says Porter. 'There was a smile on people's faces for the first time in a while. We trained differently. Steve was very much into skill work, training with the ball. Peter had a lovely manner about him. But we'd dug ourselves into quite a deep hole.'

When Perryman arrived, Watford were bottom of the table with just nine points from 13 games. Under the new manager, they won three and drew five but were still in the relegation zone.

Because the league was being

Perryman was followed as manager by...

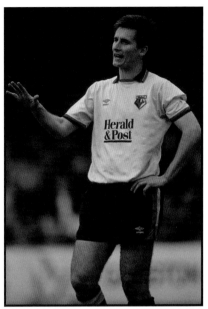

...his centre-half and captain, Roeder.

restructured, only two teams were to be relegated at the end of the season, meaning it would be harder to go down than stay up if they could put a half-decent run together.

But the new year was terrible. They kept losing and by mid-March were destined for the drop. A 3-0 defeat at home to fellow strugglers Blackburn Rovers seemed to spell the end.

'Someone threw a dustbin onto the pitch from the so-called family stand at that game,' says Perryman. 'That was the lowest point of all. That was when I started to think that this was my problem as much as anyone else's. We weren't turning it around quickly enough.'

Perryman had been a promising manager at Brentford before taking the Watford job. 'Before I went there, I had seen a couple of Watford's games and I knew that division and I felt that things

couldn't get any worse. I thought they were certainly good enough to stay up.

'First of all you want the players to start enjoying themselves in training and to play without that fear you have when you are at the bottom of the league. But it took a long time to turn things around. I decided to move Gary Penrice on. He was a very bubbly character but I felt that some of the people who can be so 'up' can also be very down. I also felt he was being tapped up so I let him go and used the money to bring in Peter Nicholas, who was tried and tested, a Welsh warrior.'

Glenn Roeder had been edged out of the team in Lee's final days but found himself back in favour with Perryman.

'Colin Lee had basically tried to retire me,' he says. 'He gave me the chance to coach the reserves, to pacify me, and he brought in Keith Dublin and Joe McLaughlin. When Steve and Peter came in, they said they wanted to change the formation and play me alongside two young central defenders, Barry Ashby and David Holdsworth.

'I was a good talker on the pitch. I didn't shut up for 90 minutes and I could play deep as a sweeper, mop up any mistakes and organise them.'

Holdsworth got injured before the plan could be tested so Roeder, Dublin and Ashby played together and began to form a good understanding at the heart of the defence.

Paul Wilkinson was used as a lone striker and towards the end of the season, Perryman brought old favourite Nigel Callaghan in on loan.

As spring wore on, they still needed snookers to avoid dropping into the Third Division. 'Even though things looked bleak, Steve and Peter were very upbeat,' says Porter. 'They gave us this belief that we would be okay.'

A run of good results meant that Watford hauled themselves up the rock face inch by inch. With two games to go, they needed one win to survive.

The penultimate match was at the Manor Ground, Oxford. 'I'd been at Oxford as a player,' says Perryman. 'It was a tight little ground, held about

A Hornet Houdini act

Colin Lee was sacked after a 1-0 defeat at Newcastle United on November 24, which left the Hornets rooted to the foot of the table. With just two wins from 17 games, they were seven points adrift of Charlton Athletic.

Although Perryman halted the decline briefly, a long, cold winter set in and by mid-March it looked like the fight was over.

A 3-0 defeat against Blackburn, who were also in trouble, seemed to spell the end.

Watford got an unlikely late winner at Middlesbrough and suddenly things started to pick up. By taking 23 points from a possible 30 they managed to pull off an escape that had looked unlikely. Almost half their points for the season came from that ten-game run.

March		Pos
23	Middlesbrough A 2-1	24th
30	Port Vale A 0-0	24th
April		
1	**Leicester City H 1-0**	**24th**
6	Swindon Town A 2-1	23rd
13	**Wolves H 3-1**	**23rd**
16	Notts County A 0-1	23rd
20	**Charlton Athletic H 2-1**	**23rd**
23	**West Brom H 1-1**	**23rd**
27	Portsmouth A 1-0	21st
May		
4	Oxford United A 1-0	19th
11	**Bristol City H 2-3**	**20th**

MARCH 19

		P	W	D	L	F	A	Pts
19	Blackburn	35	10	7	18	37	49	37
20	Portsmouth	36	9	10	17	42	59	37
21	Leicester City	34	10	6	18	45	67	36
22	West Brom	34	8	11	15	40	46	35
23	Hull City	34	7	10	17	46	72	31
24	**Watford**	**35**	**5**	**13**	**17**	**30**	**50**	**28**

END OF THE SEASON

		P	W	D	L	F	A	Pts
19	Blackburn	46	14	10	22	51	66	52
20	**Watford**	**46**	**12**	**15**	**19**	**45**	**59**	**51**
21	Swindon Town	46	12	14	20	65	73	50
22	Leicester City	46	14	8	24	60	83	50
23	West Brom	46	10	18	18	52	61	48
24	Hull City	46	10	15	21	57	85	45

nine thousand at a push, and it wasn't, in fairness, the most daunting of places to go.

'But the pitch had a hell of a slope and I felt that would be crucial.'

More than 3,000 Watford fans made the trip and packed every inch of the tiny terrace allocated to away fans.

David James had played for the England under-21 team in Turkey in midweek. It had crossed Perryman's mind to pull him out of the squad but he decided the trip might do his young keeper good.

'I felt we were always in control of the game,' says Roeder. 'We were well organised and quite composed by that stage of the season. We had our destiny in our own hands. What seems an absolutely nightmarish and dangerous situation for the supporters watching is not so bad when you're actually out there, dealing with it.

'But we did it by the skin of our teeth. It wasn't a case that we were drowning. We had drowned. But somehow we came back to life.'

Wilkinson got the crucial goal, which sparked incredible celebrations.

'It felt as good as a promotion, it really did,' says Perryman. 'Everyone thought we were going down and the vultures were out for our best players, but we rallied together really well in a tough situation and that is something the players should be proud of.'

James, Gibbs, Drysdale (Denton 83), Dublin, Ashby, Roeder, Nicholas, Wilkinson (Callaghan 85), Butler, Porter, Falconer
Manager Steve Perryman
Scorer Wilkinson 59
Attendance 8,436

A much-maligned chairman?

It's not a fashionable point of view to speak in favour of former chairman, Jack Petchey. But, like his successor Glenn Roeder, Steve Perryman has nothing but praise for him.

'I'd meet Petchey once a month and those dates were set in stone, a year in advance,' says Perryman. 'He made minutes of every meeting and I was given a list of action points. He ran the club like a business. He was very shrewd. He once read about Glenn Hoddle saying that sports massage in France had added two years to his career and he wanted me to check it out and report back.

'He once did something very clever. He said to me "If you had £500,000 for a striker, who would it be? Don't get excited, you haven't got it, but suppose you did?"

'I would have to look into it and answer it. I came up with a list and said I thought that Paul Furlong at Enfield was a decent player and that he'd cost about £140,000.

'Eventually Furlong went to Coventry for about £140,000. So, he assessed my judgement of a player without having to buy anyone.

'In the end, we got Furlong for £250,000 and I joked that if he'd backed me earlier I could have saved him ninety thousand.

'People knocked Jack but he was never anything other than straight with me. He didn't promise anything he couldn't deliver. He said there was little or no money for the team. I am not sure he was a great football fan but from a business point of view he taught me a lot. And he built two new stands and didn't get the club into financial trouble.'

1-0

12 minutes
Nigel Callaghan nods home after Blissett hooks the ball back across the penalty area.

2-0

23 minutes
Another Callaghan header. He outjumps Barry Venison to meet Jenkins' deep cross.

3-0

26 minutes
Les Taylor plays a perfectly-weighted ball over the top for Blissett, who races onto it to slot in.

4-0

32 minutes
Sunderland, all at sea at the back, fail to clear and Jenkins takes full advantage to grab his first.

Total football brings

 WATFORD.............. 8 SUNDERLAND................ 0

Division One, Saturday September 25 1982

The First Division season was only 29 days old and here were Watford administering the sort of hammering a newly-promoted side might have dreaded.

Sunderland were torn apart by a team that was rampant and yet almost unaware of its own strength.

Graham Taylor's insistence that his men would attack without mercy, for fear of being taught a lesson by sides that were supposedly superior, meant there was the possibility someone might be on the end of a humiliating defeat.

This was one of only two occasions when Watford have scored eight goals in a match since the Second World War – the other was an 8-0 League Cup win over Darlington in 1987.

And this remains Watford's biggest ever win in the Football League.

Sunderland were mauled, overrun

and demoralised but they didn't start too badly. With a young Ally McCoist up front, they could have scored at least twice before Watford took the lead.

Steve Terry was making his first appearance in Division One and as he lost his man a couple of times, he could have been forgiven for having flashbacks to his nightmare Watford debut, a 5-0 hammering at Sunderland's Roker Park two years earlier.

But once Nigel Callaghan had scored two headed goals and Luther Blissett and Ross Jenkins had added the third and fourth with just over half an hour gone, the result was beyond doubt.

At half-time, the manager refused to let his players sit down. Perhaps it was because he sensed a massacre or maybe he feared his team would not know how to handle the situation ahead of them. It was not in Watford's nature to take

5-0

58 minutes

A perfect long pass from Bolton, first-time cross from Callaghan and a Blissett header.

6-0

71 minutes

Blissett's cross from the left beats the defender and is deftly steered into the net by Jenkins.

7-0

83 minutes

Sunderland fall apart under more pressure. Blissett dives in at the far post to head home.

8-0

88 minutes

Blissett finds space in six-yard box, controls and prods his fourth. The rout is complete.

total annihilation

the foot off the pedal. Taylor certainly didn't want them relaxing and letting Sunderland back into the match, so he made them jog on the spot for ten minutes until it was time to go back out.

Taylor had been particularly tough on his squad in the run-up to the game. The previous week they had been poor at Nottingham Forest, so he had them running all week until their heads were about to drop. Then, just when the players wondered if they could cope with any more, he took them to a hotel and treated them to a full English breakfast and a couple of pints.

It was the equivalent of caging a pack of tigers for a week and denying them food, then giving them a sniff of prime steak before sending them into the arena.

The second half offered more of the same. The fifth goal was poetry in motion. Watch it on YouTube. Watford rob Sunderland's attackers in their own area and play their way out of trouble. The ball is worked to Ian Bolton, tight on the right-hand touchline deep in his own half. He sends an inch-perfect long pass sailing high down the line with his first touch.

It beats the Sunderland full back and lands in front of Callaghan with such precision that the winger doesn't even need to break his stride. It was like the ball had been parachuted to safety.

Callaghan crosses first time and

Another goal for Blissett. Another chance to pick the ball out of the net for Chris Turner.

Blissett heads firmly past Chris Turner. Three touches and the ball has travelled 90 yards in one direction and 20 yards in another. Three touches, and Sunderland may as well not have been on the pitch.

Blissett completed his first senior hat-trick and added a fourth for good measure. Even the electronic score-board joined in the celebrations with a message: 'Well done Luther'.

While Turner, who almost joined Watford from Sheffield Wednesday when they were in the Third Division, found his nightmare was complete, the Watford supporters must have thought they were dreaming.

RIGHT HAMMERINGS

Watford's biggest league wins

8-0 v Sunderland H Division One	1982
8-2 v Newport H Division Three South	1924
7-0 v Newport H Division Three South	1934
7-1 v Northampton H Division Three	1920
7-1 v C Palace H Division Three South	1954
7-1 v Grimsby Town H Division Three	1967

Biggest FA Cup wins

10-0 v Leighton Cee Springs	1900
10-0 v Bournemouth	1913
10-1 v Lowestoft Town	1926

Biggest League Cup win

8-0 v Darlington H	1987

WATFORD
Sherwood, Rice, Rostron, Taylor, Terry, Bolton, Callaghan, Blissett, Jenkins, Jackett, Barnes
Goals Callaghan 12, 23, Blissett 26, 58, 83, 88, Jenkins 32, 71
Manager Graham Taylor

SUNDERLAND
Turner, Venison, Munro, Atkins, Hindmarch, Nicholl, Buckley, Rowell, McCoist, Pickering, Cummins
Manager Alan Durban
Attendance 16,774

GOING UP

WATFORD............1 PLYMOUTH ARGYLE........0

Division Three, Tuesday April 15 1969

Photograph: Watford Observer

The long wait is over. Ken Furphy swigs from a champagne bottle in the directors' box after becoming the first Watford manager to lead the club into the Second Division.

If you listened to the gossip in the pubs and clubs around Watford you'd have heard a familiar story, told with all the certainty of the saloon bar. Watford don't want promotion. They keep throwing it away on purpose. Bonser doesn't want the hassle. The board don't want to pay Division Two bonuses or improve the ground.

It was nonsense, of course, but after a series of near-misses the conspiracy theory was beginning to take hold.

And as Watford's bid to reach the Second Division for the first time began to stutter again in the spring of 1969 some felt they had seen it all before.

In 1964, with Bill McGarry at the helm, Watford forced their way into the second promotion spot late in the season. There were eight games to go. They won only one of them, lost at Luton Town, of all places, on the last day of the season and missed out by just two points.

In 1967, now with Ken Furphy in charge, they were in the hunt all season. They drew their final two games but once they had played that last fixture, away at Oldham Athletic, they were still in second place.

Middlesbrough still had one game to play and, three days later, they beat Oxford United 4-1 to leapfrog the Hornets at the death. If Watford had won one of those final two matches and scored an extra two goals, they would have finished above Boro on goal average. It was that close.

The Second Division had remained tantalisingly out of reach for Watford.

Nine years after hauling themselves out of the Fourth Division, they still hadn't cracked it. Some thought this was as far as a club like Watford could go.

Furphy arrived from Workington in November 1964 and had spent five years making the place his own. His team was built from the back. He wanted his side to be sound defensively.

The arrival of Micky Walker, a goalkeeper from York City, was the final piece of the jigsaw. Walker went on to manage Norwich and Everton and his son, Ian, played for Tottenham and England. He slotted in behind a defence that was already pretty tight. Walker was the ideal safe pair of hands.

Watford only conceded seven goals at home in the league all season as they made Vicarage Road a very awkward place to visit.

At times it was not particularly inspiring stuff, particularly in the first six weeks of the season. Then someone recommended a young striker to Furphy. Barry Endean was playing parks football in the north east. Furphy took a punt and Endean coped brilliantly with the step up, scoring 18 goals in 28 matches.

Watford hit the top spot after winning 4-1 at Barrow just before Christmas and were never out of the top two. Surely this time they'd do it?

Despite going on a run of only two defeats in more than 20 games, there

		P	W	D	L	F	A	Pts
1	Watford	46	27	10	9	74	34	64
2	Swindon Town	46	27	10	9	71	35	64
3	Luton Town	46	25	11	10	74	38	61
4	Bournemouth	46	21	9	16	60	45	51

were still some worries. In mid-February, they travelled to Kenilworth Road for a game against Luton, who were also chasing promotion. 'It was snowing, so we went up there in the afternoon to have a look at the pitch,' says Tom Walley. 'Somehow they got the game on but it carried on snowing and by half-time it was coming down really heavy.'

After 63 minutes and with the score 1-1, the referee abandoned the match. It would have to be rescheduled and played again from the start. A bad omen.

The fixtures were backing up. Both Watford and Luton were playing twice a week and although neither club wanted the game to be played so late in the season, they had no choice. The match was rearranged for April 30 and would be Watford's penultimate game.

'It was like everything was set up for that to be the decider,' says Walley. 'Luton were going hell for leather for promotion as well so we wanted to avoid that at all costs.

'We were desperate to get it done before then because if we had to go up there needing a win, it would be tasty.'

Watford were due to play nine games in April, one every three days. There were three teams chasing two places, the other was Swindon Town, and nerves were getting frayed.

'It was very tight,' says Walley. 'It doesn't matter what you think, when every game is so important the stress builds up. You go into every game knowing you have to win. We did keep

winning but there weren't too many great games. Everyone is at the end of their tether when it gets that late in the season. You're under pressure and you just don't want to make silly mistakes and give points away.'

Watford got a vital 1-0 win at Swindon but with only two points for a win, it was hard to gain much of a lead.

Walley was desperate to get back up the league. He'd been at Arsenal as a youngster and felt Division Two was his natural level, at the very least.

Furphy signed Walley for £9,000 in 1967, having heard that Walley was available after a training ground flare-up with Peter Storey.

'Storey went over the top, so I grabbed him, showed the gash on my shin and said if he did it again I'd smash him,' Walley says. 'The next week I was on the transfer list. Storey was the rising star, you see. I said to my brother Ernie I was going to go back to Wales but he told me not be stupid.

'First day at Watford, we were at Cassiobury Park playing a training match and Bert Slater, the goalkeeper, was playing out on the pitch. He thought he'd sort out the new lad from Arsenal. We were marking up at a corner and he threw a punch at me. I ducked and clocked him. Furphy said: "Are you mad?" I told him that I wasn't going to take any shit. If Bert had caught me, I'd have been knocked out. I think Furphy liked me after that.'

They're up and Watford have the title in their sights after a 1-0 win over Reading.

The Plymouth match wasn't do-or-die, there were still four games to go afterwards, but recent history had taught Watford harsh lessons about how hard it was to get over the line.

It was far from a classic and the goal was barely a goal but it didn't matter. Watford had done it, they had reached the Second Division. Or, as the *Watford Observer* put it: They're up at last.

The goal, which came early in the second half, was controversial. Roy Sinclair hit a shot from distance that wrong-footed the Plymouth keeper Pat Dunne. The former Manchester United man could only punch it up onto the bar. The ball bounced down. Was it on the line or over? It was Watford's Geoff Hurst moment. Dunne said later: 'It bounced well in front of the line. I was stunned when a goal was given.' Even Sinclair had his doubts. 'To be honest I didn't think it was a goal.'

The final whistle sparked scenes of jubilation. The team and the fans celebrated together. The long wait and near-misses were forgotten and the invidious accusation that Watford did not really want promotion was at last laid to rest.

They only won one of their final four matches but Swindon failed to do enough to overhaul them. The two sides were level on points but Watford won the championships because they had a slightly better goal average.

And what about that Luton match? It was a good job it hadn't been the promotion decider because the Hatters won it 2-1, and Walley was sent off for retaliation. Even though Luton won, they missed out on promotion, making Watford's triumph even sweeter. At last. At long, long last, Watford could call themselves a Second Division club.

WATFORD
Walker, Welbourne, Williams, Eddy, Lees, Walley, Garbett, Hale, Sinclair, Endean, Scullion
Goal Sinclair
Manager Ken Furphy
....
PLYMOUTH ARGYLE
Dunne, Reeves, Neale, Saxton, Molyneux, Reynolds, Davey, Piper, Burnside, Bickie, Maher
Manager Billy Bingham
Attendance 22,515

Clough goes on holiday while his European champions are humbled

Imagine the furore there would be if the manager of a Premier League club chose to go on holiday while his team played an important League Cup tie.

Brian Clough left his assistant Peter Taylor in charge not because he was so arrogant that he thought his team could cope without him but because it was the school holidays.

Clough took his family to Majorca thinking that his Nottingham Forest team was perfectly capable of winning without him.

After all, Nottingham Forest were the reigning European champions and had reached the League Cup final three years in a row.

Graham Taylor selected John Ward, usually a centre forward, for a specific job. He told Ward to mark Forest's winger John Robertson as tightly as he could. Robertson could hurt a team with one dribble and cross, so Taylor wanted to cancel him out, hoping to make the game a clash of ten against ten.

They played Liverpool's anthem *You'll Never Walk Alone* before kick-off and it had the desired affect, whipping the crowd into a frenzy and heightening the emotion.

The first half was tight. As expected, Forest were dangerous but Watford kept going forward and eventually the

pressure began to tell. Four minutes before half-time, Kenny Burns fouled Malcolm Poskett in the penalty area and Blissett scored the penalty.

Forest didn't have time to recover before they were two behind. Ross Jenkins was dominating Larry Lloyd, in the air and on the ground, and he capitalised on a mistake to score.

Perhaps fearful of a Forest fight-back, at half-time Taylor urged Watford to keep pushing on. Jenkins scored two more before Ian Wallace managed to pull a goal back.

Clough waited until the morning to ring the club to find out the result, and apparently thought he was having his leg pulled when they told him.

Beating the European Cup holders had Watford's supporters wondering just how good their team would turn out to be.

Taylor reminded them that football has a funny habit of bringing you down to earth. In the next round, they lost 5-0 to Coventry City in a replay.

But that did nothing to dampen the memory of a night when Watford beat the team that ruled Europe.

Steele, Henderson, Harrison, Blissett, Sims, Jackett, Poskett, Ward, Jenkins, Train, Rostron.
Manager Graham Taylor
Scorers Jenkins 43, 55, 69, Blissett 41 pen
Forest scorer Wallace 74
Attendance 22,742

Heroic Holton leads from the front

WORKINGTON 0   WATFORD 1

Division Four, Saturday April 30 1960

Borough Park in Workington was no place for a party. Hardly anyone had made the trip from Hertfordshire to witness Watford clinch their first Football League promotion.

Three days later, more than 20,000 people turned up at Vicarage Road for some proper celebrations.

As much as they were there to toast the team's success and cheer them on in their final game against Walsall, the side that had won the championship, really they had come to see one man. 'We want Cliff,' they chanted over and over.

This will always be known as Cliff's team. While the names of Linton, Bell, Catleugh and Uphill will also be fondly remembered, the way Holton stood head and shoulders above them all will never be forgotten.

It is no exaggeration to say that Holton led the club out of the Fourth Division and the rest followed. He struck up a partnership with Dennis Uphill that terrified defences. That season Holton scored 42 goals in the league, while Uphill got 30.

That's not to say that promotion was a foregone conclusion. Watford were

DIVISION FOUR

End of the season

		P	W	D	L	F	A	Pts
1	Walsall	46	28	9	9	102	60	65
2	Notts County	46	26	8	12	107	69	60
3	Torquay Utd	46	26	8	12	84	58	60
4	**Watford**	**46**	**24**	**9**	**13**	**92**	**67**	**57**
5	Millwall	46	18	17	11	84	61	53
6	Northampton	46	22	9	15	85	63	53

only able to take the fourth place on offer. And it was not until the final three weeks of the season that they forced their way into the picture.

It helped that most of their final fixtures were against struggling teams from the north.

Easter was a hectic time. Watford had to play three games in four days. It was when faced with such challenges that Holton came into his own.

He scored a hat-trick in the 4-2 win over Chester on Good Friday and another three in the 5-0 thrashing of Gateshead the very next day.

Watford had been on the shoulder of Millwall for several weeks but now the Lions were really wobbling it was time to make their move.

All Watford had to do was hold their nerve. They beat Chester again, this time away, on Easter Monday then got a draw and a win over Rochdale in the space of four days.

There were now two games to go. Workington away and Walsall at home. Not wanting to leave anything to chance against the team that had proved itself the best in the division, Ron Burgess knew Watford had to finish the job at Workington.

There's an apocryphal tale about the match that has gone down in local folklore. Here is how it goes.

Concerned about the possibility of

No one has scored more goals for Watford in a single season than Cliff Holton. Here is a list of the club's top scorers.

	Season	Goals
Cliff Holton	1959-60	48
Ross Jenkins	1978-79	37
Cliff Holton	1960-61	34
Maurice Cook	1954-55	31
Luther Blissett	1982-83	30
Dai Ward	1962-63	30
Billy Jennings	1973-74	29
Luther Blissett	1984-85	28
Danny Graham	2010-11	27
Keith Mercer	1976-77	25
Charlie Livesey	1963-64	25
Cyril Thompson	1951-52	25

League, FA Cup and League Cup matches only.

coming unstuck at Borough Park, someone, rumoured to be one of the players, was sent north the day before the match to see if the result couldn't be helped along a bit. He had a bag with him, containing enough notes to make it worth Workington's while to go easy.

The player arrived at Workington's ground while the team was still training on the pitch. He studied the playing surface, uneven and rutted even by the standards of the day.

He watched the players in their hotch-potch kit. He saw the crumbling terraces and poked his head into the changing rooms, noticing the peeling paint and cracked basins. And he decided there was no way Watford would not beat them.

So he took the bag of money and decided he'd share it among his teammates as a little promotion bonus when they got the job done.

Whether there's a grain of truth in it or not, it's an entertaining yarn.

Watford did what they needed to do. Holton, who had a painkilling injection in his shoulder before the match, to numb an injury he'd picked up against Chester, scored the only goal of the game after nine minutes. He collected the ball on the edge of the area, took a couple of touches and fired it home in his trademark fashion.

What followed was scrappy but Watford held on. The nerves were

DID YOU KNOW?
Keith Burkinshaw, the Workington defender, was later assistant to Adrian Boothroyd

evident as Workington went close near the end but, as it turned out, even a draw would have been enough.

Millwall had already finished their season so it all hinged on whether Northampton Town could win at Stockport County. One of the reporters made a call to his sports desk to find out the result and relayed it to the Watford team. Stockport had won 3-0.

The atmosphere on the evening Walsall visited was electrifying. Watford had enjoyed some fleeting successes in the past, the odd cup shock here and there, but never had they had a season of such achievement.

'I still look back on that promotion at Watford with a greater sense of satisfaction than when I won the league with Arsenal,' Holton later said. 'Seeing how much it meant to the supporters and the town was tremendous. They were not used to success and so they valued it more.'

WORKINGTON
Newlands, Wilson, Brown, Burkinshaw, Tennant, Keen, McGarry, Hinchcliffe, Harburn, Gibbs, Kirkup
Manager Joe Harvey

WATFORD
Linton, Bell, Nicholas, Catleugh, Porter, Sanchez, Benning, Walker, Uphill, Holton, Gregory
Manager Ron Burgess
Scorer Holton 9
Attendance 22,515

Endean delivers the knockout blow

15 | **WATFORD....................... 1 LIVERPOOL 0**

FA Cup sixth round, Saturday February 21 1970

With the biggest cup tie in years coming up, it looked like Watford were in danger of falling apart.

They were having to fight for their lives to stave off an immediate return to Division Three. Every time they hauled themselves upwards, they slipped back into trouble again. At times they seemed unable to cope with the step up and yet in the FA Cup they had produced some of their most accomplished displays of the season.

Tom Walley, the Welshman who wasn't just the team's engine but the one who fetched and carried the coal to keep the train going, never doubted Ken Furphy.

'He had this knack of getting us very well organised for the big matches,' says Walley.

As the season drew on, Watford knew every game was going to be like a cup tie if they were to avoid the drop.

The cup was a nice diversion. Having knocked

out Bolton Wanderers and Stoke City, they scraped past Gillingham to make the sixth round for the first time since 1932, and only the second time in the club's history.

Their reward was another clash with Liverpool. Earlier in the season, Bill Shankly's Reds had knocked Watford out of the League Cup, winning 2-1 at Vicarage Road.

Eleven days before their biggest cup tie in decades, disaster struck. The influential Keith Eddy got injured.

While Walley toiled, Eddy pulled the strings in Watford's midfield, dropping back and orchestrating moves from deep. 'Eddy was a bloody good player,' says Walley. 'He could use the ball very well. When he was out, we did miss him.'

Eddy was injured at Carlisle and the Hornets crumbled, losing 5-0 and slipping into the bottom two for the umpteenth time that season.

With Liverpool on their way, the last thing

It's there! Barry Endean's header has beaten Chris Lawrence and Liverpool are out.

Watford needed was to lose arguably their most composed player.

But if there was one thing Furphy was good at, it was coming up with a plan and then executing it precisely.

He took the team away for a few days, to St Helier in Jersey, where the club's wealthy vice-chairman Harold Hutchinson owned a villa.

The squad played golf and relaxed around the swimming pool, enjoying an unusually warm spring in the Channel Islands while England saw out the last days of winter.

It wasn't all play, though. Knowing the Vicarage Road pitch would be heavy, Furphy found a sandy corner of beach and had his players running through it.

'Somehow the gaffer got me on a plane. I didn't like flying and we were on this little thing that wobbled about,' says Walley. 'We went there and we got really well organised. We went through everything, man by man, so we all knew our

jobs. Furphy was very good at that. He could get us going for specific games. It wasn't possible to do it for every game because you couldn't watch the opposition like you can now. You can get video of everyone, you can send scouts to several matches. Back then you couldn't do it.'

Liverpool were sure to be formidable opponents but the suspicion was that Bill Shankly's first great team was on the wane. After winning two league titles, in 1964 and 1966, there were now some ageing legs in the side. Furphy hoped to exploit this by playing at a high tempo and stretching the defence. The fact that

1970 FA CUP

3rd round	Bolton Wanderers A	2-1
4th round	Stoke City H	1-0
5th round	Gillingham H	2-1
6th round	Liverpool H	1-0
Semi-final	Chelsea	1-5
3rd place play-off	Manchester United	0-2

Tommy Smith, Liverpool's combative midfield player, would be missing from the line-up was a bonus.

Furphy's biggest dilemma was how to replace Eddy. Most people expected him to pick Colin Franks, the 18-year-old, who scored a sensational winner in the fourth round against Stoke.

The teenage midfielder's long-range strike caught out Gordon Banks, the England goalkeeper who had won the World Cup just four years earlier.

Although his goal had given the tabloids an excuse to use a variation on their favourite Banks of England headline, Furphy was not so sure.

Franks was young and inconsistent. Instead, he went for Mike Packer.

Walley remembers Furphy's team talk being clear and concise. 'He didn't have to say much,' he says. 'We had done a lot of work. Before we went out he said, "Don't be afraid of them. They're just men. It's a big job and they're a good team but they aren't going to want to fight like we'll fight. If we do our bit correctly, I am telling you, we can go a long way. If we stay organised, we might nick it." He gave you confidence, made you feel like you had prepared well.'

This was Furphy's finest hour. His team stuck to the task brilliantly. They hassled Liverpool, refusing to let them settle on the ball.

At half-time, it was still goalless but Furphy was wary. He knew a moment of inspiration could be Watford's undoing. The longer it went on, the clearer it became that a single goal would decide it. As it turned out, that moment of brilliance was created by the players in the gold shirts.

Stewart Scullion, whose wing play had caused problems all afternoon,

BILL SHANKLY'S PRESS CONFERENCE

I wouldn't say the best team won. I thought their goal came at the right moment for them. I thought Watford had shot their bolt. They hadn't the energy. It was more bravado that kept them going. Walley, he makes a difference to them. He's a useful player. And Lugg played well. He had such poise. But you need more than hard running in the semi-final. They could meet an awful powerful team. They could be... demoralised... aye, demoralised...

pushed the ball forward from deep, ran past three defenders and won a throw-in off Ron Yeats.

Ray Lugg took the throw and Scullion knocked it back to him. With quick thinking and even speedier feet, Lugg tapped the ball through Chris Wall's legs and sent in a perfect, arcing cross. Barry Endean, surrounded by defenders, timed his run beautifully and sent a powerful header into the net.

At the time, it was the single most important goal in the club's history and sealed a place in the semi-finals.

Endean, a barrel-chested bully of a centre forward, had come out of non-League football 18 months earlier and could be too much for many defences to handle.

The clock seemed to stand still for Furphy after that but Shankly's team had run out of ideas.

The four minutes of injury time were torture. 'I now know the meaning of the word eternity,' he said.

WATFORD
Walker, Welbourne, Williams, Lugg, Lees, Walley, Scullion, Garbett, Endean, Packer, Owen
Goal Endean 63
Manager Ken Furphy
....
LIVERPOOL
Lawrence, Lawler, Wall, Strong, Yeats, Hughes, Callaghan, Ross, Evans, St John, Graham
Manager Bill Shankly
Attendance 34,047

WHAT HAPPENED NEXT?

Unfortunately, Bill Shankly was right. Watford were demoralised in the semi-final. The other three teams in the hat were Manchester United, Chelsea and Leeds United. All of them giants, all of them capable of giving out a hiding. Watford were the team everybody else was hoping to get. Watford's match against Chelsea was played on a White Hart Lane pitch that resembled a sandpit.

In truth, the team of Peter Bonetti, John Hollins, Ron 'Chopper' Harris, Alan Hudson and Peter Osgood was too good for them.

David Webb gave Chelsea the lead after three minutes, although Watford fought back eight minutes later, when Terry Garbett scored an equaliser, and they held on until the second-half.

Osgood broke Watford's resolve just before the hour mark and then the cracks opened up.

Chelsea scored three times in eight minutes. Peter Houseman got two and Ian Hutchinson grabbed the other. Although Watford could not claim to deserve a place in the final, it was a harsh score.

Watford's cup run wasn't quite over. They went on to play the first ever third-fourth place play-off against Manchester United, the other beaten semi-finalists, The match was played at Highbury, the evening before the cup final. Only 15,000 people saw a 2-0 United win.

WATFORD......3 WEST BROMWICH ALBION......0

Division One, Saturday September 11 1982

Top of the league

Take that. Blissett smashes his second goal. Note to Ali Robertson: it's not offside.

Photograph: Press Association

For the first and only time in Watford's history, the club could stand at the very pinnacle of the game and stare down at everyone else below them.

The First Division's new boys had enjoyed an exceptional start to their debut season.

In those days, the Football League and the newspapers waited until three league matches had been played before publishing the tables. While it is possible to look back at the results and make a case that Watford topped the league ten days earlier, after winning their opening two games, that is not really the case.

Admittedly the league was still in its embryonic stages but the visit of West Bromwich Albion was already a top-of-the-table clash.

The Baggies were second, a point behind Liverpool. Watford were fourth, level on points with their guests that day. By a quarter to five, Graham Taylor's team were top of the pile.

What an extraordinary rise it was.

Just seven years earlier they had been bottom of the lot.

Going top of the table was not uppermost in the manager's mind before the game. He simply wanted Watford to build on their fine start. Albion were a tough team to beat.

Luther Blissett had started the season in midfield because of injuries to Les Taylor and Jan Lohman but he returned to the attack to partner Gerry Armstrong. Albion's central defenders, Ali Robertson and Martin Bennett didn't quite know what had hit them.

Afterwards they compared the

Watford striker favourably to their own striker Cyrille Regis, who was an England international.

West Brom were stubborn but they couldn't deal with Watford's constant pressure. As Robertson said: 'They just keep coming at you. In the end, you are just clearing your lines and getting back into position before they come at you again. They make it very difficult to play your own game.'

They held out until six minutes before half-time, when Blissett scored. Taylor added another early in the second half before Blissett gave them

From 92nd to first in seven years

When Watford were beaten 1-0 at Darlington on August 30, 1975, they sank as low as it was possible for a league club to sink. The following morning, the papers made grim reading. Mike Keen's team, who were hoping to bounce straight back after relegation the previous season, were bottom of the Fourth Division.

Three consecutive defeats without scoring a goal was their worst start to a season since 1953-54.

Just seven years later, they had

climbed 91 places in the league and sat proudly above the rest of the country.

Ross Jenkins was the only player to figure for Watford when they were both top and bottom of the league.

The centre forward was in the team that beat Hartlepool to haul themselves off the bottom of Division Four and, although he didn't feature against West Brom, he did come on as a sub the following week, when the table-toppers lost 2-0 at Nottingham Forest.

DIVISION FOUR

August 30, 1975

		P	W	D	L	F	A	Pts
19	Crewe	3	0	2	1	4	6	2
20	Bradford City	3	0	2	1	1	2	2
21	Scunthorpe	3	0	1	2	0	3	1
22	Southport	3	0	1	2	0	3	1
23	Workington	3	0	0	3	2	7	0
24	**Watford**	**3**	**0**	**0**	**3**	**0**	**4**	**0**

DIVISION ONE

September 11, 1982

		P	W	D	L	F	A	Pts
1	Watford	5	4	0	1	11	3	12
2	Man United	5	4	0	1	12	5	12
3	Man City	5	4	0	1	6	3	12
4	Liverpool	5	3	2	0	11	6	11
5	West Brom	5	3	0	2	11	6	9
6	Stoke City	5	3	0	2	10	7	9

a comfortable advantage to see out the remainder of the match.

With three points in their grasp, Watford needed results at Anfield and Old Trafford to go their way.

Liverpool, who were a point ahead before the match, were hosting Luton Town, while Manchester United, level on points and goal difference with Watford, were playing Ipswich Town.

When the final scores were read out, United had beaten Ipswich 3-1 while Liverpool were held to a 3-3 draw by the Hatters.

Incredibly, Watford were top of the Football League on goal difference ahead of the two Manchester clubs. The margins were tiny, but an Ipswich goal and a draw for their biggest rivals were enough for the Hornets.

Elton John had delayed a trip to the West Indies so he could see the Hornets in action. He flew out of the country knowing that his club, the one he had bought when it was a struggling Fourth Division team best known for midweek greyhound racing, could go no higher. They were ahead of all of English football's illustrious names.

That evening, Graham Taylor, Bertie Mee and their wives went to see the Proms at the Royal Albert Hall. Taylor, the manager of the best football team in England at that moment – remember the league table never lies – was prouder than he had ever been. He calls it the happiest night of his life as he stood alongside his wife, singing

Jerusalem with everything he had.

The stirring adaptation of William Blake's poem took on extra meaning. His team, his Watford, were the finest in England's green and pleasant land.

With no midweek fixtures to follow, Watford's supporters could bask in the glory for a full week. How many schoolchildren cut out the league table from one of the papers and stuck it on their exercise books?

There is one Watford fan – perhaps more than one – who laminated a clipping of that league table and carried it in his wallet for years. You know who you are.

The following week, Watford faced Nottingham Forest. When the two sides had met two years earlier, Forest had been reigning European champions.

Now, in his programme notes, the great Brian Clough was welcoming the league leaders to the City Ground.

And those league leaders were us, little Watford. Wasn't it amazing? Wasn't it surreal?

WATFORD
Sherwood, Rice, Rostron, Taylor, Bolton, Jackett, Callaghan, Blissett, Armstrong, Lohman, Barnes
Goals Blissett 39, 68, Taylor 54
Manager Graham Taylor

WEST BROMWICH ALBION
Grew, Batson, Whitehead, Zondervan, Bennett, Robertson, Jol, Brown, Regis, Owen, Eastoe
Manager Ron Wylie
Attendance 17,603

OH DEAR...

WATFORD.............. 2 LEEDS UNITED 1

Coca-Cola Cup third round, November 10 1992

The old Vicarage Road terrace deserved one last hurrah, a final send-off before being bulldozed and replaced with a smart new stand.

She had looked out upon many a famous night but was due to be pulled down at the end of the season.

Her shallow steps didn't offer a great view. The lack of a roof meant that the supporters got wet when it rained and the passion and fervour they created evaporated on the breeze.

But it was home and it was welcoming the same way a shabby old sofa can be. Everyone had their favourite spot. You were one of the North East boys or maybe you headed to the North West corner. The faces gathered under the scoreboard that had looked so achingly, science-fiction cool when it first went up in the late Seventies but was now endearingly dated, like a neglected Pacman machine in a video game arcade.

With the team bobbing around in Division One, Watford needed a decent cup draw to create one of those special evenings. A last chance to dance on the terrace, an exhilarating if sometimes anxiety-inducing experience that simply cannot be replicated in the seats.

Once Leeds had beaten Scunthorpe United, it was confirmed. The reigning league champions were coming to town for a Coca-Cola Cup tie.

The excitement was palpable on the approach to the ground. There was a buzz in the crisp, cold air, queues at the turnstiles, and an eagerness to get inside and be part of the hubbub.

Leeds had not started the season well. Their away form was shaky and they had been involved in several Uefa Champions League matches.

'Howard Wilkinson was the Leeds manager and they were very good at set pieces,' says Steve Perryman, the Watford boss. 'We went away to a hotel in Waltham Abbey the day before the game and did a couple of training sessions concentrating on defending against free-kicks and corners. I felt it might come down to who was better at them. We also did a session on the morning of the game.'

For Andy Hessenthaler, the game was the biggest occasion of his career. A year earlier, he'd been playing for non-league Redbridge Forest.

'This is what I had been waiting for,' he says. 'At the time, it was the biggest crowd I'd ever played in front of. When you play non-league, you dream of being involved in big matches like this but you're never sure how it's going to

CANTONA

Eric Cantona ran half the length of the pitch and had only Perry Suckling to beat.

affect you. I was going to be up against Gordon Strachan and Gary McAllister in midfield. They were the champions. I was determined not to be daunted by them. I liked to play at a high tempo but we started at a pace that we hadn't played at all season. We were really up for it. They had so many individuals who could cause you problems that you had to forget their pedigree and try to beat the man you were facing. We rolled our sleeves up and we outworked them.

'Early on, Trevor Putney put in a crunching tackle on Gary Speed and turned to us and clenched his fists. That set the tone.'

Although Watford had started well, they came perilously close to conceding in the 17th minute.

A sloppy pass in the centre circle was intercepted by Eric Cantona, the brilliant, mercurial Frenchman who had been the driving force behind the Leeds title triumph.

Cantona broke forward stealthily, his senses awakened now he had the ball. He was clear through on goal with just the goalkeeper to beat. This was going to be the opening goal. Surely.

Perry Suckling, the Watford keeper, was suddenly all that stood between Cantona and the goal.

'Cantona had a great touch and he had the art of dropping his shoulder and making you commit and then rolling the ball the other side,' says Suckling. 'Really, he could make a goalkeeper look a bit silly.

'When I was a kid, I was at Coventry with Steve Ogrizovic, and he was able to play the attacker at his own game. He would drop his shoulder and make it look like he was going to dive, which would make the striker's mind up for him. As Cantona came forward, I was trying to be big, making sure I didn't do anything rash. Time was on my side and the pressure was all on him.

'He was brilliant because he could take the ball on while looking you in the eye. I took my eye off the ball, looked at him and half read the situation and blocked his shot. When you think about critical moments in games, that was one because things went in our favour after that. We should have been one down but I'd stopped it and the crowd went mad, as if we'd scored a goal.'

'It was a great stop by our goalkeeper,' says Perryman. 'Cantona was waiting for Perry to do something but he didn't panic, he stayed calm and called his bluff.'

Watford were on top for the rest of the half but couldn't score. Perryman feared their chance was slipping by.

But nine minutes into the second half, Watford got the breakthrough. They won a free-kick on the edge of the box and David Holdsworth ran between Jon Newsome and Chris Whyte to head home from Putney's free kick. All the work on set-pieces had paid off.

Watford continued to attack and won a penalty when Whyte fouled Paul Furlong in the area. Jason Drysdale blasted the spot kick past John Lukic.

'The celebrations when Jason scored

Photograph: Steve Riding

The final whistle has gone. Watford have knocked the league champions out of the cup.

were fantastic,' says Hessenthaler. 'We all jumped on him and we were right in front of the fans.'

By now the Hornets were good value for their 2-0 lead. All they had to do was hang on. Gary McAllister set up a very tense finale when he curled in a superb shot from the edge of the box.

'I picked the ball out of the net and kicked it upfield thinking that this could be a very long seven or eight minutes,' says Suckling.

Watford saw it through and when the final whistle blew, the players ran towards the Vicarage Road terrace and allowed the celebrations to linger.

'It wasn't exactly a hotbed, Vicarage Road, but that night it was really intense,' says Suckling.

Back in the dressing room, the goalkeeper was just taking his boots off when Elton John came in. 'He stood and clapped everyone, then he came up to me and said "Nice save, Perry." It was the first time I'd ever met him.'

For a surreal split-second, as the goalkeeper let the rock star's praise sink in a thought crossed his mind: 'Elton John knows who I am.'

It had been five years since Watford had been in the top flight. The Premier League was in its infancy and football was about to change for ever.

Leeds were the league champions, an impressive and imposing team, but these were days when the giants of the English game at least deigned to walk the same earth as the rest of us.

Leeds had been dumped out of the cup fairly and squarely, not because

they had replaced half their team with youngsters wearing squad numbers double their age. This was an giantkilling in the true sense of the word. There were no excuses.

And what of Eric Cantona? This game turned out to be his last for Leeds before he joined Manchester United, and led the Old Trafford club to their first championship in a generation.

In the next round, Watford were hammered 6-1 by Blackburn Rovers at Ewood Park, with Alan Shearer in unstoppable form.

But that didn't take the shine off the feat of beating Leeds. The official gate was given as just over 18,000. But if you were on the terrace that night, unable to move your hands from your sides at times, you'll perhaps doubt that figure.

It was a magical night, one that seems to stand as the gateway between two distinct eras in the game's history. A night when we all stood and danced together. And, as the terrace emptied, an impromptu conga started that led out into the street.

WATFORD
Suckling, Putney, Drysdale, Dublin, Holdsworth, Ashby, Hessenthaler, Nogan (Butler), Furlong, Porter, Lavin
Goals Holdsworth 54, Drysdale 72 pen
Manager Steve Perryman

LEEDS UNITED
Lukic, Newsome (Rocastle), Kerr, Wallace, Fairclough, Whyte, Strachan, Cantona, Chapman, McAllister, Speed
Goal McAllister 83
Manager Howard Wilkinson
Attendance 18,035

CHAMPIONS

FULHAM ....1 WATFORD....................2

Division Two, Saturday May 2 1998

Jason Lee after scoring the goal that clinched the Second Division championship.

'We beat Bournemouth on the Tuesday night to keep ourselves in with a chance of winning the championship,' says Jason Lee. 'The manager had us in the following day to start the build-up to the Fulham game. Graham gave us a bit of a speech. He said that we'd done well to win promotion but to go up as champions would be special.

'It sounds obvious but it really hit home. He said we'd put in too much work and got too close not to give it everything. There's a big difference between just going up and winning the title. We would be remembered as the team that won a trophy for the club and that would stay with us.'

The trophy wasn't quite there for the taking. Watford were relying on Bristol City slipping up at Preston.

Taylor didn't focus on the importance of the result too often but on this occasion he reminded his players that they needed to win. The match was vital to Fulham too. They needed a draw to make sure they made the play-offs.

Lee arrived from Nottingham Forest in the summer and loved playing for Taylor's team. 'We played with quite a strange system, certainly for the Second Division,' he says. 'We had full-backs who were more like wingers. Tommy Mooney was at centre half and he didn't look out of place. Richard Johnson and Micah Hyde went together perfectly in midfield. Ronnie Rosenthal had a bit of guile that most teams couldn't handle.

The emphasis was on attacking and creating chances. As a centre forward I loved it. Gifton Noel-Williams was just coming through and you could see how much Graham liked working with him.

'I'd been at Forest where they had a fitness coach but Graham was so far in advance of what they were doing. We got so fit and so powerful. We never eased off in matches.

'Gifton and I worked well together. I tried to help his game. He had such great physique I couldn't believe he was only 17. There was a running joke that I had three kids at 26 and he had three with one on the way.'

But Lee and Taylor had a bumpy relationship at times. 'When I signed, I agreed to move down to London because the manager had this rule about the players living within a certain distance of the training ground,' he says.

'Being from London I thought it would be easy but the reality was that it wasn't. My children were settled at school. Graham and I didn't fall out but he wasn't too happy that I was the one player who hadn't relocated. I pointed out I could have moved somewhere within the range and spent an hour and a half on the M25 every day.'

Having decided against moving, Lee sensed that he might be on his way from Watford in the summer. 'I really enjoyed the season but it was a strange one. I did have an inkling the Fulham match might be my last game,' he says. As it turned out, Lee stayed all summer and scored the winner at Portsmouth on the opening day of the following season before being sold to Chesterfield. His instincts had been correct. 'I didn't want to leave but I thought, if Graham was going to move me on, I wanted to win the championship first.'

Watford's fans were ready to party on the banks of the Thames. Their team was hungry to get their hands on some silverware.

'We had this new kit, blue and grey stripes,' Lee says. 'We'd already seen it and I don't think the lads were too impressed. What I remember most about it was how tight the shorts were. I was looking around to see if there were any slightly larger ones.'

For Taylor there was the added

motivation of getting one over on his very good friend John Ward, the Bristol City manager.

'You can't influence what happens somewhere else,' says Lee. 'But you get a feeling from the crowd. They take great delight in letting you know. As players, you're supposed to say "Oh, we were concentrating on what we were doing," which, of course, we were, but when your own fortune hinges on what's going on in another game it's impossible to block it out.'

In the first ten minutes, Bristol City fell behind, got themselves back on terms and then conceded again.

'It was tough to get into the game,' says Lee. 'Fulham played a completely different way to us and it took a while for us to get going. We were playing a high tempo, trying to get forward and then they were getting the ball, trying to pass it and it took the sting out of us.'

Ten minutes before half-time, Noel-Williams opened the scoring. 'We had something to lose now,' says Lee. 'I've seen it a million times before. Graham said all the right things about not sitting back, not settling for what we had got and to keep playing aggressively, to keep going forwards.

'But no matter what the manager says, there's a fear factor. Instinctively, you want protect what you've got.'

Fulham equalised but Watford still had one hand on the trophy, as long as Bristol City didn't equalise at Preston.

Five minutes after Beardsley's goal,

Lee had the chance to win the title for the Hornets. 'It came after quite a nice bit of build-up play,' he says. 'I didn't catch it the cleanest. I caught it well enough but it wasn't a sweet strike. The feeling of relief when I saw it go in was fantastic. I'd got my goal and hopefully that would be enough.

'When the final whistle went, the fans came on the pitch and it was about getting to the dressing room with a stitch of clothing on you. I gave my shirt away but they'd have done well to get the shorts off me.

'It was only afterwards I got to reflect on it and realised that I scored the goal that won the championship.

'The medal is nice to have. It's a tiny thing. My son can't believe it's a proper medal – he's won bigger ones playing kids football.'

For only the third time in their history, Watford had won a cup to put in their trophy cabinet.

FULHAM
Taylor, Lawrence, Brevett, Smith (Trollope 76), Coleman, Blake, Beardsley, Bracewell, Moody, Peschisolido (Thorpe 72), Collins
Goal Beardsley 61
Manager Kevin Keegan

....

WATFORD
Chamberlain, Bazeley, Kennedy, Lee, Millen, Mooney, Noel-Williams (Robinson 68), Hyde, Palmer (Gibbs 26), Johnson, Hazan
Goals Noel-Williams 35, Lee 71
Manager Graham Taylor
Attendance 17,114

How they stood

Before kick-off: Tied on points but Robins are top on goals scored.

	F	A	Pts
1 Bristol City	68	37	85
2 Watford	**65**	**40**	**85**

3.05pm Lee Ashcroft gives Preston the lead after five minutes, while it's still 0-0 in West London.

1 Watford	**65**	**40**	**86**
2 Bristol City	68	38	85

3.09pm Sean McCarthy levels at Deepdale and the trophy is back in Bristol City's hands.

1 Bristol City	69	38	86
2 Watford	**65**	**40**	**86**

3.10pm City's joy is shortlived as David Eyres fires Preston ahead a minute later.

1 Watford	**65**	**40**	**86**
2 Bristol City	69	39	85

3.35pm The title is bound for Watford as Noel-Williams opens the scoring at Craven Cottage

1 Watford	**66**	**40**	**88**
2 Bristol City	69	39	85

4.16pm Beardsley equalises for Fulham. Watford are top, but City only need to level at Preston to leapfrog them.

1 Watford	**66**	**41**	**86**
2 Bristol City	69	39	85

4.51pm The final whistle blows and the championship is in the bag.

1 Watford	**67**	**41**	**88**
2 Bristol City	69	39	85

Everyone is just about decent. The cans of Skol are open. Let the celebrations begin.

At last. At long, long last...

The clock said 9.26pm when the final whistle went. After 91 years, Watford could finally call themselves a First Division club.

Promotion had been on the cards since the early part of the spring but a sticky run in early April meant all the usual doubts came flooding back.

Graham Taylor steadied the ship and urged his players to reach out and grab their slice of history.

Vicarage Road was all set for one of those special Tuesday nights under lights when Wrexham came to visit.

The Welsh side were unlikely to be a pushover because they were in danger of slipping into the bottom three.

A sense of anticipation surrounded Watford. Even the cover of the match programme seemed to be loaded with metaphor. Gerry Armstrong and Steve Sims looked as if they were queuing for admittance to the First Division. With games against Leicester and Derby still to go, everyone expected Watford to do enough in their last three matches but no one was counting their chickens.

It was with beautiful symmetry that

Divsion Two 1981-82

		P	W	D	L	F	A	Pts
1	Luton Town	42	25	13	4	86	46	88
2	**Watford**	**42**	**23**	**11**	**8**	**76**	**42**	**80**
3	Norwich City	42	22	5	15	64	50	71
4	Sheff Weds	42	20	10	12	55	51	70
5	QPR	42	21	6	15	65	43	69
6	Barnsley	42	19	10	13	59	41	67

the two goals which completed the Hornets' run from the Fourth Division to the First came from Ross Jenkins, one of the few who had been there every step of the way.

The anxiety in the final minutes was agonising. One-nil up with so much at stake, it was one of the rare occasions when Taylor was happy to see his team run down the clock.

In the last minute, as Watford played for time on the right wing, Jenkins got the ball in the box and turned to smash a low shot towards the far post.

The Wrexham goalkeeper's clumsy attempt to gather the powerfully-struck ball was calamitous. It bounced off his arms and in.

That sealed it. The journey had taken five years and, although there had been the odd bump along the way, for the most part it had been pure joy, the most glorious period in the club's history.

Little did Watford's fans realise but this was not the end of the journey, it was just a new beginning.

The club's status had been altered for good. The lower divisions would no longer be considered Watford's natural habitat. No wonder the party in the pond lasted well into the night.

Sherwood, Rice, Rostron, Taylor, Sims, Bolton, Callaghan, Blissett, Jenkins, Lohman, Barnes
Manager Graham Taylor
Scorers Jenkins 33, 89
Attendance 20,028

10 WATFORD .... 7 SOUTHAMPTON 1

Watford win 7-5 on aggregate

The impossible comeback

Southampton's manager, Lawrie McMenemy was spotted behind the main stand after the match with his head in his hands.

He wasn't even angry that his team had managed to throw away a 4-0 first leg lead. He was simply shellshocked.

Graham Taylor admired McMenemy. When he was Grimsby manager he took the players to the fisheries and introduced them to the workers and tried to drum up support. It sparked in Taylor the idea to make Watford an integral part of the local community.

Watford had been horribly exposed at The Dell. They weren't just beaten, they were swatted aside with ease.

But Taylor refused to give up. He told his team they were to treat the tie as if it was a league game. They'd lost away but they could still get three points from the home game.

Taylor was simply trying to get something worthwhile out of the match because all hope of reaching the third round had gone.

In football, you can never give up hope. If you don't believe in the impossible, what's the point in playing?

Perhaps if Watford could get one goal they could get two. If they could get two maybe they could score a third. And if that happened, Southampton might begin to panic. Crazy talk. It was absolute madness to think a miracle was on the cards?

So why did Taylor, when asked by a young fan on the morning of the match what the score would be, reply, 7-1?

The manager's programme notes were upbeat. He promised his team would have a go. They did more than that. Much more.

Thinking the tie was dead, the Saints rested a few players. Kevin Keegan did not play. It was only after the game that it emerged that he had picked up a knock during Saturday's match. Was he really injured or did it just make sense to say he was rather than admit they'd rested their best player?

Watford set about their task with a sense of purpose. Ten minutes passed before Malcolm Poskett got the first. Ten minutes before half-time Ray Train fired a second.

1980-81 LEAGUE CUP

1st round, 1st leg	Millwall H	2-1
1st round 2nd leg	Millwall A	2-0
2nd round 1st leg	Southampton A	0-4
2nd round 2nd leg	Southampton H	7-1
3rd round	Sheffield Wednesday A	2-1
4th round	Nottingham Forest H	4-1
5th round	Coventry City H	2-2
Replay	Coventry City A	0-5

They were halfway there but still had no right to get back into the tie. All Southampton had to do was shut up shop for the second 45 minutes.

But Martin Patching got a third and suddenly Watford were in business.

Disaster struck at the other end when the ball bounced off Steve Sims and went in. It was back to square one.

A brave fight had been stopped in its tracks.

However, within a minute, Watford had made it 4-1. They were given a penalty and Ian Bolton blasted it home.

Seven minutes from time, Ross Jenkins scored a fifth, which was enough to force extra-time. By now, word had spread and people were arriving at Vicarage Road so they could say they had witnessed it.

The teenage substitute Nigel Callaghan scored a superb goal with his first touch of the game and Poskett rounded it off with his second goal.

Seven-one. Could the Watford fans believe what they had seen?

It set the tone for a decade when it seemed nothing was impossible.

Steele, Henderson, Jackett, Patching, Sims, Bolton, Blissett, Poskett, Jenkins, Train (Callaghan 92), Rostron
Manager Graham Taylor
Scorers Poskett 10, 115, Train 35, Patching 67, Bolton 74 pen, Jenkins 83, Callaghan 93
Southampton scorer Sims og 73
Attendance 15,992

A QUESTION OF STYLE

Watford's cup upsets and great strides forward in the league led to much debate about their style of play. Speaking to the BBC's John Motson, Graham Taylor was clear.

Taylor: We keep getting asked this about the style of play. I don't really know what the style of play is. What we do is we want to go forward and we want to get the ball in the box as often as possible.

If you say to me will I change my attitude and approach to the game I will say quite emphatically 'no'.

As regards our style, I'll leave it to the experts to decide what style we play. We've been described in certain quarters as a kick and rush side. I find that quite amazing that people in the game say we're just a kick and rush side.

If it is as simple as that then I think everyone ought to kick and rush it but you know as well as I do, John, that it's not as simple as that.

Motson: But it may be more sophisticated in the First Division is the point I am making.

More sophisticated? I hate that word being used where football is concerned. Football is a simple game. It is not a sophisticated game It's a game for the man on the terraces. It's a game to excite the people. I know that the man on the terrace when he sees something that creates excitement, and that is usually in and around the penalty box, will take great interest. He is not interested, in my opinion, in watching people play 15 or 16 consecutive passes in their own half.

Ten years of hurt, 29 minutes of joy

9 | LUTON TOWN .... 0 WATFORD 4

Division Two, Saturday October 4 1997

So what if Luton were ravaged by injuries and had to call up understudies from the reserve team. All is fair in love and local derbies.

Apart from an Anglo-Italian Cup win over the Hatters in 1993, it had been ten years, five months and thirteen days since Watford had got the better of their rivals in a league game.

With Luton currently enjoying a spell in non-league obscurity, they are no more relevant to the Hornets now than St Albans City or Chesham United, and it is easy to forget how much these fixtures used to mean.

The frustration that had built over a decade was becoming unbearable. Luton seemed to hold some kind of hex over Watford.

Both clubs had endured a frustrating season in the Second Division after being relegated together in 1996. Luton lost in the play-offs, Watford stalled in mid-table. The pressure was now on both clubs to win promotion.

Graham Taylor had been convinced to return as team manager after a year spent upstairs overseeing Kenny Jack-

ett. Taylor's first priority was to get the Hornets out of the Second Division.

He dramatically reshaped the team. There were several new signings, such as Micah Hyde, Peter Kennedy, Jason Lee and Ronnie Rosenthal. And he wanted the team to play a fluid, attacking style with three central defenders and wing backs who looked to get forward at every opportunity.

Tommy Mooney, a forward, was asked to play as a central defender with Robert Page and Keith Millen.

'We played Arsenal in a testimonial match for Les Simmons at the end of the previous season and Graham threw it at me then,' says Mooney. 'He asked me just before the game to play at the back and I thought he was joking. He said it was something he wanted to look at for the next season.

'I was playing up against Thierry Henry and I must have done okay because when we came back for pre-season he had decided we were going to play with three at the back.'

Watford started the season strongly and were already top of the table by the

Peter Kennedy lashes home his second goal, and Watford's fourth.

time the trip to Kenilworth Road came round.

In the days leading up to the game, the players were under no illusion about how much it meant to the supporters to beat Luton.

'I knew what it was all about,' says Mooney. 'I'd played in a few derby defeats, including one when I was up front with Jamie Moralee – which wound me up because he wasn't the easiest to play alongside.

'Jamie was the opposite of me, really. He didn't care whether we won or lost and that drove me mad. Losing didn't hurt him the way it hurt me.

'I'd seen how hard the fans took it when we'd lost 4-2 to Luton at home.'

Alec Chamberlain had spent five happy years at Kenilworth Road and when he first joined Watford he wondered if he'd be accepted. Now he was concerned about what sort of reception he'd get on his return.

'I'd been back with Sunderland and we'd been beaten,' he says. 'I was now playing for the enemy but I got a nice reception when we first went out.'

Peter Kennedy says: 'I knew the game was important but it wasn't until I got to the ground and saw the tight pitch and felt the atmosphere that I realised what it meant to people.

'It's the only derby I've played in that had that intensity.'

In their red and black stripes, Watford looked like Milan and played like them too. They attacked relentlessly, barely allowing Luton a chance to breathe.

After five minutes Richard Johnson blasted the first goal. After 19 minutes, Dai Thomas doubled the lead, finishing

---

LUTON TOWN
Davis, McGowan (Douglas 35), Harvey, Waddock, Small, White, Gray, McLaren, Oldfield, Thorpe, Davies (James 35)
Manager Lennie Lawrence

WATFORD
Chamberlain, Gibbs, Kennedy, Page, Millen, Mooney, Slater, Palmer, Thomas, Johnson, Rosenthal (Noel-Williams 81)
Goals Johnson 5, Thomas 19, Kennedy 27, 29
Manager Graham Taylor
Attendance 9,041

Thomas didn't last long at Watford but he'll always be remembered for his goal at Luton.

from close range at the second attempt. Watford's supporters, packed into the decrepit Oak Road end, could barely contain their glee.

The untamed centre forward Thomas, who was as much of a handful off the pitch as he was on it, took his shirt off and ran the whole length of the pitch in celebration.

Taylor was irritated and rebuked the Welshman afterwards. He didn't want his players to pour oil on the flames. The atmosphere among the home fans was already turning sour.

Kennedy then hit Luton with a left and a right. The cheers had barely died down following his first goal when he struck his second.

'I don't think I'd ever scored with my right foot.' says the Northern Irishman, who had a sweet left foot but who joked that his right was for little more than balancing on.

'After my second I ran all the way down the whole length of the pitch to celebrate with the Watford fans,' he says. 'I don't know why I did that. It was the sort of thing Graham hated. He didn't want his players overdoing it or rubbing it in. I looked across at the bench and thought he was going to kill me.'

With less than half an hour on the clock, Luton were down and out. Ten years of bitter frustration erased in 29 dazzling minutes.

While the travelling fans danced and sang, the Luton supporters turned on their team and their manager, Lennie Lawrence. The atmosphere on three sides of the ground was ugly.

At half-time, the anger spilled over and there were scuffles in the corner as some Luton fans tried to make their way to the away enclosure to wipe the smiles off the Watford supporters' faces.

A couple of idiots tried to climb into Lawrence's dug-out and police horses were brought into the stadium in an attempt to calm things down.

In the dressing room, Taylor had to

give one of his more challenging team talks. The game was over but he didn't want his team to take their foot off the gas. But nor did he want the situation to boil over.

Kennedy recalls the manager saying jokingly: 'Don't score again because it's going to go bonkers.' But Mooney's memory is of Taylor telling his men to go out and score another four.

Steve Palmer says: 'Graham said it was a test for us. The game was won, so what were we going to do? The task was to keep control of the game.'

When they went out for the second half, Chamberlain became aware that he would have to run towards the end of the ground where the Luton supporters sat. 'They could quite easily have given me a lot of abuse,' he says.

'But they were great. Watford's fans might not want to hear that but they were very nice to me and I really appreciated that because it must've been horrible for them, 4-0 down at home to their bitterest rivals.'

The second half was a non-event on the pitch but the party continued at the Oak Road end. 'Ten years, but it was worth the wait,' rang out as the Hornets fans sang loud and proud, although anyone who says they weren't a little concerned about running the gauntlet back to the coach or car afterwards is probably lying.

So what if Luton were in utter disarray? So what if it was completely one-sided for the first 45 minutes and no contest for the second? So what if the result didn't clinch promotion or knock them out of a cup?

It was the biggest win over Luton in the club's history. A mauling, a massacre a day to make the faces of Hatters everywhere flush red with embarrassment. And it was very, very good fun.

The Hatters are hammered

5 minutes
With his back to goal, Ronnie Rosenthal holds the ball up and lays it to **Richard Johnson**, who drives in a low shot from outside the penalty area that wrong-foots Luton keeper Kelvin Davis.

19 minutes
Barrel-chested Welsh striker **Dai Thomas** creates havoc in the six-yard box. He shouts 'mine' as the ball arrives in the area. That fools the Luton defenders into leaving it. Thomas's first shot is parried but he stabs home the rebound.

27 minutes
Watford lay seige to the Luton penalty area. The Hatters clear a couple of times but the ball drops to **Peter Kennedy**, who hits a sweet half-volley.

29 minutes
Luton Town are on the ropes now. Heads lolling, punch-drunk from the relentless onslaught. **Kennedy** intercepts a poor pass and heads towards goal. Cutting inside onto his right foot, he picks his spot in the far corner.

Photograph: Watford Observer

A moment to savour. The sun is shining. The pitch is immaculate. Pat Rice leads the Watford team out before their First Division debut. The Hornets have finally arrived.

8   WATFORD .... 2 EVERTON 0

Division One, Saturday August 28 1982

'**W**ell! Here we are, all of us in the First Division! What a challenge and opportunity we now face. How shall we manage? The number of times I have been asked that question since last May!

'We must not play and support in awe of the glorious names and teams we shall meet, but accept the responsibility, make sure we believe in ourselves and play and support as well as we can.

'We must settle ourselves down, without losing the feeling of excitement of operating in the big league and then go about making certain Watford's place in Division One is assured for years to come.'

Graham Taylor's programme notes

Gerry Armstrong had been the star of Northern Ireland's summer, scoring the goal that defeated the hosts Spain in the World Cup. Now he was to make history for Watford.

It was a day for breaking new ground. Watford's first game in Division One was against a team they had never faced before.

Who knew what to expect? After all the excitement of the journey, and a long summer of anticipation, who was to say the whole experience might not be a fleeting one?

Perhaps reaching the destination would turn out to be a disappointment. That was what made it so electrifying

for Watford's supporters. They were confident their team could cope but they didn't know what Division One held in store for them.

The team savoured every moment. They walked out onto the pitch in their tracksuit jackets and enjoyed the sensation of being the men to make history.

Pat Rice, who had won the league championship and FA Cup double, says he felt every bit as much pride leading out the Hornets that day as he had lifting trophies for Arsenal.

For many, it was a first taste of life in the top flight but Taylor had trained them not to be overawed.

Watford had earned their place among the elite and they were not going to stand on ceremony.

With Les Taylor not fully fit, Luther Blissett played in midfield with Armstrong taking his place up front alongside Ross Jenkins.

The stage was now set for Armstrong to give the newspaper reporters the story they wanted to write.

After 22 minutes, he scored, stabbing home from close range after Nigel Callaghan's free-kick had bounced around in the Everton box.

Armstrong had scored in the First Division before, for Tottenham, and he'd just come back

from a World Cup but he says it wasn't until some years later that he realised the scale of what he'd done.

'I came back to Watford to watch a match when Graham was back as the manager and we were walking up the steps in the hospitality area in the Rous stand,' he says. 'There was a big photo of me scoring that goal and it caused me to sort of stop and take a second look. Graham turned to me and said: "That was a moment in time, Gerry. There can only be one first goal in the top division and you scored it."'

Everton looked like they were still on their summer holidays at times but take nothing away from Watford. They started the way they intended to go on.

The second goal came when Neville Southall caught Pat Rice's misdirected cross and carried it back over the line. 'I'd totally shanked it,' says Rice.

'I'd already turned to run back thinking, what an idiot, when I heard the crowd roar. Big Neville had taken it over the line. Was I claiming it as my goal? Too right I was.'

The history boys

The team that started Watford's first game in the top division.

1	Steve Sherwood
2	Pat Rice
3	Wilf Rostron
4	Luther Blissett
5	Ian Bolton
6	Kenny Jackett
7	Nigel Callaghan
8	Gerry Armstrong
9	Ross Jenkins
10	Jan Lohman
11	John Barnes

Goals Armstrong 22, Rice 66

Everton Southall, Borrows, Bailey, Higgins, Wright, Heath, McMahon (Richardson 72), Johnson, Sharp, King, Sheedy.
Attendance 19,630

WATFORD...........3 KAISERSLAUTERN...........0

Watford win 4-3 on aggregate

Comeback kids stun the German giants

Ian Richardson and Jimmy Gilligan took their place in the tunnel. The Kaiserslautern players lined up alongside them. Outside, Vicarage Road reverberated to an alien hum.

The two teenagers had played here scores of times for the reserves but it felt different tonight.

Gilligan leaned forward and said to his reserve team strike-partner: 'We will win this tonight.'

Richardson, at 5ft 7in the small, speedy poacher to Gilligan's beefy target man, couldn't help but notice how big the Kaiserslautern players were. Great strapping hulks of men. He swallowed hard, took a deep breath and the line of gold-shirted players in front of him headed out onto the pitch.

A fortnight earlier, Watford's introduction to European football had brought a mild sense of disappointment. The team bore little relation to the

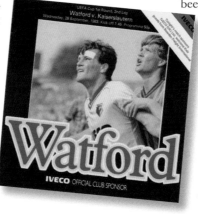

one that qualified for the Uefa Cup. Luther Blissett, Ross Jenkins and Gerry Armstrong had all gone. Pat Rice's legs had gone. Ian Bolton was not the same player he had been.

Graham Taylor had no choice but to throw teenagers in at the deep end. The likes of Charlie Palmer, Richard Jobson and Gilligan played in West Germany.

And it was Gilligan who entered the record books by scoring Watford's first goal in Europe. The game ended in a 3-1 defeat, although if Jan Lohman's strike had not been disallowed for offside, the balance of the tie would have been very different.

The common belief was that Watford's Uefa Cup run would be ending here. They needed to win the second leg 2-0 to reach the next round. Against an experienced team, that looked a tall order.

Ian Richardson (lying on his back) is congratulated by Gilligan after scoring his second.

Between the two first legs, Watford suffered yet more injuries. Taylor was down to the barest bones.

Eight of the side that lined up to play in Vicarage Road's first European fixture were aged 21 or under.

Richardson was making his first team debut. Palmer, the right back, only his sixth start.

Kaiserslautern, on the other hand, were seasoned European campaigners. They had a World Cup winner in their ranks, the towering Hans-Peter Briegel.

And they thought they had the tie won. The Germans had scoffed when they heard what Taylor had said after the first leg. 'We've seen what it's like to play here, now they have to come to Vicarage Road and experience that.'

John Ward, Taylor's first team coach, watched the Kaiserslautern players arrive and get off the bus.

He was irritated to see they were wearing an assortment of tracksuits, t-shirts and jeans rather than official club suits. Their casual dress hinted at a casual manner. He told the players: 'They think they've got this won here.'

Richardson barely had time to be nervous. He had been sent off playing for the reserves at Millwall just two days earlier. When Taylor asked to see him on the morning of the match, he thought he was going to get a telling off. Instead, Taylor told him he'd be making his first team debut that evening.

Lohman had failed a fitness test on the morning of the game and Taylor was forced to rejig his team yet again

It meant putting Richardson and Gilligan together up front. They had terrorised defences for the juniors in the South East Counties league and for the reserves in the Football Combination but this was the Uefa Cup.

Taylor refused to be daunted by the odds stacked against him and his young team. They had lost away from home

John Barnes fires in a shot as Vicarage Road hosts a European tie for the first time.

and were left with a mountain to climb. All they could do was give it a go.

He thought back three years to the match against Southampton, a night when they made the impossible possible. No one gave them a chance then, either. So he implored the supporters to remember the spirit of Southampton and to arrive at Vicarage Road in a positive mood.

Taylor wanted to bring a dash of European élan to south west Hertfordshire. He urged supporters to bring flags, scarves and banners to make it a truly Continental occasion. For their part, the club handed out hundreds of plastic horns to add to the atmosphere.

By kick-off time, there was a crackle of electricity in the air.

Taylor knew that an early goal was of paramount importance but, as usual, he did not stress that need to the players in case they failed to make the breakthrough and became disheartened.

For the manager, attitude and desire, commitment and hard work were the standards by which he judged his team, rather than goals and results.

With such a young, inexperienced team at his disposal he could afford to urge them to throw caution to the wind. They had absolutely nothing to lose. If they lost 2-0, who could criticise them?

Perhaps Kaiserslauten really did think they had finished the job in their home leg. They looked completely unprepared for the all-out assault of the first ten minutes.

Four minutes had been played when Steve Sherwood launched a long goal kick upfield. It was knocked forward for John Barnes to flick deftly with his head into the path of Richardson, who had anticipated superbly and was already on the move. The 19-year-old controlled the ball neatly, took it another stride forwards and slotted it delicately but defiantly into the far corner.

Cue pandemonium on the terraces.

Watford continued to bombard the Germans. They played with such pace and aggression, seeking to attack every time they had the ball.

The second goal came when Charlie Palmer broke forward and sent in a low cross from the right-hand side of the Kaiserslautern penalty area. The ball hit Werner Melzer and flew in.

Inside ten minutes, Watford had levelled the aggregate scores – and had the benefit of an away goal. In a way, it could have been the worst possible start. It would surely spark the visitors into life. All Kaiserslautern had to do was score and the wind would be taken out of Watford's sails.

The remainder of the first half saw the Hornets continue to attack but in the second half things were more edgy. Suddenly the thought of what they had to lose seemed to spread through the team. Even the third goal did not entirely ease the nerves.

Jobson, who had been playing non-league football for Burton Albion a year earlier, crossed for Richardson, who slid in, made contact with the ball and lay on his back watching it loop perfectly over the goalkeeper.

Watford now led 4-3 on aggregate but knew that if they conceded now, it would be all square again.

Taylor sent Ward over to the far side of the pitch to coax and cajole the players on Watford's right-hand side. He crouched down in front of the Shrodells stand, yelling at Palmer and Nigel Callaghan to keep things tight and watch for danger, all the time fearing that he'd be in trouble with the referee for leaving the bench.

The clock ticked down agonisingly slowly and Kaiserslautern by no means accepted their fate without a fight but eventually the referee blew the final whistle and Watford reached the second round of the Uefa Cup.

Taylor was full of praise for his young team. 'This is the greatest result of my career. Perhaps not the greatest performance but certainly the best re-sult. We had seven players unavailable for selection. We've tried very hard not to bleat about the injuries but this is a very different Watford team from the team that qualified for Europe. Really, they are just kids.'

Explaining his decision to replace Lohman, a midfielder, with Richardson, a striker, he said: 'Ian has got natural pace and he's a goalscorer. On a man-to-man situation I felt it was worth us having a go. But perhaps I ought to tell the truth and say he was the only one I'd got left.

'I told the players that they could do it. I believe that every team that rep-resents me can win. On reflection, of course, we shouldn't have had a chance tonight.'

Sherwood, Palmer, Rostron, Jobson, Terry, Bolton, Callaghan, Richardson, Gilligan, Jackett, Barnes
Manager Graham Taylor
Scorers Richardson 4, 56, Melzer og 9,
Attendance 21,457

'Like lambs to

Friday lunchtime at Liverpool's Lime Street station. The Watford players arrive wearing their club tracksuits. Graham Taylor liked to travel to away games by train if it was possible. It was quicker and more comfortable than the coach and, having been to Sunderland and back three days earlier, he wanted to give his players every help because their bumpy introduction to the Premiership was not about to get any easier. Their next stop was Anfield.

The players walked across the station concourse and out to where the coach that would take them on to the hotel was parked. 'We had to walk past the taxi rank,' says Tommy Mooney. 'All the taxi drivers waiting for their jobs were standing at the front of the line of taxis, leaning on the bonnet, chatting, as they do. I was at the front, walking next to Richard Johnson. Knowing the Scousers, I knew they wouldn't let us pass without saying something.'

Mooney braced himself. And then it came, in the thickest Scouse accent you've ever heard. 'Like lambs to the slaughter, boys, lambs to the slaughter…' Then came the laughter.

'We smiled and tried to laugh it off but when we were out of earshot,

I turned to Johnno and said "I hope they're not right but there's every chance they could be."'

Already, Watford had learned that the Premiership could exact a cruel and twisted form of justice. The opening match at home to Wimbledon had been such a whirlwind of emotions. A goal down after ten minutes, level and a man up seven minutes later when Dean Blackwell was sent off for a cynical foul on Michel Ngonge and Peter Kennedy hammered home the penalty. Watford fell behind again before half-time but an equaliser from Ngonge with 19 minutes to go offered hope of a fairytale finish.

Richard Johnson had been immense in midfield but with 12 minutes to go he made a mess of things in the area. He tried to chest the ball back to Chris Day, who failed to commit himself. Johnson's desperate attempt to clear the ball was sliced high into the roof of his own net. It was an undeserved blow and one that would have the experts on Match of the Day shaking their heads and muttering about naïve defending. Then came a perfunctory defeat at Sunderland, another promoted team but one whose faces fitted better than Watford's. Taylor complained that the

the slaughter....'

referee, Jeff Winter, was on first-name terms with their players.

And so to Anfield and certain defeat. This was Liverpool's first home game of the season and the atmosphere was bristling. After a summer starved of their beloved Reds this was another new dawn, and a chance to give a newly-promoted side a footballing lesson.

Watford were without their goal-keeper Alec Chamberlain, who had dislocated a finger during the pre-season trip to the Isle of Man. 'I tried to play with a splint but Graham was not keen,' says Chamberlain. 'I said I was fit but we did some finishing and one hit my hand and it was very sore.'

Paul Robinson and Micah Hyde had missed the Wimbledon and Sunderland matches but the sight of them warming up offered a glimmer of hope. Eight of the team that had won the play-off final at Wembley were back together.

For Mooney, this was the realisation of a childhood fantasy. 'The last time I'd even been to Anfield was as a kid, wearing a Liverpool tracksuit, on the stadium tour,' he says. 'To go there wearing the number nine shirt was incredible. This was everything I'd wanted to do.' Kennedy was a Liverpool supporter as a child too and he had to fight the urge to just stand and take in the sight of the stadium filling up when they went out for their warm-up.

Only someone with the emotional responses of a stone statue could have been unmoved when they began to play the famous anthem *You'll Never Walk Alone*. Steve Palmer admits he was welling up. 'Normally the away fans boo it but the Watford fans sang along,' says Mooney. 'That was fantastic. The Watford fans know how special that song is and they didn't just respect it, they joined in. The atmosphere was absolutely incredible. I've played there since and it's never been the same. It was the first home game of their season and there was all that hope, optimism and excitement.'

But Watford were not there to roll over for their hosts and Liverpool made the terrible mistake of beginning the match in lackadaisical fashion, all loose passes and admonishing body language.

For all their stature and history, Liverpool have a tendency to allow their confidence to become arrogance at times. The attitude among the fans can transmit to the players. 'Come on lads, we should be beating these.'

After ten minutes they had a wake-up call when Johnson stung Sander Westerveld's palms with a searing shot. The warning went unheeded.

Four minutes later, Watford were given a free-kick on the right-hand side. Peter Kennedy took it left-footed and the unusually flighted ball bounced around, causing chaos. It hit a Liverpool defender and a Watford attacker and squirmed across the area. Dominic Matteo swung a boot at it but he was beaten by both Robert Page and Mark Williams, who were fighting for the same ball. It fell to Mooney, unmarked in the six-yard box, and he had the simple task of turning it home. A quick glance across to the linesman to check he wasn't offside and then the celebrations began.

Mooney's dream was complete. 'I was shouting "I can't believe I've scored in front of the Kop," over and over. I still get ribbed about it now,' he says. 'That goal epitomised what we were all about. We were braver than they were, more committed than they were. Williams and Page almost tackled each other going for that ball. They both got there before any Liverpool players. That was how much we wanted it.'

A goal up after quarter of an hour meant nothing. This was dangerous territory for the division's newcomers because Liverpool would surely be stung into action. The onslaught never came. Watford kept chasing, challenging and forcing mistakes. Expensive players signed for sums beyond Watford's wildest dreams were made to look cumbersome and ordinary.

Then the steady drizzle became a torrential downpour. Oddly, the sun never quite disappeared, despite the rain. The romantics might be tempted to believe they saw a rainbow in the sky above the city but that would be stretching things.

At one point the rain was so heavy the ball was beginning to snag on the wet turf. Mooney turned to the referee, Alan Wilkie, and joked: 'Don't you dare call this off. I'll find out where you live.' Wilkie replied: 'There's plenty of football left in this.'

He was not wrong. In the second half, the pitch began to dry out and the surface became slick.

This coincided with Liverpool's best spell. They began to pass the ball with pace and a little verve, stretching Watford's disciplined formation almost, but not quite, to breaking point.

Every man in a golden shirt stuck to his task with defiance. There were heroes all over the pitch but the man between the posts, Chris Day, was inspired. He had been criticised for his hesitancy against Wimbledon but on this occasion he was flawless. Alec Chamberlain, watching

DID YOU KNOW?
Watford had never secured a league point at either Anfield or Goodison Park until today. Their record at Everton and Liverpool had been played 12, lost 12

in the stands, frustrated to miss such a big game because of injury, was willing his young understudy to keep them out. Day was superb. Alert, eager to organise the defence, never slow to take responsibility. He stopped shots and claimed crosses. He pushed his defenders out of the way in order to get to the ball. 'It was a brilliant performance,' says Chamberlain. 'It was a hard day because he had to cope with all sorts of weather. Bright sun one minute, torrential rain the next. They are always the most difficult conditions for a goalkeeper but he was totally in the zone that day.'

Even when Richard Johnson was injured after a strong challenge by Steven Gerrard early in the second half, Watford's focus was not disrupted. Houllier brought on Karl-Heinz Riedle, the German international forward, with half an hour to go. It was the sort of substitution that could have deflated the Hornets had they allowed it to. After an hour of Watford holding out, Liverpool still had more to throw at them.

Liverpool had chances, of course, but Day was equal to them. He stopped a great shot from Jamie Redknapp and another from Patrik Berger.

Robinson threw his body in front of Robbie Fowler as the Liverpool striker was about to take aim, and blocked the ball. It was desperate stuff at times but Watford must have been encouraged by the fact that Liverpool's defence at the other end had only a fraction of their commitment or courage.

Mooney continued to cause problems, bumping and bullying their centre halves, whose response to the whole-hearted assault they were subjected to failed to live up to the finest traditions of Hansen and Lawrenson. Towards the end, Palmer was allowed to stroll forward with the ball. They backed off him until he had a shooting opportunity and although Westerveld stopped it, the way in which Watford had imposed themselves on their illustrious opponents, forcing them to retreat in fear, said everything about the way the visitors had taken control of the match.

As the clock counted down Watford's supporters grew impossibly nervous while Liverpool's became exasperated. Those final ten minutes seemed to last for ever. And when the final whistle went, ninety minutes of tension was released with a booming chorus of 'We are Premier League' from the away supporters in the Anfield Road stand.

If your eyes had been trained on the bench, you'd have seen the private reaction of the architect of another extraordinary result. Graham Taylor applauded the Kop, shook Gérard Houllier's hand, put his glasses in their case, snapped the lid shut and then allowed himself to clench his fist. This was not a great, triumphant fist in the air, more a small gesture to himself. After everything that had happened with England and Wolverhampton Wanderers, Graham Taylor was back at the top.

Liverpool 0 Watford 1

Photograph: Press Association

Tommy Mooney is mobbed by his team-mates after scoring the early goal at Anfeld.

The players savoured things a little longer. They celebrated with their supporters but as they turned to walk off the pitch they must have been almost bursting with pride. The Kop, home of arguably the most discerning football supporters in the country, was still packed. The majority had stayed to the end to applaud the Watford players from the pitch. 'To be clapped off the pitch by the Liverpool fans was absolutely amazing,' says Robinson. 'It was one of those times when you couldn't quite believe what was happening. When I was a kid, Liverpool were the best team in the country by miles. We'd just beaten them and they were clapping us.'

Back in the dressing room, Johnson's knee had already been strapped. He had an ice pack on it to keep the swelling down. He'd at least been spared the ordeal of having to watch the last ten minutes hoping his team-mates would hold on.

As soon as Mooney opened the door, he went straight to Johnson. They both said the same thing at the same time, mimicking the taxi driver's Scouse accent from the previous day. 'Like lambs to the slaughter, boys, lambs to the slaughter…'

LIVERPOOL
Westerveld, Matteo, Hyypia, Carragher, Heggem (Song 81), Berger, Redknapp, Gerrard (Thompson 57), Smicer (Riedle 62), Fowler, Camara
Manager Gérard Houllier

WATFORD
Day, Lyttle, Kennedy, Palmer, Page, Robinson, Ngonge (Foley 69), Hyde, Mooney, Johnson (Easton 52), Williams
Goal Mooney 14
Manager Graham Taylor
Attendance 44,174

MANCHESTER UNITED ......1 WATFORD 2

Blissett's curtain call at the Theatre of Dreams

This was the cup upset that made the football world sit up and take notice of Elton John. Suddenly they could see that there was more to the rock star than flamboyant clothes and outrageous glasses.

Watford had started their campaign in the Third Division well. They were second in the table and goals were flowing. Luther Blissett and Ross Jenkins had struck up a partnership that was beginning to yield a lot of fruit. With the season a couple of months old, they already had 20 goals between them.

Twenty-year-old Blissett came off the bench to score both goals that knocked Second Division Newcastle United out in the previous round. When the draw for the third round was made, Graham Taylor said: 'We've hooked the biggest fish left in the competition, now we've got to land it.'

Watford went about the job methodically. Bertie Mee, Taylor's assistant, watched United and identified their threats. No one dared to say it beforehand but this was not a vintage United side. They had not long recovered from a season in the Second Division and were finding it hard to turn a run of draws into victories. Even so, they had some dangerous players. Steve Coppell on the wing and Joe Jordan the powerful centre forward, who was a sort of rich man's Ross Jenkins, had to be stopped. And Old Trafford in the late Seventies was not a place for the faint-hearted. It was cavernous, noisy and intimidating.

The first half did not go to plan. For a team that wanted to ruffle feathers, Watford showed too much respect and five minutes before the break Jordan scored. As Taylor would later say: 'In the Third Division you challenge for every ball as if you believe that ball is rightfully yours. You have to take charge of the game. Just because we are up against a First Division team, some of them international players, does not mean we should change our approach. That is what I told them at half-time.'

Alan Garner put it differently. 'We got a rollocking at half-time and the boss told us they were nothing special.'

The second half was a different story. Within a minute, Watford were level.

Blissett ran into the box, between the defenders, and connected sweetly with Bobby Downes's cross to head past Paddy Roche.

From then on, Watford feared no one. They were full of running and made Old Trafford's big pitch work in their favour, dragging United's defenders wide and creating space. Mee's plan to isolate Coppell worked perfectly.

Blissett's second was another header. Brian Pollard broke clear on the right and played the ball to Jenkins, who had made a run towards the corner, stretching United's defence again. They worked the ball to Booth who had time and space to send in a neat cross for Blissett to meet.

'What was so pleasing about that goal was that it was something we worked on in training,' says Blissett. 'We worked on certain moves like that so that everyone knew where they should be and what runs to make. What was so good about it was that something we'd worked on in training came off against a First Division side. It showed me that these players were not that much bet-

1978-79 LEAGUE CUP

1st round, 1st leg	Brentford H	4-0
1st round, 2nd leg	Brentford A	3-1
2nd round	Newcastle United H	2-1
3rd round	Manchester United A	2-1
4th round	Exeter City A	2-0
5th round	Stoke City A	0-0
Replay	Stoke City H	2-1
Semi-final, 1st leg	Nottingham Forest A	1-3
Semi-final, 2nd leg	Nottingham Forest H	0-0

ter than us. We were just as fit, if not fitter, and we were well organised and our manager had come up with something that Manchester United couldn't stop and we'd executed it well.'

Taylor confided in *The Watford Observer*: 'I wouldn't want this repeated nationally, but we are as good as Manchester United. The difference between Division One players and lower division players is marginal.'

Watford weren't quite home and dry. United came at them repeatedly in the closing quarter of an hour and would have equalised five mintues from the end but for a remarkable save from Andy Rankin.

Gordon McQueen, whose header Rankin saved, was convinced he had scored. 'It was one of the most incredible saves I have ever seen. I placed that header so well. I knew it was a goal, then that green thing with a hand on the end of it got there and pushed it away.'

After the match, Watford's supporters, all 2,300 of them, were held back until the stadium was empty and the surrounding roads clear of United fans. As they celebrated, the public address system played *Candle in the Wind* and the fans began to sing along. Perhaps it wasn't the most triumphant song in the chairman's back catalogue but it was a nice touch.

Up in the stand, Elton was doing a television interview. Wearing a huge dog's-tooth check baker boy hat on his head, bushy sideburns and an earring,

Blissett, number eight, scores against the team he supported as a boy. United are stunned.

but with an understated black suit and tie, Elton looked almost shy, a far cry from his exuberant on-stage persona. One of the directors, Geoff Smith, said that the chairman had suffered in his seat, barely able to watch, as his team sought to hold on.

'It's a great reflection on the players, Graham and the staff,' said the chairman. 'They have come out of the Fourth Division, now they're in the Third and they come to Old Trafford and play like that. I was petrified at the end. I thought the referee was never going to blow the whistle. Bertie Mee said to me "Wait till you go to a cup final, you won't be able to stand it."'

The Watford Observer hailed it as the club's best ever result. United's manager Dave Sexton made a prediction. He said that Watford would make it to the First Division but that Blissett would be the only player to go all the way with them. Sexton wasn't quite right. Of the side that conquered United, Ian Bolton and Jenkins also made it to the top flight.

As the for the League Cup, the reward for knocking out Manchester

United was a trip to St James' Park. Not the one in Newcastle, the Hornets had already knocked them out, but the one in Exeter.

A trip to another Third Division side was neither glamorous nor lucrative but it offered a great chance of further progress. Watford saw them off and then earned an excellent goalless draw at Stoke City before beating the Second Division high-flyers in a replay. The run came to an end at the semi-final stage when they found Nottingham Forest too strong at the City Ground.

MANCHESTER UNITED
Roche, Albiston, Houston, B Greenhoff (McCreery 9), McQueen, Buchan, Coppell, J Greenhoff, Jordan, McIlroy, Grimes
Goal Joe Jordan 40
Manager Dave Sexton

WATFORD
Rankin, Stirk, Harrison, Booth, Joslyn, Bolton, Pollard, Blissett, Jenkins, Garner, Downes
Goals Blissett 46, 71
Manager Graham Taylor
Attendance 40,534

LEEDS UNITED .... 0 WATFORD 3

Boothroyd's bus arrives in the Premiership

When Watford returned for pre-season training in July, Adrian Boothroyd called his squad together for a meeting.

The players entered the room to find the chairs had been arranged two by two, with an aisle down the middle, like the seats on a bus.

There was one seat at the front, for the driver. Boothroyd sat down in it and said: 'This bus is going to the Premiership, who's coming with me?'

Seeing as Watford had only just avoided relegation in May, most of the players thought their manager was barmy but slowly they began to take their seats.

'It took courage to do that in front of a group of players who didn't know him that well,' says Jay DeMerit, who had felt unsettled when Ray Lewington was sacked. 'Ray was the manager who took me from Northwood. It was strange going in one day and hearing your boss is no longer there.

'The lads were talking and when we heard who the new manager was, I will be honest, everyone was saying, who the heck is Aidy Boothroyd? I even got on the computer to look him up and find out who he was and there wasn't a lot of information out there.

'Immediately his attitude was infectious. We were tipped for relegation but he was looking completely the other way. He was talking about promotion. Maybe people thought he was mad but he was so driven and for a while, that drive really worked.

'We had a sports psychologist who got us to focus on what we wanted to achieve. That really brought us together and it was that togetherness that got us promoted. Everyone wanted the same thing. The only other time I have experienced that was when I played for the USA and we beat Spain in the Confederations Cup.'

Boothroyd enjoyed financial backing his predecessor could only have dreamed of. His first few signings were questionable (remember Junior, Martin Devaney, Adam Griffiths or Sietes?) but later he hit upon Marlon King, Darius Henderson and Matthew Spring, who helped transform the team.

The rookie manager traded in self-belief and that transmitted itself to the players. The style of play was direct but it wasn't without a touch of finesse.

While some of the tactics were unlikely to win friends among the purists, they were adept at winning matches.

'We were a winning team,' says the captain, Gavin Mahon. 'Everything was focused on winning matches. We broke the season down into blocks of six games and the manager asked us to set a points target. If we met it, we were treated to a night out as a group. One time we all got laptops.

'It made us concentrate on the short term and take each game as it came. And if we lost a game that we thought we should have won it gave us an extra incentive.'

Having qualified for the play-offs, Boothroyd reset the counter to zero.

'We had played 46 games but our mentality was we had to forget how we got there, now we had to win three games,' says DeMerit.

'When we reached the final, there was such a sense of belief that this was our time, I don't think many teams would have beaten us.'

Watford went to Cardiff a few days before the final and familiarised themselves with the Millennium Stadium.

'We had this feeling that Leeds thought they had already won it,' says DeMerit. 'That was the sense we had. We used that to our advantage and it really spurred us on.'

Before the match, Marlon King wanted to know the Leeds team. As captain, Mahon was able to give him the news he wanted.

'There had been a question mark about Paul Butler, their centre half, and whether he'd be fit,' says Mahon.

'Marlon really fancied playing against him because he knew him and he'd done well against him before. He knew he could run Butler into the ground. You should have seen the look on Marlon's face when I told him Butler was in. That was probably worth a goal to us.'

In the tunnel, Watford's players were loud and aggressive. They were shouting and bouncing on their toes. Mahon looked across at their opponents and thought: 'I know which team I'd rather be captain of.'

HOW THE 2005-06 SEASON UNFOLDED

August				
6	Preston North End	H	L	1-2
9	Plymouth Argyle	A	D	3-3
12	Cardiff City	A	W	3-1
20	Burnley	H	W	3-1
27	Reading	H	D	0-0
29	Derby County	A	W	2-1
September				
10	Stoke City	A	W	3-0
13	Norwich City	H	W	2-1
17	Sheffield United	H	L	2-3
24	Crewe Alexandra	A	D	0-0
28	Coventry City	A	L	1-3
October				
1	Leeds United	H	D	0-0
15	Leicester City	H	L	1-2
18	Sheffield Wednesday	A	D	1-1
22	Ipswich Town	A	W	1-0
29	Wolverhampton Wanderers	H	W	3-1
November				
1	Queens Park Rangers	H	W	3-1
5	Hull City	A	W	2-1
19	Sheffield Wednesday	H	W	2-1
22	Leicester City	A	D	2-2
26	Preston North End	A	D	1-1
December				
3	Brighton & Hove Albion	H	D	1-1
10	Plymouth Argyle	H	D	1-1
17	Burnley	A	L	1-4
26	Southampton	H	W	3-0

Jay DeMerit sends his powerful header flying into the net to open the scoring.

That confidence coursed through every vein and sinew of the Watford players. There was an indomitable spirit about the team that it was evident Leeds could not muster.

Watford were gung-ho, they were swashbuckling and exuberant, in fact, they displayed qualities to match the finest teams produced in the club's history. Leeds were crushed. Saddled with debt, there was so much riding on the outcome of this one match for the Yorkshire club.

Their financial situation implored them to reach for the riches on offer. Watford were driven by something

28	Millwall	A	D	0-0
31	Crystal Palace	H	L	1-2
January				
2	Luton Town	A	W	2-1
14	Stoke City	H	W	1-0
21	Norwich City	A	W	3-2
28	Crewe Alexandra	H	W	4-1
February				
6	Sheffield United	A	W	4-1
11	Coventry City	H	W	4-0
14	Leeds United	A	L	1-2
18	Brighton & Hove Albion	A	W	1-0
25	Cardiff City	H	W	2-1
March				
4	Derby County	H	D	2-2

11	Reading	A	D	0-0
20	Southampton	A	W	3-1
25	Millwall	H	L	0-2
31	Crystal Palace	A	L	1-3
April				
9	Luton Town	H	D	1-1
14	Wolverhampton Wanderers	A	D	1-1
17	Ipswich Town	H	W	2-1
22	Queens Park Rangers	A	W	2-1
30	Hull City	H	D	0-0
Play-offs				
May				
6	Crystal Palace	A	W	3-0
9	Crystal Palace	H	D	0-0
21	Leeds United		W	3-0

plainer, purer and simpler – desire.

Boothroyd worked the touchline like a master puppeteer. He instructed, he cajoled, he made notes. He was in his element. Little over a year ago, he had been a coach at Leeds, working under Kevin Blackwell. Now he was able to put his knowledge of their strengths and weaknesses to good use. Boothroyd, already hailed as one of the game's most talented young managers, was in his element.

The early exchanges were tense. The Millennium Stadium had none of the history or shabby chic of the old Wembley but it was an imposing arena which kept the atmosphere bubbling like the lid on a pan of boiling water.

Matches like this can turn on instinctive decisions. Watford won a corner, which Ashley Young prepared to swing into the penalty area.

'Normally, I would make a run to the near post,' says DeMerit. 'That was my move but for some reason I sensed that Rob Hulse knew what I was going to do so I mixed up. I backed off then ran around in a loop.'

The ball curled into the box and time seemed to stand still for DeMerit. 'All I can see is the ball,' he says. 'I am not looking at anyone or thinking about anything. I am just going for that ball.

'Malky blocked off his guy so I could get through and I can still see it now, flying into the net.

'That was the goal we were looking for. There had been a bit of uneasiness in the Leeds crowd and that goal really deflated them. Then their team start-ed to lose something, while it gave us something to build on.

'I often think back at how crazy this game is. It's amazing to think "What if?" What if I had stuck with my normal run? What if I hadn't decided to go round the back? What if my header had gone over the bar or the keeper had saved it? What if we hadn't scored first? Every game hinges on hundreds of thousands of moments like that.'

Watford survived a penalty appeal late in the first half when Ben Foster nudged Paul Butler and after the break they tightened their grip on the game.

There was more than a touch of good fortune about the second goal.

A long throw from Mahon was seized on by James Chambers who turned and fired a shot which spun off Eddie Lewis, slipped from Neil Sullivan's grasp and rolled in near the post.

With six minutes left, Shaun Derry hauled Marlon King down in the box and Darius Henderson thumped home the penalty. For the third time, Watford had reached the top flight.

Gavin Mahon, the captain, lifted the trophy with his manager. 'Aidy was such a huge part of what we achieved,' he says. 'We had been relegation favourites at the start of the season and when he started talking about promotion there were a few people who thought he was mad. But he had a vision. He was very single-minded and he was very good at getting across to the players what he wanted. It was a very exciting thing to be a part of.'

It took DeMerit a while to come

to terms with what he had achieved. The American had come to Europe to try to make it as a footballer. 'A couple of years earlier, I'd been playing non-league. I used to go to the pub to watch Premiership games on TV. To be honest, it didn't sink in until the fixture list came out and I saw the dates against Manchester United and Arsenal.'

A few weeks later, Mahon and his wife went to see Elton John in concert at Worcestershire cricket ground. During the season, Elton would often ring Boothroyd after a game and sometimes the manager would put Mahon on the phone for a chat.

Elton arranged for Mahon and his wife to sit in the front row and to go backstage before the encore to say

hello. 'We went and met him and he tried to get me to go on stage but I wasn't having any of that,' says Mahon. 'The thing that struck me was how much it meant to him that his team had been successful. That felt pretty special.'

LEEDS UNITED
Sullivan, Kelly, Butler, Gregan (Bakke 84), Kilgallon, Richardson (Blake 45), Miller (Healy 62), Derry, Douglas, Lewis, Hulse
Manager Kevin Blackwell

WATFORD
Foster, Doyley, Mackay, DeMerit, Stewart, Chambers (Bangura 72), Mahon, Spring, Young, King, Henderson
Goals DeMerit 25, Sullivan og 57, Henderson 84 penalty
Manager Aidy Boothroyd
Attendance 64,736

LEVSKI

Even after the stunning comeback against Kaiserslautern, few people gave Watford's young team any chance of making further progress in the Uefa Cup. The European adventure would surely be curtailed in Sofia. A trip behind the Iron Curtain would have been daunting for more seasoned European campaigners, let alone a bunch of teenagers, some with only a handful of first team appearances behind them.

Watford had blown their chance in the first leg at Vicarage Road. Graham Taylor had said before that match that they would need to take a two-goal lead with them to Bulgaria if they were to have any chance. After a 1-1 draw, the manager subtly qualified that statement, insisting that Watford could score in Sofia. The question was whether they could do enough.

When the draw for the second round was made, Watford were pulled out of the hat second, meaning that they were due to play the away leg first. However, Sofia's other team, CSKA, were also drawn at home in the European Cup, against AS Roma. The European Cup took

precedence and the rules stated Watford's tie would have to be switched.

That presented a slight handicap to Watford's chances. Going away from home first is always assumed to be an advantage in a two-legged tie. Watford would have battled to hold out for a draw, or they'd have settled for a slender defeat, perhaps the opportunity to pinch a valuable away goal would present itself. And then they'd come back to Vicarage Road knowing exactly what they had to do.

Watford had ample opportunity to win the home leg handsomely. In the 12th minute, Nigel Callaghan had a penalty saved by Borislav Mikhailov. The goalkeeper moved very early but the French referee, Georges Konrath did not instruct a re-take. Five minutes later, John Barnes limped off with an injury, something that Taylor later thought was a blessing in disguise.

Wilf Rostron scored with a superb shot just before half-time but Watford spurned chance after chance before falling to the sucker punch when Russi Gotchev equalised after 74 minutes.

The second leg would

> **Did you know?**
> Levski's goalkeeper Borislav Mikhailov played for Reading from 1995 to 1997.

SPARKED OUT

....

be played in the national Vasil Levski stadium, a vast concrete bowl that would hold 60,000 whistling, jeering Bulgarians. In contrast to CSKA, the army team, Levski Spartak were the people's football club, named after a Bulgarian revolutionary and national hero called Vasil Levski, who sought to free the country from Ottoman rule in the 19th century.

The country was part of the Eastern Bloc, a satellite state of the Soviet Union. In the late 1960s Levski Sofia were forced to merge with Spartak Sofia and the team was placed under the control of the interior ministry. It was a move that was deeply unpopular with the club's supporters but ordinary Bulgarians still preferred them to CSKA.

Watford's directors were welcomed warmly when they got to Sofia but Eddie Plumley, the secretary, couldn't help noticing that the directors he was introduced to were different to the 'directors' he'd welcomed to Vicarage Road. Travel to the West was tightly restricted and sportsmen and women were hugely privileged to see what life was like on the other side of the Berlin Wall. Many took the opportunity to fill their suitcases with clothes and electri-

cal equipment and there were rumours, difficult to verify, that Levski's players had been on a shopping trip during their trip to Hertfordshire.

Some of Watford's players were in for a culture shock in Sofia. What little they saw of the city was grey and foreboding. There were long queues at the shops for everyday items such as bread and vegetables. The country was years, if not decades, behind Western Europe.

The night before the match, Watford trained at the stadium and were watched by 10,000 Levski fans who booed and jeered throughout.

Watford's team was again patched up and the formation was tweaked slightly. John Barnes was fit again and Taylor gambled on the fact that Levski would not have seen much of him in the first leg. They would, perhaps, be unaware of the danger he could cause. Barnes, Callaghan and Ian Richardson played as a front three, with the two wingers dropping deeper at times to avoid being man-marked. With Kenny Jackett still injured and Les Taylor recovering from an operation, the manager had few options. He put Richard Jobson with Ian Bolton and Wilf Rostron in

ANNOUNCEMENTS

WANTED
PROFESSIONAL FOOTBALLERS

Many vacancies now available at First Division Football Club for men (or women) aged between 18 and 80 and prepared to work on Saturday. Some playing experience desirable but preference will be given to those with two arms and two legs in good working order! Apply in writing in the first instance to: G. Taylor, Vicarage Road Stadium, Watford

Graham Taylor's advert appeared in the classified pages of *The Times* in November 1983.

Injury crisis? What crisis?

Watford's injury problems were getting beyond a joke but Graham Taylor was determined not to sulk about it. With eight first-teamers on the treatment table he considered fitting Billy Hails' physiotherapy room with a revolving door.

Instead, he placed an advert in *The Times* appealing for new players. 'We had this incredible run of injuries,' says Taylor. 'It was very concerning. I was questioning myself and my methods. Had they all been soft-muscle injuries I'd have worried about our preparation but it seemed to be just a run of terrible luck.

'We would get someone fit and then someone else would get a knock. One or two of the injuries turned out to be long-term. It meant we had to play with half a reserve team in Europe.'

Taylor decided to draw attention to Watford's plight but wanted to do it in a light-hearted way, rather than whine about his misfortune.

He said: 'Instead of trotting out the same excuses for our mixed bag of results, I thought we could poke fun at ourselves. We are a happy club and if you cannot laugh at yourself then you may as well pack it in.'

The decision to run the advert turned out to be a public relations masterstroke.

Watford received hundreds of letters, many of them in the same jovial spirit as Taylor's advert.

There were pensioners, children, a few who were suspected of being Luton supporters on a sabotage mission and someone who said that finishing second in a Subbuteo league with his friends made him the ideal candidate. Someone even sent in a photo of their dog, Sheba, dribbling a football.

Watford's response was to invite a dozen or so of the best applicants (including Sheba) to appear in a special team photograph taken at Vicarage Road.

the middle. At the back, 19-year-old Neil Price, never a shrinking violet, was given his debut.

As it turned out, the pairing of Bolton and Rostron added just the right steel to Watford's midfield. The battle for control in the middle of the pitch got ugly at times and Bolton admitted he winced at of some of the challenges but the extraordinary circumstances demanded the Watford players gave as good as they were getting because the referee was offering little protection.

If the booing during their training session had been off-putting, it was nothing compared to the atmosphere that awaited the Watford players when they took to the field. It was intense. Flares burned brightly all over the terraces. The whistling and catcalling was so noisy the players found it difficult to hear above the din.

As soon as the match kicked off, Levski's players signalled their intentions. In the first couple of minutes Bolton, Jobson and Rostron were on the receiving end of some aggressive challenges. The Levski players were not concerned about going in over the top of the ball.

Strangely, the referee was slow to punish the Levski players but quick to give them a penalty. After five minutes Iskrenov broke clear and played the ball towards Plamen Tsvetkov. Jobson rushed across to meet him and the Bulgarian crashed into the Watford player and went down. Emil Spassov scored from the penalty spot.

Watford could have been intimidated out of the match before it had even begun but three minutes later, Callaghan scored a phenomenal goal, striking sweetly from 25 yards. For the first time, the Bulgarian crowd fell silent.

After half an hour, Jobson conceded another penalty, this one every bit as harsh as the first. Again it was Tsvetkov who ran into Jobson and fell over. For Jobson this was something he had not experienced before. 'In England, we didn't have diving like that,' he says. 'To have a player run into you and go down because you hold your ground wouldn't happen in the English league. But here they were getting penalties for it.'

This time, though, the woodwork came to Watford's rescue. Spassov fired his kick against the bar. Jobson can remember thinking then that things might turn in Watford's favour.

1983-84 UEFA CUP

1st round, 1st leg	Kaiserslautern A	1-3
1st round, 2nd leg	Kaiserslautern H	3-0
2nd round, 1st leg	Levski Spartak H	1-1
2nd round, 2nd leg	Levski Spartak A	3-1
3rd round, 1st leg	Sparta Prague H	2-3
3rd round, 2nd leg	Sparta Prague A	0-4

Watford's conquerers, Sparta Prague, were drawn against the Croatians Hajduk Split in the quarter-finals. They lost 2-1 on aggregate. Tottenham Hotspur won the trophy, beating the Belgians Anderlecht in a penalty shoot-out at White Hart Lane after both legs ended 1-1. Mark Falco, who joined Watford in 1986, scored one of the penalties.

They did, but not without a fight. Price remembers Bolton telling him to go in as hard as he could on the Bulgarian winger. All over the pitch there was a battle but slowly, Watford managed to impose themselves.

Levski had hit the bar, the post and they'd had two penalties but Watford were beginning to frustrate them. Maybe they were used to teams retreating into their shells after being subjected to such treatment.

Rostron caught one of the Levski players with an elbow. 'We jumped for the ball and I caught him accidentally,' says Rostron. 'He was going mad. I'd split his head and he was pointing to the blood but it was completely accidental.'

Levski continued to create chances in the second half but Watford held firm. Steve Sherwood made a couple of saves to keep them in it.

In the first period of extra-time Watford continued to live dangerously but a combination of good fortune and heroism thwarted Levski.

Watford kept going. Five minutes from the end of extra-time, they won a corner. Callaghan went across to take it but was being pelted with things by the crowd. He daren't look round but when a glass bottle smashed at his feet on the athletics track he ran onto the field and protested to the referee. Steve Sims told him to stop worrying and to get on with it. Callaghan's corner was flicked on by Sims and Rostron dived in at the far post to head it into the net.

The crowd became even fiercer and the Levski players opted for outright brutality. Ian Richardson was chopped down three times in quick succession by three different players. John Barnes got the ball on the left wing and headed for the corner to kill time, though mindful that missiles were landing on the edges

BIGGEST CROWDS

A list of the top ten biggest crowds Watford have played in front of in competitive fixtures.

100,0000	**Wembley**			
Everton	0-2	FA Cup final	1984
76,032	**Old Trafford**			
Man United	0-4	Premiership	2007
70,343	**Wembley**			
Bolton	2-0	Play-off final	1999
64,736	**Millennium Stadium**			
Leeds United	3-0	Play-off-final	2006
63,498	**Old Trafford**			
Man United	1-1	FA Cup	1969
60,018	**Emirates Stadium**			
Arsenal	0-3	Premiership	2006
60,000	**Levski Stadium**			
Levski Spartak	1-1	Uefa Cup	1983
57,879	**St James' Park**			
Newcastle	0-5	FA Cup	1932
55,209	**White Hart Lane**			
Chelsea	1-5	FA Cup	1970
55,188	**Old Trafford**			
Man United	1-4	Premiership	1999

Vicarage Road's biggest crowd is 34,099 for a cup tie against Manchester United in 1969. It is 59th in the list of biggest gates.

of the pitch. He knew the Levski defenders were going to try to hack him down too but as one of them lunged at him his feet were quick enough to avoid the tackle and skip past with the ball. Suddenly he had time and space to pick out Jobson at the far post, who laid it back for Richardson to score.

It was an extraordinary result, one the *Daily Telegraph* called 'possibly the most impressive and most unlikely result by an English team in Europe'.

Taylor said after the match: 'We shouldn't have had a prayer tonight. We could have lost 4-1 but then again we could have won the home leg 4-1.'

The third round draw was not kind to Watford. In fact, it was horrible. Taylor hoped to avoid another team from the Eastern Bloc because he knew the away leg would be played in the depth of their winter.

Sparta Prague were a different proposition to both Kaiserslautern and Levski Spartak. At the time Taylor described them as possibly the most accomplished club side to visit Vicarage Road. Watford fell 2-0 behind in the first leg and although they fought back to 2-2 they conceded again in the last minute. The away leg, played on an ice rink of a pitch in Prague, was no contest. Sparta Prague scored three times in the first 11 minutes and got a fourth just before half-time.

Had Watford managed to reach the quarter-finals, their new signings George Reilly, Maurice Johnston,

David Bardsley and Lee Sinnott, who all played their part in the run to the FA Cup final, would have been eligible to play. They had joined the club after the deadline for European registration.

Who knows how the competition would have panned out? It is worth noting that Nottingham Forest reached the semi-finals where they lost to the Belgian side, Anderlecht. Having won the first leg 2-0, Forest were beaten 3-0 in Brussels. The Belgians were given a controversial penalty and Forest had a goal disallowed. Years later it emerged that the club's president had bribed the referee.

Speculating on how Watford might have fared is academic. But despite the heavy defeat in Prague, the club broke new ground in the autumn of 1983. And the victory in Sofia has to go down as the most remarkable triumph against the odds the club has ever enjoyed.

LEVSKI SPARTAK
Michailov, Nikolov, Balevski, Petrov, Iliev (Tchavdarov 107), Tsvetkov, Gotchev (Valev 81), Sirakov, Kurdov, Spassov, Iskrenov
Goal Spassov 5 penalty
Manager Vasil Metodiev

WATFORD
Sherwood, Palmer, Price, Jobson, Sims, Franklin, Callaghan, Richardson, Barnes, Bolton, Rostron
Goals Callaghan 8, Rostron 115, Richardson 117
Manager Graham Taylor
Attendance 60,000

2 Que sera, sera, whatever will be, will be

We're going to Wem-ber-lee

PLYMOUTH ARGYLE 0   WATFORD.............1

Villa Park, Saturday April 14 1984

The intoxicating rush of an FA Cup run is unlike anything else. The excitement is contagious. You set out in January in hope more than expectation and you take whatever the draw throws at you, dreaming that maybe this year will be your year.

As the rounds go by and you find your team is still standing you allow yourself to think ahead. What if this really is our time?

Perhaps it was written in the stars that Watford would reach the FA Cup final in 1984. Before the draw for the third round was even made, Graham Taylor told Elton John to keep cup final day clear.

The chairman was about to embark on a long European tour but he made sure there wasn't a concert on Saturday, May 19.

Watford knocked Luton out in the third round replay, then skipped past Charlton Athletic and brushed aside the previous season's finalists Brighton to reach the last eight, by which time Wembley was on everyone's mind.

Most of the First Division giants had been knocked out. Manchester United, the holders, lost at Bournemouth. Liverpool, Arsenal and Tottenham were also sent packing early on.

And Watford kept going. In the sixth round they faced a potentially awkward tie, a trip to face a bruising Birmingham City side.

That moment of genius from John Barnes helped them make light work of the Blues.

The Twin Towers of Wembley, just ten miles away from Vicarage Road as the crow flies, were now looming large.

All they needed now was a touch of good fortune in the semi-final draw and they could make it to Wembley.

Into the FA's velvet bag alongside

Maurice Johnston had started the season playing for Partick Thistle in the Scottish First Division. Now he was all set to make an FA Cup final appearance at Wembley Stadium.

Watford went Everton, Southampton or Sheffield Wednesday and Derby or Plymouth Argyle.

Derby were labouring in Division Two and Plymouth were struggling in the Third Division. It was obvious who everyone wanted and Watford pulled out the plum, like little Jack Horner.

Things got even better when the West Country side knocked Derby out in their replay at the Baseball Ground.

That was until it dawned on the Watford players that the pressure would all be on them. So often the giant-killer, now they would be the favourites and the nation would be rooting for the underdogs.

By now, cup fever had spread through the town. There was a rush for tickets. Supporters hunted high and low for the ticket stubs that would enable them to apply for a ticket for Villa Park. The Hornets Shop was doing a roaring trade in souvenirs. Shop windows were decorated in red, yellow and black. Children made replica FA Cups from cereal packets and tin foil.

And slowly the tension began to ramp up. Watford had traded for so long on upsetting the odds. Now they were there to be shot at.

A week before the semi-final, they were hammered 6-1 at Carrow Road by Norwich City. It was a humiliating capitulation, a day when nothing went right. Steve Sherwood, the goalkeeper, was nursing an injured finger and had kept quiet the extent to which it was troubling him. Several players were a booking away from missing the big cup tie and no one wanted to pick up an injury and find they were ruled out.

Graham Taylor refused to dwell on the Norwich defeat. Instead he had a selection problem to solve. Kenny Jackett, so important to the team's midfield, was out of action and Taylor had to decide how to fill the gap.

The manager opted to move Wilf Rostron into midfield and play Neil Price at left-back. Price had spent time on loan at Plymouth earlier in the season and their manager's request to allow him to play in an earlier round of the FA Cup had been rejected by Taylor. Now he was lining up against his temporary former team-mates.

The atmosphere inside Villa Park was brilliantly vibrant. Watford's bright yellow and red competed with Plymouth's deep green. The vast Holte End terrace was divided in two with both sets of supporters vying to be the loudest.

Fourteen years had passed since

PLYMOUTH ARGYLE
Crudgington, Nisbet, Uzzell, Harrison, Smith, Cooper, Hodges, Phillips, Tynan, Staniforth, Rogers
Manager John Hore

WATFORD
Sherwood, Bardsley, Price, Taylor, Terry (Jobson 81), Sinnott, Callaghan, Johnston, Reilly, Rostron, Barnes
Goal Reilly 14
Manager Graham Taylor
Attendance 43,858

Watford's only other FA Cup semi-final, that deflating defeat at White Hart Lane against Chelsea. Everything felt different now but if Watford's fans thought they had one foot in the final before a ball was kicked, they were mistaken.

It is arguably the case that more hinged on this match than any other in the club's history up to this point.

Victory would mean an appearance in the FA Cup final – the most-watched club game in the world. Back then more people tuned in to watch the Wembley showdown than watched the European Cup final.

But it was easy to overlook the lack of experience in a Watford team that was expected to breeze past Plymouth.

None of them had played in an FA Cup semi-final. Only Wilf Rostron had got as far as the sixth round before. They were young and they were in new territory.

The opening exchanges were untidy. Neither side settled and Watford did little to suggest they deserved to be two divisions above their opponents.

In the 14th minute, Rostron won the ball on the halfway line and John Barnes picked it up, turning away from two Argyle players. He sped down the flank, his route to the byline seemingly marked by a long trail of toilet paper thrown on the pitch.

The pace of his run had Plymouth gasping. Two defenders shadowed him but neither was able to get in an effective block. Barnes sent the ball into the box and George Reilly, who had burst forward from a deep position, got in front of the defender and connected with the perfectly-flighted cross. Reilly's header flew in at the near post.

The goal did little to settle Watford down. They even had the ball in the net again a few minutes later but the referee ruled out a fine Nigel Callaghan shot for offside.

Plymouth didn't threaten much but while it was 1-0 Watford were living on the edge. The second half was just as tense, although Taylor felt that Watford always had enough to score again if it had come to it.

Perhaps knowing what was at stake was stifling the Hornets. Les Taylor, who could run all day and most of the night, got cramp just five minutes into the second half and had to grit his teeth

THE CUP SEMI-FINALS

FA CUP

1970	v Chelsea	White Hart Lane	1-5
1984	v Plymouth	Villa Park	1-0
1987	v Tottenham	Villa Park	1-4
2003	v Southampton	Villa Park	1-2
2007	v Man United	Villa Park	1-4

LEAGUE CUP

1979	v Nottm Forest	(1-3, 0-0)	1-3
2005	v Liverpool	(0-1, 0-1)	0-2

just to get through the game. 'It was a really difficult game but not because Plymouth were giving us the runaround or anything,' he says. 'It was an emotional day. There'd been a lot of build-up to it, you're playing in your first semi-final and you just wanted to reach Wembley so badly.'

Late on, Steve Terry got a bad knock on his knee and had to go off. Reilly dropped back to fill in at centre half.

Watford survived a couple of scares at the end. Reilly got his legs in the way of one shot and then came the moment when the whole stadium seemed to hold its breath.

Kevin Hodges sent a shot across the penalty area towards Sherwood's far post. The ball had beaten the Watford goalkeeper and was on its way.

Everyone in green was willing the ball to bounce in. Everyone in yellow was urging it to go the other way. In the end, the will of the yellows won and the Hornets breathed a sigh of relief.

As Price says: 'Every time I'm in Plymouth they bring that shot up and say that if it had bounced the other way and gone in they'd have won. But I remind them that it didn't.'

When the final whistle went there was first a sense of relief, then unbridled joy. For the first time in the club's history, Watford were going to Wembley. It had been close, just a moment of sublime wing play from Barnes had separated the teams, but it was enough.

As Taylor later reflected, reaching Wembley turned out to be the summit. The six-year journey from the depths of the Fourth Division to the FA Cup final had been as exhilarating.

Has there been a prouder day in the club's history?

WHAT HAPPENED NEXT?

Watford lost the FA Cup final, 2-0 to Everton at Wembley. The match will always be remembered as a bittersweet experience for the Hornets. The pride of playing in English football's showpiece occasion, the culmination of the season, has rarely been matched.

But the disappointment of seeing a young team lose brought tears to the eyes.

No Watford supporter will ever be persuaded that Everton's second goal was fair. Andy Gray jumped at Steve Sherwood and headed the keeper's arm. Sherwood spilled the ball and it bounced into the net.

It was a horrible, unjust moment. Losing at Wembley was one thing but having the game killed off in such circumstances stung.

Graham Taylor was proud to have led the team to the final and was philosophical in defeat. 'We still have something to aim at,' he said. 'We'll have to get back there and win it.'

Twenty seven years have passed since that glorious spring and we're still waiting. Maybe one day...

The road to Wembley 84

As Watford made progress through the third and fourth rounds, several big First Division clubs fell by the wayside. By the sixth round, the Hornets were second favourites to win the cup.

THIRD ROUND

Aston Villa	1-1	Norwich City
Blackburn Rovers	1-0	Chelsea
Blackpool	2-1	Manchester City
Bolton	0-3	Sunderland
Bournemouth	2-1	Manchester United
Brighton	2-0	Swansea City
Burnley	0-0	Oxford United
Cambridge United	0-3	Derby County
Cardiff City	0-3	Ipswich Town
Carlisle United	1-1	Swindon Town
Colchester United	0-1	Charlton Athletic
Coventry City	1-1	Wolves
Crystal Palace	1-0	Leicester City
Darlington	4-1	Maidstone United
Fulham	0-0	Tottenham
Gillingham	5-3	Brentford
Huddersfield Town	2-1	QPR
Leeds United	1-1	Scunthorpe United
Liverpool	4-0	Newcastle
Luton Town	2-2	Watford
Middlesbrough	3-2	Arsenal
Nottm Forest	1-2	Southampton
Notts County	2-2	Bristol City
Plymouth Argyle	2-2	Newport County
Portsmouth	2-1	Grimsby Town
Rochdale	1-4	Telford United
Rotherham United	0-0	West Brom
Sheffield United	1-1	Birmingham City
Sheffield Wednesday	1-0	Barnsley
Shrewsbury Town	3-0	Oldham Athletic
Stoke City	0-2	Everton
West Ham	1-0	Wigan Athletic

REPLAYS

Birmingham City	2-0	Sheffield United
Bristol City	0-2	Notts County
Newport County	0-1	Plymouth Argyle
Norwich City	3-0	Aston Villa
Oxford United	2-1	Burnley
Scunthorpe United	1-1	Leeds United
Swindon Town	3-1	Carlisle United
Tottenham	2-0	Fulham
Watford	4-3	Luton Town
West Brom	3-0	Rotherham Utd
Wolves	1-1	Coventry City

SECOND REPLAYS

Coventry City	3-0	Wolves
Scunthorpe United	4-2	Leeds United

FOURTH ROUND

Brighton	2-0	Liverpool
Charlton Athletic	0-2	Watford
Crystal Palace	1-1	West Ham
Derby County	3-2	Telford United
Everton	0-0	Gillingham
Huddersfield Town	1-2	Notts County
Middlesbrough	2-0	Bournemouth
Oxford United	2-1	Blackpool
Plymouth Argyle	2-1	Darlington
Portsmouth	0-1	Southampton
Sheffield Wednesday	3-2	Coventry City
Shrewsbury Town	2-0	Ipswich Town
Sunderland	1-2	Birmingham City
Swindon Town	1-2	Blackburn Rovers
Tottenham	0-0	Norwich City
West Brom	1-0	Scunthorpe United

REPLAYS

Gillingham	0-0	Everton
Norwich City	2-1	Tottenham
West Ham	2-0	Crystal Palace

SECOND REPLAY

Gillingham	0-3	Everton

FIFTH ROUND

Birmingham City	3-0	West Ham United
Blackburn Rovers	0-1	Southampton
Derby County	2-1	Norwich City
Everton	3-0	Shrewsbury Town
Notts County	1-0	Middlesbrough
Oxford United	0-3	Sheffield Wednesday
Watford	3-1	Brighton
West Brom	0-1	Plymouth Argyle

SIXTH ROUND

Birmingham City	1-3	Watford
Notts County	1-2	Everton
Plymouth Argyle	0-0	Derby County
Sheffield Wednesday	0-0	Southampton

REPLAYS

Derby County	0-1	Plymouth Argyle
Southampton	5-1	Sheffield Wednesday

SEMI-FINALS

Everton	1-0	Southampton
at Highbury		*after extra time*
Plymouth Argyle	0-1	Watford
at Villa Park		

'I knew I'd hit it well. There was a shout, then the crowd roared and I knew it was in.'
Nick Wright

BOLTON WANDERERS .... 0 WATFORD 2

For most of the Nineties, the Premiership looked like it had slammed its doors shut to the likes of Watford. But they were about to burst their way in.

Having reached the play-off final, it was the prospect of going to Wembley that was initially so thrilling. The idea of winning a golden ticket allowing entry to the exhalted, almost unreal world of the Premiership was secondary.

'There was a lot of excitement about the fact we were going to Wembley,' says Nick Wright. 'But after a couple of days it was clear we weren't going there to enjoy it. We were going there to do a job. We had a hard week. There was a lot of running, then some recovery time and then we worked on set-pieces.'

Watford were in a perfect position. They approached Wembley with the magical combination of incredible form and underdog status. They had also beaten Bolton home and away in the league. Confidence was high, but Taylor ensured nothing was left to chance in the preparations.

Steve Palmer says: 'My over-riding memory is of Graham trying to get everything organised early on. Tickets for the players' families can become a real pain so they were sorted early so we could minimise the emotion in the couple of days leading up to the game.'

Wembley Stadium was the perfect stage for a moment of genius from Nick Wright.

The squad made a trip to Wembley to familiarise themselves with the place. They checked out the dressing rooms and the tunnel. 'Graham told us to go onto the pitch and check out the areas where we'd be hoping to make a difference,' says Allan Smart.

'I went to visualise putting the ball in the net. Peter Kennedy went to look at the corners, because he'd be taking a lot of the set-pieces. Graham wanted us to feel relaxed about the place and get the fact that it was Wembley out of our system before the day.'

Over the course of the week, the manager asked each player to prepare a speech to give to his team-mates. One that sticks in Smart's mind was by Alon Hazan. 'Manchester United had just beaten Barcelona in the Champions League final with those two late goals,' says Smart. 'Alon's speech was very moving. At the end he asked us if we wanted to be United or Barcelona.'

There were no surprises when the manager named the starting line-up at the hotel on the morning of the match. Paul Robinson was back from suspension and regained his place.

'Graham didn't name the subs,' says Smart. 'I knew that his two changes in the run-in had been myself and Alon Hazan but until it was announced I was like a cat on a hot tin roof. I had to ask Robert Page to go and find out from the gaffer if I'd be on the bench.'

The team boarded the coach and made their way through a sea of red and yellow. 'We went from Watford to Stanmore and Kingsbury and it was yellow all the way,' says Palmer. 'It was a great trip but I was very conscious of the fact that I didn't want to get distracted from the job I had to do. If I found myself getting caught up in it all I said "No, come on, concentrate on what you're going there to do.""

Palmer had played at Wembley before, in the Varsity match for Cambridge University, but doesn't feel that experience counted for much. 'It was not the same at all. You can't compare the two occasions in any way.'

When they first caught sight of the twin towers, Tommy Mooney thought back to all the childhood visits he'd made with his father. 'When I was growing up, we'd go to internationals and cup finals as often as my dad could afford,' he says.

'On that day, I really wasn't thinking about promotion. I just wanted to play at Wembley, win at Wembley. To me, if you could do that, no matter what else happened, your career was worthwhile.'

Before the match, the players noted that their approach differed to Bolton's. The Trotters arrived in tracksuits and were trying to treat it as if it were just another game. For Watford, it was a cup final. There was a sense of occasion.

'I am not sure Bolton's way would have worked for us,' says Chamberlain. 'We knew what it all meant and I think it would have been a mistake to try to take all that emotion out of it.

'Before the match, we went onto the pitch and I remember talking to Bob Wilson and feeling that I wasn't really there. I was just nodding along to what he was saying, really. I just wanted to get my kit on, warm up, touch the ball and get on with it.'

Taylor gave his final team talk and the Watford players readied themselves to go out into the tunnel. The psychological battle started here. 'Ciaran Cosgrave wanted us to go out late, to make them wait for us,' says Palmer.

'I still believe part of winning the match was done in that tunnel,' says Wright. 'We were very controlled but we were loud and quite aggressive. They had international players but they were very quiet.'

Then came the moment the hairs stood up on the back of seventy thousand necks. Fireworks and Fat Boy Slim. The arrival of the two teams.

'That was incredible,' says Palmer. 'I knew I wanted to be able to remember that so I was making an effort to look around and take it all in. Whenever I hear *Right Here, Right Now* by Fat Boy Slim I am taken back to that moment.'

The early exchanges went Bolton's way. The fact the opposition had the better chances suited Chamberlain.

'Before the game, I caught sight of myself in a mirror and I was as white as a sheet,' he says. 'Bolton had some good chances early on. Robbo made a bit of a mistake and they had that shot that went past me but went wide. When I made a save from Eidur Gudjohnsen I really felt I was in the match. A free kick hit the wall and he turned and hit it

What happened to the Wembley heroes?

'If we win on Monday, some of them might never play outside the Premiership again...' Graham Taylor knew that the play-off final could change the lives of some of his players.

But it didn't quite turn out like that. The play-off triumph didn't transform many careers.

Of the 14 players involved in the final, only Paul Robinson went on to play regularly in the Premiership, for West Brom and Bolton, although Mooney was successful with Birmingham City.

Darren Bazeley decided to join Wolves and ended his career without playing a Premiership match.

Injuries struck Peter Kennedy, Nick Wright and Richard Johnson.

'I was due to have a knee operation a few days after the final,' says Kennedy. 'When Allan Smart scored the second goal, I jumped up and when I landed my knee collapsed under me. Robbo came and lifted me up. Two days later I was on the operating table but it was a constant niggle. I had three or four operations while I was at Watford, plus I had a back problem in the Premier League season.'

Johnson got injured playing against Liverpool. At one point, Leeds United were very interested in signing him but the injuries scuppered the move.

Wright's career should have progressed after that Wembley goal but it proved to be the peak.

'I am so pleased for Nicky that he scored that goal and can look back at that,' says Kennedy. 'He was a really great lad and such a good player but he hardly played again.'

Wright had injured his groin in the days leading up to the Wembley match. 'During training, I went to shoot and Micah clipped me from behind and I did a bit of an air shot,' he says. 'I felt something go in my groin. I had a few painkillers and anti-inflammatories because there was no way I was going to miss out on playing at Wembley. I got through the game and then went to speak to the physio, who did an x-ray.

'I had played with a fractured piece of bone in my pelvis. It was an avulsion fracture, where the tendon had pulled a piece of the bone away. If we'd known, I probably wouldn't have played.

'I missed pre-season and had some groin problems that were related. I was only getting through half a game at a time and I couldn't sprint. I had a hernia operation and felt I'd recovered. I played a couple of reserve games and felt strong.

'In December, we played Birmingham in the FA Cup and when I was taken off the crowd booed. I'd done well even though it hadn't been a good team performance. I thought I was on the way back.

'Graham Taylor wanted me to play the next reserve game to get a bit more match fitness so I could be fully fit for the next Premiership game.

'It was against Coventry reserves and after about three minutes, I went past the full back and Dominic Foley played me in. The turf was wet, the ball ran on and I collided with Steve Ogrizovic. My leg turned sideways. I tried to play on but it was clearly something serious.

'The physio told me I'd be out for three weeks. Three years later I retired without making a proper comeback.

'It was a horrible time but it taught me a lot about myself. I was trying everything to get fit but I couldn't get the strength back in my knee. I couldn't sprint or bend it fully. I played a few times in the reserves but was only at 80 per cent.

'It wasn't a consolation at the time but I do have that game and that goal to look back on. Over the years, I've met Watford fans who named their children born around that time Nick or Nicky.

'Most players don't get to experience what I did. It's an awesome thing. You know you have done something that means a lot to the supporters.'

on the volley and I had to react quickly. I felt like I'd made a real contribution to the game and it settled me down.'

It wasn't just the goalkeeper who was eager to get into his stride. 'For the first ten minutes, I was running up and down, covering a lot of ground but I didn't get a touch of the ball,' says Wright. 'I was waiting for the game to settle into a rhythm. Darren Bazeley was playing behind me and he loved to get forward and he was getting a lot of the ball, so I was doing a lot of dropping back to cover as he went forward.'

But Wright's moment would come.

As the first half drew to a close, Watford won a corner after Bazeley had burst into the Bolton penalty area. Kennedy went over to take it. 'We had a few corner routines but I was trying to deliver the ball into a dangerous area and hopefully one of our players would get on the end of it,' he says.

Wright took up his position on the edge of the six-yard box. 'The manager wanted me there because the theory was I'd be able to pick up the ball if it was headed clear by a defender,' he says.

Kennedy's curling delivery was very awkward for Bolton to deal with. It was swinging towards the goal but the keeper was prevented from coming out for it because of the bodies in his way. Instead, Andy Todd headed it out.

The ball fell to where Wright was lurking. 'GT said that Nicky was there for a reason, and he was,' says Mooney. 'It wasn't luck. We worked very hard on

LETTER TO THE EDITOR

Shortly after Watford had clinched the Second Division title ahead of Bristol City, Graham Taylor splashed out a modest sum on two forwards from relegated Carlisle United. On June 12, 1998, a letter from a supporter was printed in the *Watford Observer*. We've spared the writer the embarrassment of naming him but we wonder how he felt as he celebrated the win over Bolton less than a year later?

WHEN Watford FC put the season ticket prices up for the new season, the fans were given a couple of reasons for the increase. The first was to fund the pitch and stadium redevelopment, which looks like it could be a sound investment for the future of the club.

The second reason was for the funding of new players and GT promised that Premiership players would be top of the list, so who the hell are Allan Smart and Nick Wright?

While Bristol City have spent £2.2m on Ade Akinbiyi and Tony Thorpe, which proves their intention for the new season, we spend £175,000 on a couple of Carlisle rejects. I have paid £210 for my new season ticket and these are not the quality of players I have paid to watch and I am sure everyone else felt the same way when they found out about the new signings.

set-pieces and felt we had the edge on most teams.'

For the Watford supporters, time seemed to stand still. All eyes were fixed on the little red-haired figure in yellow as he flung himself in the air.

'Usually if the ball fell to me there, I'd have laid it back to Robbo,' says Wright. 'But there was no one there, so I did what I did.'

He dismisses the suggestion that his athletic overhead kick was simply a speculative effort to get it back into the goalmouth. 'I was not helping it back on,' he says. 'I was aiming for goal. It was an instinctive thing. I am not saying I picked my spot but I was trying to hit it towards goal with enough force and good technique.

'All I was thinking was get a good contact on the ball and get it on target. If I did that, it would have a chance.'

As Wright fell to the floor, he could tell his connection had been sweet. As he landed, he peered through the forest of legs between him and the goal.

'I didn't see it go in,' he says. 'I was waiting to see the net ripple. There was a shout of "it's in" and then the crowd roared and that's when I knew.

'I turned and sprinted towards where my parents were sitting in the crowd, but I didn't get there because Robbo rugby tackled me. Then Michel Ngonge was on top of me telling me he loved me. Then the whole team piled on.

'And then you realise you are one-nil up but you still have the game to play.

You have to calm yourself down and regain your focus very quickly.'

The second half was just as tight but Watford seemed to play with more composure. For Mooney, it evolved into a strangely frustrating game. 'I had been such a big part of the run-in but we played a slightly different way in the final,' he says. 'Darren got a lot of the ball on the right and between him and Nicky, they gave Robbie Elliott a hard time. We didn't get as much down the left, so I wasn't as involved.'

With 15 minutes to go, Taylor put Smart on in place of Ngonge. 'I can't remember a word he told me just before I went on,' says the Scot. 'There's a shot on the video of him talking to me but I was just thinking about getting on there and getting a touch of the ball.

'I'd not been on long when Peter got down the left and shanked one and I gave him a bit of stick for it.'

With three minutes to go, Wright was substituted. By now, the Watford fans were whistling for full time.

Two minutes were all that remained when Smart made a crunching tackle on Scott Sellars in his own half.

A couple of years earlier, Smart broke his ankle playing for Carlisle in the Auto Windscreens Shield final at Wembley. But he didn't think twice about going into the challenge hard.

'I was a bit lucky there because I went into it with absolutely everything. I don't think either me or Sellars even touched the ball,' he says. 'I got the

Let's get this party started. Robinson and Wright celebrate promotion at Wembley.

break and Micah Hyde got the ball. My leg was killing me but all I thought about was getting up and getting forward.'

Hyde played it on to Kennedy, who was in plenty of space on the left. This time, Kennedy's pass was so well-placed, he may as well have delivered it on a silver platter.

'Peter's pass was absolutely perfect,' says Smart. 'The gaffer said to me that he knew Micah would make the pass, he knew Peter would play the right ball but he wasn't sure what I was going to do.'

Smart had several options and time to think, so often the enemy of a striker in a pressure situation. 'I knew I was going to take it first time,' he says. 'I just wanted to strike it cleanly. I reached the ball at full tilt and hit it hard.'

'It wasn't a conventional finish, with the outside of the boot, but it was a lovely finish,' says Wright, who ran half the length of the pitch to celebrate with his old Carlisle team-mate.

That sealed it. Bolton were out on their feet. 'After the second goal, the body language of the Bolton players was destroyed,' says Chamberlain.

'I asked the referee about five times in the last couple of minutes how long there was to go,' says Palmer. 'Then there were the celebrations, getting the cup and taking it down to the end where our supporters were. I sat on the pitch by myself and just took it all in.

'Looking back, it's hard to separate what you actually remember and what is a sort of second-hand memory from what you've seen in photos and on the video. A few days after the match, I watched the television coverage and when the second goal goes in the camera pans up to the Watford crowd and there's a dad going absolutely crazy and his daughter is looking up at him, slightly embarrassed. I thought that was great. It meant so much to him, he'd completely lost it.'

The team had surfed a wave of positive vibes. As Smart says: 'Ciaran Cosgrave didn't score a goal or make a tackle but he hit us at the right time. He must have thought he was the messiah after two months with us.'

Watford were in the Premiership. Of course, the question of whether they could survive followed with indecent haste.

Taylor had done it again. And two relative unknowns from Carlisle scored the goals to take them there.

'Wrighty had a real bee in his bonnet all season about the guy who wrote to the paper,' says Smart. 'He came in one day saying "Have you seen what this bloke said?" I used to say to him that the fella had a point.'

Taylor signed the pair after they'd impressed for Carlisle at Vicarage Road. 'We were getting relegated and they were going up but we outplayed them,' says Wright. 'We lost but Graham came into our dressing room, shook our hands and said we hadn't deserved to lose.'

They took a little time to settle. 'People thought we were strike partners but we'd never played as a front two for Carlisle,' says Smart. 'I don't know if Graham intended to play us together but if he did, we soon put him off the idea. We played up front together in

pre-season and I said to Wrighty as we came off "We've had a shocker there. We look like we've never seen each other before." As the season went on we established our roles.

'After the game, we had to do the media and when we got to the dressing room everyone was changed and had gone to the bar. Nicky and I ended up in the big bath together with a beer, just the two of us, one on each side. "Look at us now, two blokes from Carlisle." We wondered if the fella who wrote to the paper was out there celebrating.

But the architect of it all was Taylor, the man who had repeated history.

The Premiership turned out not to be the dream destination we'd hoped it would be. But the journey was magical, a dizzying head rush when everything came together perfectly.

And that is why Watford's victory at the home of football has to be considered the greatest ever. Well, for the time being, anyway...

BOLTON WANDERERS
Banks, Cox (Hansen 89), Elliott, Frandsen, A Todd, M Todd, Johansen (Sellars 66), Jensen, Gudjohnsen, Taylor, Gardner
Manager Colin Todd

WATFORD
Chamberlain, Bazeley, Kennedy, Page, Palmer, Robinson, Ngonge (Smart 75), Hyde, Mooney, Johnson, Wright (Hazon 87)
Goals Wright 38, Smart 89
Manager Graham Taylor
Attendance 70,343

Statistics & matches

The managers

38	Graham Taylor 1977-87
16	Graham Taylor 1998-2001
8	Aidy Boothroyd
8	Glenn Roeder
8	Aidy Boothroyd
5	Steve Perryman
4	Malky Mackay
4	Ron Burgess
3	Ken Furphy
2	Steve Harrison
2	Gianluca Vialli
1	Bill McGarry
1	Mike Keen

The top goalscorers

Luther Blissett 22
Nigel Callaghan 17
Ross Jenkins 12
John Barnes 10
Gary Porter 8
Gerry Armstrong 6
George Reilly 6
Tommy Mooney 6
Heidar Helguson 6
Maurice Johnston 5
Peter Kennedy 5
Gifton Noel-Williams 5
Danny Graham 5

The venues

Home (Vicarage Road) 52
Away 46
Wembley 1
Millennium Stadium 1

Here's to the next 100 great Watford wins.

These are the 100 greatest Watford wins listed in chronological order, with their position in book in the right-hand column, so you can read about the games in the order they happened if you wish.

1959-60 – Division Four			No.
Birmingham City (FA)	H	2-1	40
Southampton (FA)	H	1-0	77
Workington	A	1-0	16
1961-62 – Division Three			
QPR	H	3-2	84
1963-64 – Division Three			
Colchester United	H	3-2	74
1967-68 – Division Three			
Grimsby Town	H	7-1	99
1968-69 – Division Three			
Plymouth Argyle	H	1-0	18
1969-70 – Division Two			
Liverpool (FA)	H	1-0	15
1976-77 – Division Four			
Huddersfield Town	H	2-0	89
1977-78 – Division Four			
Stockport County	A	3-1	58
Southport	H	3-2	43
1978-79 – Division Three			
Manchester United (LC)	A	2-1	5
Hull City	H	4-0	27
1979-80 – Division Two			
Wolves (FA)	A	3-0	76
1980-81 – Division Two			
Southampton (LC)	H	7-1	10
Nottingham Forest (LC)	H	4-1	17
1981-82 – Division Two			
Newcastle United	A	1-0	88
Chelsea	A	3-1	49
Manchester United (FA)	H	1-0	68
West Ham United (FA)	H	2-0	93
Derby County	H	6-1	81
Wrexham	H	2-0	11
1982-83 – Division One			
Everton	H	2-0	8
Southampton	A	4-1	63
West Brom	H	3-0	14
Sunderland	H	8-0	19
Tottenham Hotspur	A	1-0	23
Arsenal	A	4-2	39
Luton Town	H	5-2	98
Liverpool	H	2-1	25

1983-84 – Division One			No.
Kaiserslautern (Uefa)	H	3-0	7
Levski Spartak (Uefa)	A	3-1	3
Wolves	A	5-0	94
Luton Town (FA)	H	4-3	55
Notts County	A	5-3	83
Birmingham City (FA)	A	3-1	30
Plymouth Argyle (FA)	N	1-0	2

1984-85 – Division One			
West Brom (LC)	H	4-1	79
Tottenham Hotspur	A	5-1	33
Manchester United	H	5-1	32

1985-86 – Division One			
Arsenal	H	3-0	50
Chelsea	A	5-1	73

1986-87 – Division One			
Manchester United	H	1-0	46
Liverpool	H	2-0	60
Luton Town	A	2-0	71
Arsenal (FA)	A	3-1	21
Everton	H	2-1	64

1988-89 – Division Two			
Newcastle (FA)	H	1-0	67

1989-90 – Division Two			
Bradford City	H	7-2	96

1990-91 – Division Two			
Middlesbrough	A	2-1	42
Oxford United	A	1-0	20

1991-92 – Division Two			
Millwall	A	4-0	57

1992-93 – Division One			
Leeds United (LC)	H	2-1	13
Newcastle	H	1-0	62

1993-94 – Division One			
Bolton Wanderers	H	4-3	29
Peterborough United	A	4-3	38
Southend United	H	3-0	92
Portsmouth	H	1-0	90
Crystal Palace	A	2-0	86

1994-95 – Division One			
Wolves	H	2-1	78
Tottenham Hotspur (LC)	A	3-2	97

1995-96 – Division One			
Millwall	A	2-1	95
Grimsby Town	H	6-3	80
Norwich City	A	2-1	69

1997-98 – Division Two			
Luton Town	A	4-0	9

1997-98 – Division Two			No.
Southend United	A	3-0	82
Bournemouth	H	2-1	34
Fulham	A	2-1	12

1998-99 – Division One			
Bristol City	A	4-1	75
Sunderland	H	2-1	44
Tranmere Rovers	H	2-1	22
Port Vale	A	2-1	54
Birmingham City	H	1-0	37
Birmingham City	A	0-1	24
Bolton Wanderers	N	2-0	1

1999-2000 – Premiership			
Liverpool	A	1-0	6
Chelsea	H	1-0	35

2000-01 – Division One			
Blackburn Rovers	A	4-3	45

2001-02 – Division One			
Bradford City (LC)	H	4-1	85
Charlton Athletic (LC)	H	3-2	65

2002-03 – Division One			
Coventry City	H	5-2	91
Sheffield United	A	2-1	31
Sunderland (FA)	A	1-0	72
Burnley (FA)	H	2-0	51
Burnley	A	7-4	61

2004-05 – Championship			
Southampton (LC)	H	5-2	52
Portsmouth (LC)	H	3-0	41

2005-06 – Championship			
Sheffield United	A	4-1	66
Crystal Palace	A	3-0	26
Leeds United	N	3-0	4

2006-07 – Premiership			
Middlesbrough	H	2-0	56
West Ham United (FA)	A	1-0	53
Plymouth Argyle (FA)	A	1-0	47

2007-08 – Championship			
Southampton	H	3-2	70
Crystal Palace	A	2-0	59

2008-09 – Championship			
Southampton	A	3-0	87

2009-10 – Championship			
QPR	H	3-1	36

2010-11 – Championship			
Norwich City	A	3-2	100
Millwall	A	6-1	28
QPR	A	3-1	48